Cosmic Critiques

Cosmic Critiques

HOW & WHY TEN SCIENCE FICTION STORIES WORK

Isaac Asimov

& Martin H. Greenberg

commentaries by Ansen Dibell

Writer's
Digest
Books

Cincinnati, Ohio

Cosmic Critiques. Copyright © 1990 by Isaac Asimov and Martin
H. Greenberg. Printed and bound in the United States of America.
All rights reserved. No part of this book may be reproduced in
any form or by any electronic or mechanical means including
information storage and retrieval systems without permission in
writing from the publisher, except by a reviewer, who may quote
brief passages in a review. Published by Writer's Digest Books, an
imprint of F&W Publications, Inc., 1507 Dana Avenue, Cincinnati,
Ohio 45207. First edition.

94 93 92 91 90   5 4 3 2 1

Library of Congress Cataloging in Publication Data

Cosmic critiques : how & why ten science fiction stories work /
    [compiled by] Isaac Asimov & Martin H. Greenberg;
    commentaries by Ansen Dibell.
      p.   cm.
    ISBN 0-89879-394-7
    1. Science fiction — Technique. 2. Science fiction, American.
3. Science fiction, English.   I. Asimov, Isaac.
II. Greenberg, Martin Harry.   III. Dibell, Ansen.
PN3377.5.S3C6   1990
809.3'8762 — dc20   89-27822
                                                              CIP

The following page constitutes an extension of this copyright page.

Contents

Advice

by Isaac Asimov

Over the years, hundreds of aspiring young writers have written to me asking for advice on "how to get started." I presume other aged and toil-worn writers get the same request.

I am always most reluctant to offer the advice that is so eagerly requested. For one thing, I don't feel wise enough. I'm not sure that my own success is the result of wisdom or talent. It may be the result of nothing more than dumb luck.

On the other hand, I don't like to refuse the advice either. I always have the uneasy feeling that those who are contemplating careers as writers suspect that I have somehow discovered the key to writing success; that it can be expressed in a short sentence; that I have carefully written it down on a slip of paper and put it in a safe-deposit box; and that if I don't give it out to anyone who asks it is just because I am a selfish hound who wants to hug his success to himself and allow no one else a chance at it.

This is simply not so, of course, but in order to avoid having people think it's so, I suppose I have no choice but to give you my idea of what the route to writing success might be.

In the first place, you must like to write; you must want to write; you must feel that you would rather write than anything else you can think of. (I was once asked, given my choice between writing and sex, which I would choose. My answer was: "Well, I can write for twelve hours at a stretch without getting too tired.")

If you don't like to write, but think that writing would be a good idea because it will make you rich and famous, or because it will make it possible for you to lead a glamorous life, or because it means you can set your own hours and take long vacations, then, please—forget about it and do something else.

Most writers, even those who actually sell some of the things they write, don't become rich and famous or any of those other good things. To be a writer is to learn to face disappointment and frustration most of the time (I'd be lying if I told you anything else) and the only way of surviving this is to enjoy the actual process of writing, to find a pleasure in the thing itself. A callous editor, or an unsympathetic reading public, may deprive you of material success, but they can't take away your pleasure.

Suppose, then, that I'm talking to people who want to write, who really want to write, and who fully intend to keep on writing even if they make few or no sales. If that should be you, the question is: how do you go about it?

The simplest answer is that you write. *You can't just sit around thinking about writing. You can't wait for inspiration to strike. You can't hang on while your brain ripens and fills with genius. I assure you none of that will happen.*

You know *that none of that will happen if you want to learn to ride a bicycle. Just picturing the bicycle and imagining that you are riding it will do you no good. You've got to get on, wobble, fall off, and get on again. It will be an uncomfortable process, but eventually you will learn to ride a bicycle.*

The analogy is, of course, a strained one. You know exactly what you are aiming for when you want to learn to ride a bicycle. You want to learn how to speed ahead and make turns, start and stop, without falling off or hurting yourself. In short, you want to learn to keep your balance. You know you have succeeded in learning this when you no longer fall off, or even wobble.

Writing is far more subtle. Writing is not just a matter of putting words on paper. We can all do that. That would be like keeping our balance on a bicycle; we want to ride on a high-wire with it; we want to climb walls and leap gaps with it.

Or to put it into writing terms — you don't just want to scribble; what you want to do is to write well. *You want to put the right words on paper in the right order. That's the kind of circus trick we are after.*

But how do you learn to do that? How can you even possibly recognize that you have succeeded? In fact, to put it as concisely as possible: What is *good writing, anyway?*

A Supreme Court justice, I am told, was once asked to define "pornography." He thought a while and admitted he couldn't think of a good airtight legal definition, and then he said, "But I know it when I see it."

And that's how it is with good writing. You may not be able to define it; you may not be able to describe it; you may not be able to tell anyone how to go about producing it — but you sure know it when you see it.

Clearly, then, the essential training process for any writer involves more than taking courses on how to write, or reading books on how to write, or asking established writers for clever shortcuts they may have stumbled upon. What an ambitious young writer must do, more than anything else, is to read the good writers.

You can find the good writers easily enough. They are the ones whose writing moves you, whose writing you find clear and forceful, whose writing is a pleasure to read, whose writing in sizable quantities does not become cloying or wearisome. Believe me, you'll know it when you see it.

Suppose you read those writers carefully, observe what they do and try to answer such questions as: "Now why did he say that in just that way?" or "Why didn't he make thus-and-so clear at this point, instead of letting the reader remain doubtful?" In that case, you will be learning the tricks of the trade after all. It's just that those tricks can't be put into a single sentence or, perhaps, into any number of sentences. Rather they become a feeling *that you have — a feeling for the right word, for the right touch, for the right order of presentation, of when to end a scene, and whether to snap it off cleanly or allow it to dwindle slowly.*

You will never learn it all — but on the other hand, you may, with experience, develop entirely new devices of your own. You may, given enough talent, surpass those you read as models and serve as a new standard for others.

Naturally, we must be selective in choosing our good writers. We all want to read the great classic writers of all time, but if what we want to do, in particular, is to write science fiction, then reading Homer, Sophocles, Shakespeare and Goethe isn't quite enough. You also have to read science fiction as written by the masters in the field.

And that's what we have tried to supply you with in this collection. There are ten stories by ten different authors, each representing a different type of science fiction and each with a commentary which may serve as a guide for you—though we would always encourage independent thought too, since each prospective writer is an individual who must, when all is done, carve his own road to Valhalla.

To some, true science fiction is "hard science fiction," that is, stories that feature authentic scientific knowledge and depend upon it for plot development and for plot resolution. It is, perhaps, the opposite pole of "cyberpunk" [see Pat Cadigan's "Rock On," page 28] and I am, myself, much given to it.

Naturally, in writing hard science fiction, it helps a good deal to have a thorough grounding in science. This does not necessarily mean graduate degrees in it, however, though some science fiction writers do possess such things. Frederik Pohl, for instance, never went to college and is entirely self-educated in science — and can write hard science fiction with the best of us. Therefore, if your ambition is to write this variety of science fiction, don't give it up just because you feel your formal education is insufficient.

Larry Niven's "Neutron Star," which I have introduced several times in several anthologies, is a classic hard science fiction story that won the science fiction Hugo award. I said to him once (filled, as I was, with envy), "Gee, Larry, I could have written that story. I wrote an essay on tides once . . ."

"I know," said Larry. "I read that essay. That's what gave me the idea for the story."

I could have chewed nails.

— Isaac Asimov

Neutron Star

Larry Niven

The *Skydiver* dropped out of hyperspace an even million miles above the neutron star. I needed a minute to place myself against the stellar background, and another to find the distortion Sonya Laskin had mentioned before she died. It was to my left, an area the apparent size of the Earth's moon. I swung the ship around to face it.

Curdled stars, muddled stars, stars that had been stirred with a spoon.

The neutron star was in the center, of course, though I couldn't see it and hadn't expected to. It was only eleven miles across, and cool. A billion years had passed since BVS-1 burned by fusion fire. Millions of years, at least, since the cataclysmic two weeks during which BVS-1 was an X-ray star, burning at a temperature of five billion degrees Kelvin. Now it showed only by its mass.

The ship began to turn by itself. I felt the pressure of the fusion drive. Without help from me my faithful metal watchdog was putting me in a hyperbolic orbit that would take me within one mile of the neutron star's surface. Twenty-four hours to fall, twenty-four hours to rise . . . and during that time something would try to kill me. As something had killed the Laskins.

The same type of autopilot, with the same program, had chosen the Laskins' orbit. It had not caused their ship to collide with the star. I could trust the autopilot. I could even change its program.

I really ought to.

How did I get myself into this hole?

The drive went off after ten minutes of maneuvering. My orbit was established, in more ways than one. I knew what would happen if I tried to back out now.

All I'd done was walk into a drugstore to get a new battery for my lighter!

Right in the middle of the store, surrounded by three floors of sales counters, was the new 2603 Sinclair intrasystem yacht. I'd come for a battery, but I stayed to admire. It was a beautiful job, small and sleek and streamlined and blatantly different from anything that'd ever been built. I wouldn't have flown it for anything but I had to admit it was pretty. I ducked my head through the door to look at the control panel. You never saw so many dials. When I pulled my head out, all the customers were looking in the same direction. The place had gone startlingly quiet.

I can't blame them for staring. A number of aliens were in the store, mainly shopping for souvenirs, but they were staring too. A puppeteer is unique. Imagine a headless, three-legged centaur wearing two Cecil the Seasick Sea Serpent puppets on its arms, and you'll have something like the right picture. But the arms are weaving necks, and the puppets are real heads, flat and brainless, with wide flexible lips. The brain is under a bony hump set between the bases of the necks. This puppeteer wore only its own coat of brown hair, with a mane that extended all the way up its spine to form a thick mat over the brain. I'm told that the way they wear the mane indicates their status in society, but to me it could have been anything from a dock worker to a jeweler to the president of General Products.

I watched with the rest as it came across the floor, not because I'd never seen a puppeteer but because there is something beautiful about the dainty way they move on those slender legs and tiny hooves. I watched it come straight toward me, closer and closer. It stopped a foot away, looked me over, and said, "You are Beowulf Shaeffer, former chief pilot for Nakamura Lines."

Its voice was a beautiful contralto with not a trace of accent. A puppeteer's mouths are not only the most flexible speech organs around, but also the most sensitive hands. The tongues are forked and pointed; the wide, thick lips have little fingerlike knobs along the rims. Imagine a watchmaker with a sense of taste in his fingertips . . .

I cleared my throat. "That's right."

It considered me from two directions. "You would be interested in a high-paying job?"

"I'd be fascinated by a high-paying job."

"I am our equivalent of the regional president of General Products. Please come with me, and we will discuss this elsewhere."

I followed it into a displacement booth. Eyes followed me all the way. It was embarrassing, being accosted in a public drugstore by a two-headed monster. Maybe the puppeteer knew it. Maybe it was testing me to see how badly I needed money.

My need was great. Eight months had passed since Nakamura Lines folded. For some time before that I had been living very high on the hog, knowing that my back pay would cover my debts. I never saw that back pay. It was quite a crash, Nakamura Lines. Respectable middle-aged businessmen took to leaving their hotel windows without their lift belts. Me, I kept spending. If I'd started living frugally, my creditors would have done some checking . . . and I'd have ended in debtor's prison.

The puppeteer dialed thirteen fast digits with its tongue. A moment later we were elsewhere. Air puffed out when I opened the booth door, and I swallowed to pop my ears.

"We are on the roof of the General Products building." The rich contralto voice thrilled along my nerves, and I had to remind myself that it was an alien speaking, not a lovely woman. "You must examine this spacecraft while we discuss your assignment."

I stepped outside a little cautiously, but it wasn't the windy season. The roof was at ground level. That's the way we build on We Made It. Maybe it has something to do with the fifteen-hundred-mile-an-hour winds we get in summer and winter, when the planet's axis of rotation runs through its primary, Procyon. The winds are our planet's only tourist attraction, and it would be a shame to slow them down by planting skyscrapers in their path. The bare, square concrete roof was surrounded by endless square miles of desert, not like the deserts of other inhabited worlds, but an utterly lifeless expanse of fine sand just crying to be planted with ornamental cactus. We've tried that. The wind blows the plants away.

The ship lay on the sand beyond the roof. It was a No. 2 General Products hull: a cylinder three hundred feet long and twenty feet through, pointed at both ends and with a slight wasp-waist constriction near the tail. For some reason it was lying on its side, with the landing shocks still folded in at the tail.

Ever notice how all ships have begun to look the same? A good ninety-five percent of today's spacecraft are built around one of the four General Products hulls. It's easier and safer to build that way, but somehow all ships end as they began: mass-produced look-alikes.

The hulls are delivered fully transparent, and you use paint where you feel like it. Most of this particular hull had been left transparent. Only the nose had been painted, around the lifesystem. There was no major reaction drive. A series of retractable attitude jets had been mounted in the sides, and the hull was pierced with smaller holes, square and round, for observational instruments. I could see them gleaming through the hull.

The puppeteer was moving toward the nose, but something made me turn toward the stern for a closer look at the landing shocks. They were bent. Behind the curved transparent hull panels some tremendous pressure had forced the metal to flow like warm wax, back and into the pointed stern.

"What did this?" I asked.

"We do not know. We wish strenuously to find out."

"What do you mean?"

"Have you heard of the neutron star BVS-1?"

I had to think a moment. "First neutron star ever found, and so far the only. Someone located it two years ago, by stellar displacement."

"BVS-1 was found by the Institute of Knowledge on Jinx. We learned through a go-between that the Institute wished to explore the star. They needed a ship to do it. They had not yet sufficient money. We offered to supply them with a ship's hull, with the usual guarantees, if they would turn over to us all data they acquired through using our ship."

"Sounds fair enough." I didn't ask why they hadn't done their own exploring. Like most sentient vegetarians, puppeteers find discretion to be the *only* part of valor.

"Two humans named Peter Laskin and Sonya Laskin wished to use the ship. They intended to come within one mile of the surface in a hyperbolic orbit. At some point during their trip an unknown force apparently reached through the hull to do this to the landing shocks. The unknown force also seems to have killed the pilots."

"But that's impossible. Isn't it?"

"You see the point. Come with me." The puppeteer trotted toward the bow.

I saw the point, all right. Nothing, but nothing, can get through a General Products hull. No kind of electromagnetic energy except visible light. No kind of matter, from the smallest subatomic particle to the fastest meteor. That's what the company's advertisements claim, and the guarantee backs them up. I've never doubted it, and I've never heard of a General Products hull being damaged by a weapon or by anything else.

On the other hand, a General Products hull is as ugly as it is functional. The puppeteer-owned company could be badly hurt if it got around that something *could* get through a company hull. But I didn't see where I came in.

We rode an escalladder into the nose.

The lifesystem was in two compartments. Here the Laskins had used heat-reflective paint. In the conical control cabin the hull had been divided into windows. The relaxation room behind it was a windowless reflective silver. From the back wall of the relaxation room an access tube ran aft, opening on various instruments and the hyperdrive motors.

There were two acceleration couches in the control cabin. Both had been torn loose from their mountings and wadded into the nose like so much tissue paper, crushing the instrument panel. The backs of the crumpled couches were splashed with rust brown. Flecks of the same color were all over everything, the walls, the windows, the viewscreens. It was as if something had hit the couches from behind: something like a dozen paint-filled toy balloons striking with tremendous force.

"That's blood," I said.

"That is correct. Human circulatory fluid."

Twenty-four hours to fall.

I spent most of the first twelve hours in the relaxation room, trying to read. Nothing significant was happening, except that a few times I saw the phenomenon Sonya Laskin had mentioned in her last report. When a star went directly behind the invisible BVS-1, a halo formed. BVS-1 was heavy enough to bend light around it, displacing most stars to the sides; but when a star went directly behind the neutron star, its light was displaced to all sides at once. Result: a tiny circle which flashed once and was gone almost before the eye could catch it.

I'd known next to nothing about neutron stars the day the puppeteer picked me up. Now I was an expert. And I still had no idea what was waiting for me when I got down there.

All the matter you're ever likely to meet will be normal matter, composed of a nucleus of protons and neutrons surrounded by electrons in quantum energy states. In the heart of any star there is a second kind of matter: for there, the tremendous pressure is enough to smash the electron shells. The result is degenerate matter: nuclei forced together by pressure and gravity, but held apart by the mutual repulsion of the more or less continuous electron "gas" around them. The right circumstances may create a third type of matter.

Given: a burnt-out white dwarf with a mass greater than 1.44 times the mass of the sun—Chandrasekhar's Limit, named for an Indian-American astronomer of the nineteen hundreds. In such a mass the electron pressure alone would not be able to hold the electrons back from the nuclei. Electrons would be forced against protons—to make neutrons. In one blazing explosion most of the star would change from a compressed mass of degenerate matter to a closely packed lump of neutrons: neutronium, theoretically the densest matter possible in this universe. Most of the remaining normal and degenerate matter would be blown away by the liberated heat.

For two weeks the star would give off X-rays as its core temperature dropped from five billion degrees Kelvin to five hundred million. After that it would be a light-emitting body perhaps ten to twelve miles across: the next best thing to invisible. It was not strange that BVS-1 was the first neutron star ever found.

Neither is it strange that the Institute of Knowledge on Jinx would have spent a good deal of time and trouble looking. Until BVS-1 was found, neutronium and neutron stars were only theories. The examination of an actual neutron star could be of tremendous importance. Neutron stars might give us the key to true gravity control.

Mass of BVS-1: 1.3 times the mass of Sol, approx.

Diameter of BVS-1 (estimated): eleven miles of neutronium, covered by half a mile of degenerate matter, covered by maybe twelve feet of ordinary matter.

Nothing else was known of the tiny hidden star until the Laskins went in to look. Now the Institute knew one thing more: the star's spin.

"A mass that large can distort space by its rotation," said the puppeteer. "The Laskins' projected hyperbola was twisted across itself in such a way that we can deduce the star's period of rotation to be two minutes twenty-seven seconds."

The bar was somewhere in the General Products building. I don't know just where, and with the transfer booths it doesn't matter. I kept staring at the puppeteer bartender. Naturally only a puppeteer would be served by a puppeteer bartender, since any biped life form would resent knowing that his drink had been made with somebody's mouth. I had already decided to get dinner somewhere else.

"I see your problem," I said. "Your sales will suffer if it gets out that something can reach through one of your hulls and smash a crew to bloody smears. But where do I come in?"

"We want to repeat the experiment of Sonya Laskin and Peter Laskin. We must find—"

"With me?"

"Yes. We must find out what it is that our hulls cannot stop. Naturally you may—"

"But I won't."

"We are prepared to offer one million stars."

I was tempted, but only for a moment. "Forget it."

"Naturally you will be allowed to build your own ship, starting with a No. 2 General Products hull."

"Thanks, but I'd like to go on living."

"You would dislike being confined. I find that We Made It has re-established the debtor's prison. If General Products made public your accounts—"

"Now, *just* a—"

"You owe money on the close order of five hundred thousand stars. We will pay your creditors before you leave. If you return—" I had to admire the creature's honesty in not saying "When"—"we will pay you the residue. You may be asked to speak to news commentators concerning the voyage, in which case there will be more stars."

"You say I can build my own ship?"

"Naturally. This is not a voyage of exploration. We want you to return safely."

"It's a deal," I said.

After all, the puppeteer had tried to blackmail me. What happened next would be its own fault.

They built my ship in two weeks flat. They started with a No. 2 General Products hull, just like the one around the Institute of Knowledge ship, and the lifesystem was practically a duplicate of the Laskins', but there the resemblance ended. There were no instruments to observe neutron stars. Instead, there was a fusion motor big enough for a Jinx warliner. In my ship, which I now called *Skydiver,* the drive would produce thirty gees at the safety limit. There was a laser cannon big enough to punch a hole through We Made It's moon. The puppeteer wanted me to feel safe, and now I did, for I could fight and I could run. Especially I could run.

I heard the Laskins' last broadcast through half a dozen times. Their unnamed ship had dropped out of hyperspace a million miles above BVS-1. Gravity warp would have prevented their getting closer in hyperspacc. While her husband was crawling through the access tube for an instrument check, Sonya Laskin had called the Institute of Knowledge. ". . . We can't see it yet, not by naked eye. But we can see where it is. Every time some star or other goes behind it, there's a little ring of light. Just a minute, Peter's ready to use the telescope. . . ."

Then the star's mass had cut the hyperspacial link. It was expected, and nobody had worried—then. Later, the same effect must have stopped them from escaping whatever attacked them into hyperspace.

When would-be rescuers found the ship, only the radar and the cameras were still running. They didn't tell us much. There had been no camera in the cabin. But the forward camera gave us, for one instant, a speed-blurred view of the neutron star. It was a featureless disk the orange color of perfect barbecue coals, if you know someone who can afford to burn wood. This object had been a neutron star a long time.

"There'll be no need to paint the ship," I told the president.

"You should not make such a trip with the walls transparent. You would go insane."

"I'm no flatlander. The mind-wrenching sight of naked space fills me with mild but waning interest. I want to know nothing's sneaking up behind me."

The day before I left, I sat alone in the General Products bar letting the puppeteer bartender make me drinks with his mouth. He did it well. Puppeteers were scattered around the bar in twos and threes, with a couple of men for variety, but the drinking hour had not yet arrived. The place felt empty.

I was pleased with myself. My debts were all paid, not that that would matter where I was going. I would leave with not a minicredit to my name, with nothing but the ship . . .

All told, I was well out of a sticky situation. I hoped I'd like being a rich exile.

I jumped when the newcomer sat down across from me. He was a foreigner, a middle-aged man wearing an expensive night-black business suit and a snow-white asymmetric beard. I let my face freeze and started to get up.

"Sit down, Mr. Shaeffer."

"Why?"

He told me by showing me a blue disk. An Earth government ident.

I looked it over to show I was alert, not because I'd know an ersatz from the real thing.

"My name is Sigmund Ausfaller," said the government man. "I wish to say a few words concerning your assignment on behalf of General Products."

I nodded, not saying anything.

"A record of your verbal contract was sent to us as a matter of course. I noticed some peculiar things about it. Mr. Shaeffer, will you really take such a risk for only five hundred thousand stars?"

"I'm getting twice that."

"But you only keep half of it. The rest goes to pay debts. Then there are taxes . . . But never mind. What occurred to me was that a spaceship is a spaceship, and yours is very well armed and has powerful legs. An admirable fighting ship, if you were moved to sell it."

"But it isn't mine."

"There are those who would not ask. On Canyon, for example, or the Isolationist party of Wunderland."

I said nothing.

"Or, you might be planning a career of piracy. A risky business, piracy, and I don't take the notion seriously."

I hadn't even thought about piracy. But I'd have to give up on Wunderland.

"What I would like to say is this, Mr. Shaeffer. A single entrepreneur, if he were sufficiently dishonest, could do terrible damage to the reputation of all human beings everywhere. Most species find it necessary to police the ethics of their own members, and we are no exception. It occurred to me that you might not take your ship to the neutron star at all; that you would take it elsewhere and sell it. The puppeteers do not make invulnerable war vessels. They are pacifists. Your *Skydiver* is unique.

"Hence I have asked General Products to allow me to install a remote-control bomb in the *Skydiver*. Since it is inside the hull, the hull cannot protect you. I had it installed this afternoon.

"Now, notice! If you have not reported within a week, I will set off the bomb. There are several worlds within a week's hyperspace flight of here, but all recognize the dominion of Earth. If you flee, you must leave your ship within a week, so I hardly think you will land on a nonhabitable world. Clear?"

"Clear."

"If I am wrong, you may take a lie-detector test and prove it. Then you may punch me in the nose, and I will apologize handsomely."

I shook my head. He stood up, bowed, and left me sitting there cold sober.

Four films had been taken from the Laskins' cameras. In the time left to me I ran through them several times, without seeing anything out of the way. If the ship had run through a gas cloud, the impact could have killed the Laskins. At perihelion they were moving at better than half the speed of light. But there would have been friction, and I saw no sign of heating in the films. If something alive had attacked them, the beast was invisible to radar and to an enormous range of light frequencies. If the attitude jets had fired accidentally—I was clutching at straws—the light showed on none of the films.

There would be savage magnetic forces near BVS-1, but that couldn't have done any damage. No such force could penetrate a General Products hull. Neither could heat, except in special bands of radiated light, bands visible to at least one of the puppeteer's alien customers. I hold adverse opinions on the General Products hull, but they all concern the dull anonymity of the design. Or maybe I resent the fact that General Products holds a near-monopoly on spacecraft hulls, and isn't owned by human beings. But if I'd had to trust my life to, say, the Sinclair yacht I'd seen in the drugstore, I'd have chosen jail.

Jail was one of my three choices. But I'd be there for life. Ausfaller would see to that.

Or I could run for it in the *Skydiver*. But no world within reach would have me. If I could find an undiscovered Earth-like world within a week of We Made It . . .

Fat chance. I preferred BVS-1.

I thought that flashing circle of light was getting bigger, but it flashed so seldom, I couldn't be sure. BVS-1 wouldn't show even in my telescope. I gave that up and settled for just waiting.

Waiting, I remembered a long-ago summer spent on Jinx. There were days when, unable to go outside because a dearth of clouds had spread the land with raw blue-white sunlight, we amused ourselves by filling party balloons with tap water and dropping them on the sidewalk from three stories up. They made lovely splash patterns, which dried out too fast. So we put a little ink in each balloon before filling it. Then the patterns stayed.

Sonya Laskin had been in her chair when the chairs collapsed.

Blood samples showed that it was Peter who had struck them from behind, like a water balloon dropped from a great height.

What could get through a General Products hull?

Ten hours to fall.

I unfastened the safety net and went for an inspection tour. The access tunnel was three feet wide, just right to push through in free fall. Below me was the length of the fusion tube; to the left, the laser cannon; to the right, a set of curved side tubes leading to inspection points for the gyros, the batteries and generator, the air plant, the hyperspace shunt motors. All was in order—except me. I was clumsy. My jumps were always too short or too long. There was no room to turn at the stern end, so I had to back fifty feet to a side tube.

Six hours to go, and still I couldn't find the neutron star. Probably I would see it only for an instant, passing at better than half the speed of light. Already my speed must be enormous.

Were the stars turning blue?

Two hours to go—and I was sure they were turning blue. Was my speed that high? Then the stars behind should be red. Machinery blocked the view behind me, so I used the gyros. The ship turned with peculiar sluggishness. And the stars behind were blue, not red. All around me were blue-white stars.

Imagine light falling into a savagely steep gravitational well. It won't accelerate. Light can't move faster than light. But it can gain in energy, in frequency. The light was falling on me, harder and harder as I dropped.

I told the dictaphone about it. That dictaphone was probably the best-protected item on the ship. I had already decided to earn my money by using it, just as if I expected to collect. Privately I wondered just how intense the light would get.

Skydiver had drifted back to vertical, with its axis through the neutron star, but now it faced outward. I'd thought I had the ship stopped horizontally. More clumsiness. I used the gyros. Again the ship moved mushily, until it was halfway through the swing. Then it seemed to fall automatically into place. It was as if the *Skydiver* preferred to have its axis through the neutron star.

I didn't like that.

I tried the maneuver again, and again the *Skydiver* fought back. But this time there was something else. Something was pulling at me.

So I unfastened my safety net—and fell headfirst into the nose.

The pull was light, about a tenth of a gee. It felt more like sinking through honey than falling. I climbed back into my chair, tied myself in with the net, now hanging face down, and turned on the dictaphone. I told my story in such nitpicking detail that my hypothetical listeners could not but doubt my hypothetical sanity. "I think this is what happened to the Laskins," I finished. "If the pull increases, I'll call back."

Think? I never doubted it. This strange, gentle pull was inexplicable. Something inexplicable had killed Peter and Sonya Laskin. Q.E.D.

Around the point where the neutron star must be, the stars were like smeared dots of oilpaint, smeared radially. They glared with an angry, painful light. I hung face down in the net and tried to think.

It was an hour before I was sure. The pull was increasing. And I still had an hour to fall.

Something was pulling on me, but not on the ship.

No, that was nonsense. What could reach out to me through a General Products hull? It must be the other way around. Something was pushing on the ship, pushing it off course.

If it it got worse, I could use the drive to compensate. Meanwhile, the ship was being pushed *away* from BVS-1, which was fine by me.

But if I was wrong, if the ship was not somehow being pushed away from BVS-1, the rocket motor would send the *Skydiver* crashing into eleven miles of neutronium.

And why wasn't the rocket already firing? If the ship was being pushed off course, the autopilot should be fighting back. The accelerometer was in good order. It had looked fine when I made my inspection tour down the access tube.

Could something be pushing on the ship *and* on the accelerometer, but not on me? It came down to the same impossibility: something that could reach through a General Products hull.

To hell with theory, said I to myself, said I. I'm getting out of here. To the dictaphone I said, "The pull has increased dangerously. I'm going to try to alter my orbit."

Of course, once I turned the ship outward and used the rocket, I'd be adding my own acceleration to the X-force. It would be a strain, but I could stand it for a while. If I came within a mile of BVS-1, I'd end like Sonya Laskin.

She must have waited face down in a net like mine, waited without a drive unit, waited while the pressure rose and the net cut into her flesh, waited until the net snapped and dropped her into the nose, to lie crushed and broken until the X-force tore the very chairs loose and dropped them on her.

I hit the gyros.

The gyros weren't strong enough to turn me. I tried it three times. Each time the ship rotated about fifty degrees and hung there, motionless, while the whine of the gyros went up and up. Released, the ship immediately swung back to position. I was nose down to the neutron star, and I was going to stay that way.

Half an hour to fall, and the X-force was over a gee. My sinuses were in agony. My eyes were ripe and ready to fall out. I don't know if I could have stood a cigarette, but I didn't get the chance. My pack of Fortunados had fallen out of my pocket when I dropped into the nose. There it was, four feet beyond my fingers, proof that the X-force acted on other objects besides me. Fascinating.

I couldn't take any more. If it dropped me shrieking into the neutron star, I had to use the drive. And I did. I ran the thrust up until I was approximately in free fall. The blood which had pooled in my extremities went back where it belonged. The gee dial registered one point two gee. I cursed it for a lying robot.

The soft-pack was bobbing around in the nose, and it occurred to me that a little extra nudge on the throttle would bring it to me. I tried it. The pack drifted toward me, and I reached, and like a sentient thing it speeded up to avoid my clutching hand. I snatched at it again as it went past my ear, and again it was moving too fast. That pack was going at a hell of a clip, considering that here I was practically in free fall. It dropped through the door to the relaxation room, still picking up speed, blurred and vanished as it entered the access tube. Seconds later I heard a solid *thump*.

But that was *crazy*. Already the X-force was pulling blood into my face. I pulled my lighter out, held it at arm's length and let go. It fell gently into the nose. But the pack of Fortunados had hit like I'd dropped it from a *building*.

Well.

I nudged the throttle again. The mutter of fusing hydrogen reminded me that if I tried to keep this up all the way, I might well put the General Products hull to its toughest test yet: smashing it into a neutron star at half lightspeed. I could see it now: a transparent hull containing only a few cubic inches of dwarf-star matter wedged into the tip of the nose.

At one point four gee, according to that lying gee dial, the lighter came loose and drifted toward me. I let it go. It was clearly falling when it reached the doorway. I pulled the throttle back. The loss of power jerked me violently forward, but I kept my face turned. The lighter slowed and hesitated at the entrance to the access tube. Decided to go through. I cocked my ears for the sound, then jumped as the whole ship rang like a gong.

And the accelerometer was right at the ship's center of mass. Otherwise the ship's mass would have thrown the needle off. The puppeteers were fiends for ten-decimal-point accuracy.

I favored the dictaphone with a few fast comments, then got to work reprogramming the autopilot. Luckily, what I wanted was simple. The X-force was but an X-force to me, but now I knew how it behaved. I might actually live through this.

The stars were fiercely blue, warped to streaked lines near that special point. I thought I could see it now, very small and dim and red, but it might have been imagination. In twenty minutes I'd be rounding the neutron star. The drive grumbled behind me. In effective free fall, I unfastened the safety net and pushed myself out of the chair.

A gentle push aft — and ghostly hands grasped my legs. Ten pounds of weight hung by my fingers from the back of the chair. The pressure should drop fast. I'd programmed the autopilot to reduce the thrust from two gees to zero during the next two minutes. All I had to do was be at the center of mass, in the access tube, when the thrust went to zero.

Something gripped the ship through a General Products hull. A psychokinetic life form stranded on a sun twelve miles in diameter? But how could anything alive stand such gravity?

Something might be stranded in orbit. There is life in space: outsiders and sailseeds, and maybe others we haven't found yet. For all I knew or cared, BVS-1 itself might be alive. It didn't matter. I knew what the X-force was trying to do. It was trying to pull the ship apart.

There was no pull on my fingers. I pushed aft and landed on the back wall, on bent legs. I knelt over the door, looking aft/down. When free fall came, I pulled myself through and was in the relaxation room looking down/forward into the nose.

Gravity was changing faster than I liked. The X-force was growing as zero hour approached, while the compensating rocket thrust dropped. The X-force tended to pull the ship apart; it was two gee forward at the nose, two gee backward at the tail, and diminished to zero at the center of mass. Or so I hoped. The pack and lighter had behaved as if the force pulling them had increased for every inch they moved sternward.

The back wall was fifteen feet away. I had to jump it with gravity changing in midair. I hit on my hands, bounced away. I'd jumped too late. The region of free fall was moving through the ship like a wave as the thrust dropped. It had left me behind. Now the back wall was "up" to me, and so was the access tube.

Under something less than half a gee, I jumped for the access tube. For one long moment I stared into the three-foot tunnel, stopped in midair and already beginning to fall back, as I realized that there was nothing to hang on to. Then I stuck my hands in the tube and spread them against the sides. It was all I needed. I levered myself up and started to crawl.

The dictaphone was fifty feet below, utterly unreachable. If I had anything more to say to General Products, I'd have to say it in person. Maybe I'd get the chance. Because I knew what force was trying to tear the ship apart.

It was the tide.

The motor was off, and I was at the ship's midpoint. My spread-eagled position was getting uncomfortable. It was four minutes to perihelion.

Something creaked in the cabin below me. I couldn't see what it was, but I could clearly see a red point glaring among blue radial lines, like a lantern at the bottom of a well. To the sides, between the fusion tube and the tanks and other equipment, the blue stars glared at me with a light that was almost violet. I was afraid to look too long. I actually thought they might blind me.

There must have been hundreds of gravities in the cabin. I could even feel the pressure change. The air was thin at this height, one hundred and fifty feet above the control room.

And now, almost suddenly, the red dot was more than a dot. My time was up. A red disk leapt up at me; the ship swung around me; I gasped and shut my eyes tight. Giants' hands gripped my arms and legs and head, gently but with great firmness, and tried to pull me in two. In that moment it came to me that Peter Laskin had died like this. He'd made the same guesses I had, and he'd tried to hide in the access tube. But he'd slipped . . . as I was slipping . . . From the control room came a multiple shriek of tearing metal. I tried to dig my feet into the hard tube walls. Somehow they held.

When I got my eyes open the red dot was shrinking into nothing.

The puppeteer president insisted I be put in a hospital for observation. I didn't fight the idea. My face and hands were flaming red, with blisters rising, and I ached as though I'd been beaten. Rest and tender loving care, that's what I wanted.

I was floating between a pair of sleeping plates, hideously uncomfortable, when the nurse came to announce a visitor. I knew who it was from her peculiar expression.

"What can get through a General Products hull?" I asked it.

"I hoped you would tell me." The president rested on its single back leg, holding a stick that gave off green incense-smelling smoke.

"And so I will. Gravity."

"Do not play with me, Beowulf Shaeffer. This matter is vital."

"I'm not playing. Does your world have a moon?"

"That information is classified." The puppeteers are cowards. Nobody knows where they come from, and nobody is likely to find out.

"Do you know what happens when a moon gets too close to its primary?"

"It falls apart."

"Why?"

"I do not know."

"Tides."

"What is a tide?"

Oho, said I to myself, said I. "I'm going to try to tell you. The Earth's moon is almost two thousand miles in diameter and does not rotate with respect to Earth. I want you to pick two rocks on the moon, one at the point nearest the Earth, one at the point farthest away."

"Very well."

"Now, isn't it obvious that if those rocks were left to themselves, they'd fall away from each other? They're in two different orbits, mind you, concentric orbits, one almost two thousand miles outside the other. Yet those rocks are forced to move at the same orbital speed."

"The one outside is moving faster."

"Good point. So there *is* a force trying to pull the moon apart. Gravity holds it together. Bring the moon close enough to Earth, and those two rocks would simply float away."

"I see. Then this 'tide' tried to pull your ship apart. It was powerful enough in the lifesystem of the Institute ship to pull the acceleration chairs out of their mounts."

"And to crush a human being. Picture it. The ship's nose was just seven miles from the center of BVS-1. The tail was three hundred feet farther out. Left to themselves, they'd have gone in completely different orbits. My head and feet tried to do the same thing when I got close enough."

"I see. Are you molting?"

"What?"

"I notice you are losing your outer integument in spots."

"Oh, *that*. I got a bad sunburn from exposure to starlight. It's not important."

Two heads stared at each other for an eyeblink. A shrug? The puppeteer said, "We have deposited the residue of your pay with the Bank of We Made It. One Sigmund Ausfaller, human, has frozen the account until your taxes are computed."

"Figures."

"If you will talk to reporters now, explaining what happened to the Institute ship, we will pay you ten thousand stars. We will pay cash so that you may use it immediately. It is urgent. There have been rumors."

"Bring 'em in." As an afterthought I added, "I can also tell them that your world is moonless. That should be good for a footnote somewhere."

"I do not understand." But two long necks had drawn back, and the puppeteer was watching me like a pair of pythons.

"You'd know what a tide was if you had a moon. You couldn't avoid it."

"Would you be interested in —"

"A million stars? I'd be fascinated. I'll even sign a contract if it states what we're hiding. How do *you* like being blackmailed for a change?"

Commentary

Premise: The irresistible force meets the immovable object; OR *gravity near a neutron star would be intense enough to generate catastrophic tidal pull on anything orbiting it.*

This is a hard-science story, but wonderfully humanized.

Suppose that you were in the author's position before the story was written. You've worked out an interesting theory of how gravity would operate near a neutron star, in spite of the fact that neutron stars are themselves theoretical. Where do you go from there?

First, obviously, you need a neutron star to demonstrate these gravity effects: pages and pages of mathematical calculations don't make fun reading. You need an actual neutron star that the reader can *watch*, effects the reader can *see*, to free your narrative from the tons of deadly explanation that would otherwise be required. Since no neutron star has yet been observed in our real universe (at the time of the story's writing), you need to invent a reality in which at least one demonstrably exists. *Voilà*: BVS-1. Give the theory a body. That's step one.

You could send a spaceship to explore BVS-1, discover the odd gravity, and end the story there. But it wouldn't be a very interesting story; had the *Nostromo* observed the insectoid life form in the derelict ship they find on LV 426 and then just gone home with their report and without a deadly stowaway, *Alien* would have been a pretty dull story.

So you have the freak gravity destroy the ship. More interesting, but decidedly downbeat. You up the stakes by making the ship theoretically indestructible: a No. 2 General Products hull modified for exploration and observation. And you don't destroy the ship— merely everybody aboard.

Up the odds. Make somebody's life depend on the discovery and the outcome. That's step two.

Now you've turned your story into a puzzle: not merely recounting the dry facts of gravity fields near a neutron star, but trying to solve the mystery of "what could get through a General Products hull" which no harmful force has ever been known to penetrate.

Set the irresistible force dead against the immovable object. See how much more interesting your story is getting already?

If you have a mystery, it helps to focus the investigation through a detective. And to give the detective a stake in finding out the answer, make his life depend on it. Give the character a preposterous name like Beowulf Shaeffer so that the reader will take him seriously, but not too seriously. Keep strictly to his viewpoint to heighten the tension and make us concerned about his danger. Make Shaeffer a down-and-out pilot, and have his puppeteer employer blackmail him with unpaid debts to coerce him into taking such a dreadful assignment. And have Shaeffer further blackmailed by a bomb which will be set off in a week, so that he can't prudently go somewhere—anywhere—in his specially modified new ship except into orbit around that dire neutron star. This will make him refreshingly unheroic and reluctant: not a scientist or an explorer but an Ordinary Joe willing to try *anything* to save his own skin. Someone we'll like and be rooting for.

Do you begin to see how, from an initial general concept, the story becomes more specific as it develops? See how the stakes are raised, how the main character is made an appealing person with *everything* on the line, so that finding the answer is, to him, a matter of life and death? Suspense and reader involvement are intensified and increased by every refinement that forces Shaeffer toward the Moment of Truth: when what "got" the Laskins tries to get him.

And stop to think: why are the Laskins in the story to begin with? Why not send Shaeffer out to take humanity's first close look at a neutron star (as the Laskins do) and have the rest of the story proceed just as it does from that point? The theory about gravity would have come out just as well, had the story been constructed that way. What would have been lost?

Horror writers and mystery writers know that to intensify a threat in the present, make it already have occurred at least once in the past with devastating results. Focus on the monster's *second* victim, not its first; have your murder early in the story so that the story's not only looking back, to explain that death, but forward to identify the murderer *before he/she can kill again* as will inevitably happen if the murderer isn't stopped. Science fiction writers can use the same tactic. Because the qualified and intelligent married couple, Sonya and Peter Laskin, died with such messiness that their blood is still a visible film all over their ship's cockpit, the threat to Shaeffer is undoubted.

The Laskins died. The reader therefore knows, from the beginning, that Shaeffer's death is an acute possibility.

A sudden death threat in the middle of a story isn't as breathlessly suspenseful as a death threat which exists from the very start and which each of the story's events brings steadily nearer.

That's why the story begins as it does, *in medias res*: in the middle of things, with Shaeffer already confronting the neutron star. The story could have begun later, with the long flashback section on how Shaeffer was recruited, hired, and coerced by the puppeteer worried about bad publicity if doubt were cast on the absolute safety of the drab but efficient General Products hulls. That section could have been made present action, the story then following sequentially thereafter. But the reader's sense of threat would not have been as great. Shaeffer wouldn't have been in immediate danger of death from the first moment of the story. And the story wouldn't have had so good a narrative "hook" to compel the reader to want to find out what's going to happen.

Shaeffer meets Medusa and returns to tell the tale of how gravity, acting on a 300-foot-long ship, tries to pull the ship's ends away from the middle by something resembling centrifugal force. The scientific speculation is stated. But that's not the story's end, which again is given a twist, a surprise. From the puppeteer's reactions to Shaeffer's explanation, Shaeffer deduces that the puppeteers' secret home planet must lack a moon and, through blackmail, is able to make a healthy profit, after all, on the deal. Shaeffer ends as he began: an engaging rogue.

This is a hard-science story, but one constructed and told with a whole array of narrative devices that are part of any good storyteller's grab-bag of craft options. Studying how Niven moved from concept to cliff-hanger can help you bring your own abstract premises to compellingly human life.

Science fiction, like literature generally, comes in many varieties, and any given person is sure to find that some varieties are less appealing to him (or her) than others are.

Thus, Pat Cadigan's "Rock On" is very much a story of the 1980s. It is of a variety that has come to be called "cyberpunk," in the same sense (I suppose) that some popular music is called "punk rock."

Such stories use the street language, slang and metaphors of the 1980s and seem to be related to the rock-and-drug subculture of the present day.

I, myself, aged survivor of an older time that I am, find myself out of sympathy with cyberpunk. It doesn't mean such stories are bad; on the contrary, they can be very good. It's just that, for purely subjective reasons, I neither enjoy reading them, nor would I dream of trying to write them.

You, too, may have your subjective bents, and the importance is this: If you don't like to read a particular type of science fiction, you are very likely to find yourself unable to write that particular type with any degree of expertise. Don't break your heart trying to do what you don't enjoy just because it is fashionable; the chances of success would be minimal.

— Isaac Asimov

Rock On

Pat Cadigan

Rain woke me. I thought, shit, here I am, Lady Rain-in-the-Face, because that's where it was hitting, right in the old face. Sat up and saw I was still on Newbury Street. See beautiful downtown Boston. Was Newbury Street downtown? In the middle of the night, did it matter? No, it did not. And not a soul in sight. Like everybody said, let's get Gina drunk and while she's passed out, we'll all move to Vermont. Do I love New England? A great place to live, but you wouldn't want to visit here.

I smeared my hair out of my eyes and wondered if anyone was looking for me now. Hey, anybody shy a forty-year-old rock 'n' roll sinner?

I scuttled into the doorway of one of those quaint old buildings where there was a shop with the entrance below ground level. A little awning kept the rain off but pissed water down in a maddening beat. Wrung the water out of my wrap pants and my hair and just sat being damp. Cold, too, I guess, but I didn't feel that so much.

Sat a long time with my chin on my knees: you know, it made me feel like a kid again. When I started nodding my head, I began to pick up on something. Just primal but I tap into that amazing well. Man-O-War, if you could see me now. By the time the blueboys found me, I was rocking pretty good.

And that was the punchline. I'd never tried to get up and leave, but if I had, I'd have found I was locked into place in a sticky field. Made to catch the b&e kids in the act until the blueboys could get around to coming out and getting them. I'd been sitting in a trap and digging it. The story of my life.

They were nice to me. Led me, read me, dried me out. Fined me a hundred, sent me on my way in time for breakfast.

Awful time to see and be seen, righteous awful. For the first three hours after you get up, people can tell whether you've got a broken heart or not. The solution is, either you get up *real* early so your camouflage is in place by the time everybody else is out, or you don't go to bed. Don't go to bed ought to work all the time, but it doesn't. Sometimes when you don't go to bed, people can see whether you've got a broken heart all day long. I schlepped it, searching for an uncrowded breakfast bar and not looking at anyone who was looking at me. But I had this urge to stop random pedestrians and say, Yeah, yeah, it's true, but it was rock 'n' roll broke my poor old heart, not a person, don't cry for me or I'll pop your chocks.

I went around and up and down and all over until I found Tremont Street. It had been the pounder with that group from the Detroit Crater—the name was gone but the malady lingered on—anyway, him; he'd been the one told me Tremont had the best breakfast bars in the world, especially when you were coming off a bottle drunk you couldn't remember.

When the c'muters cleared out some, I found a space at a Greek hole in the wall. We shut down 10:30 A.M. sharp, get the hell out when you're done, counter service only, take it or shake it. I like a place with Attitude. I folded a seat down and asked for coffee and a feta cheese omelet. Came with home fries from the home fries mountain in a corner of the grill (no microwave *garbazhe,* hoo-ray). They shot my retinas before they even brought my coffee, and while I was pouring the cream, they checked my credit. Was that badass? It was badass. Did I care? I did not. No waste, no machines when a human could do it, and real food, none of this edible polyester that slips clear through you so you can stay looking like a famine victim, my deah.

They came in when I was half finished with the omelet. Went all night by the look and sound of them, but I didn't check their faces for broken hearts. Made me nervous but I thought, well, they're tired; who's going to notice this old lady? Nobody.

Wrong again. I became visible to them right after they got their retinas shot. Seventeen-year-old boy with tattooed cheeks and a forked tongue leaned forward and hissed like a snake.

"Sssssssinner."

The other four with him perked right up. "Where?" "Whose?" "In here?"

"Rock 'n' roll sssssssinner."

The lady identified me. She bore much resemblance to nobody at all, and if she had a heart it wasn't even sprained a little. With a sinner, she was probably Madame Magnifica. "Gina," she said, with all confidence.

My left eye tic'd. Oh, please. Feta cheese on my knees. What the hell, I thought, I'll nod, they'll nod, I'll eat, I'll go. And then somebody whispered the word, *reward*.

I dropped my fork and ran.

Safe enough, I figured. Were they all going to chase me before they got their Greek breakfasts? No, they were not. They sent the lady after me.

She was much the younger, and she tackled me in the middle of a crosswalk when the light changed. A car hopped over us, its undercarriage just ruffling the top of her hard copper hair.

"Just come back and finish your omelet. Or we'll buy you another."

"No."

She yanked me up and pulled me out of the street. "Come on." People were staring, but Tremont's full of theaters. You see that here, live theater; you can still get it. She put a bring-along on my wrist and brought me along, back to the breakfast bar, where they'd sold the rest of my omelet at a discount to a bum. The lady and her group made room for me among themselves and brought me another cup of coffee.

"How can you eat and drink with a forked tongue?" I asked Tattooed Cheeks. He showed me. A little appliance underneath, like a *zipper*. The Featherweight to the left of the big boy on the lady's other side leaned over and frowned at me.

"Give us one good reason why we shouldn't turn you in for Man-O-War's reward."

I shook my head. "I'm through. This sinner's been absolved."

"You're legally bound by contract," said the lady. "But we could c'noodle something. Buy Man-O-War out, sue on your behalf for non-fulfillment. We're Misbegotten. Oley." She pointed at herself. "Pidge." That was the silent type next to her. "Percy." The big boy. "Krait." Mr. Tongue. "Gus." Featherweight. "We'll take care of you."

I shook my head again. "If you're going to turn me in, turn me in and collect. The credit ought to buy you the best sinner ever there was."

"We can be good to you."

"I don't have it anymore. It's gone. All my rock 'n' roll sins have been forgiven."

"Untrue," said the big boy. Automatically, I started to picture on him and shut it down hard. "Man-O-War would have thrown you out if it were gone. You wouldn't have to run."

"I didn't want to tell him. Leave me alone. I just want to go and sin no more, see? Play with yourselves, I'm not helping." I grabbed the counter with both hands and held on. So what were they going to do, pop me one and carry me off?

As a matter of fact, they did.

In the beginning, I thought, and the echo effect was stupendous. *In the beginning . . . the beginning . . . the beginning . . . .*

In the beginning, the sinner was not human. I know because I'm old enough to remember.

They were all there, little more than phantoms. Misbegotten. Where do they get those names? I'm old enough to remember. Oingo-Boingo and Bow-Wow-Wow. Forty, did I say? Oooh, just a little past, a little close to a lot. Old rockers never die, they just keep rocking on. I never saw The Who; Moon was dead before I was born. But I remember, barely old enough to stand, rocking in my mother's arms while thousands screamed and clapped and danced in their seats. *Start me up . . . if you start me up, I'll never stop . . .* 763 Strings did a rendition for elevator and dentist's office, I remember that, too. And that wasn't the worst of it.

They hung on the memories, pulling more from me, turning me inside out. *Are you experienced?* On a record of my father's because he'd died too, before my parents even met, and nobody else ever dared ask that question. *Are you experienced? . . . Well, I am.*

(Well, *I* am.)

Five against one and I couldn't push them away. Only, can you call it rape when you know you're going to like it? Well, if I couldn't get away, then I'd give them the ride of their lives. *Jerkin' Crocus didn't kill me but she sure came near. . . .*

The big boy faded in first, big and wild and too much badass to him. I reached out, held him tight, showing him. The beat from the night in the rain, I gave it to him, fed it to his heart and made him live it. Then came the lady, putting down the bass theme. She jittered, but mostly in the right places.

Now the Krait, and he was slithering around the sound, in and out. Never mind the tattooed cheeks, he wasn't just flash for the fools. He knew; you wouldn't have thought it, but he knew.

Featherweight and the silent type, melody and first harmony. Bad. Featherweight was a disaster, didn't know where to go or what to do when he got there, but he was pitching ahead like the S.S. *Suicide.*

Christ. If they had to rape me, couldn't they have provided someone upright? The other four kept on, refusing to lose it, and I would have to make the best of it for all of us. Derivative, unoriginal — Featherweight did not rock. It was a crime, but all I could do was take them and shake them. Rock gods in the hands of an angry sinner.

They were never better. Small change getting a glimpse of what it was like to be big bucks. Hadn't been for Featherweight, they might have gotten all the way there. More groups now than ever there was, all of them sure that if they just got the right sinner with them, they'd rock the moon down out of the sky.

We maybe vibrated it a little before we were done. Poor old Featherweight.

I gave them better than they deserved, and they knew that too. So when I begged out, they showed me respect at last and went. Their techies were gentle with me, taking the plugs from my head, my poor old throbbing abused brokenhearted sinning head, and covered up the sockets. I had to sleep and they let me. I hear the man say, "That's a take, righteously. We'll rush it into distribution. Where in *hell* did you find that sinner?"

"Synthesizer," I muttered, already asleep. "The actual word, my boy, is synthesizer."

Crazy old dreams. I was back with Man-O-War in the big CA, leaving him again, and it was mostly as it happened, but you know dreams. His living room was half outdoors, half indoors, the walls all busted out. You know dreams; I didn't think it was strange.

Man-O-War was mostly undressed, like he'd forgotten to finish. Oh, that *never* happened. Man-O-War forget a sequin or a bead? He loved to act it out, just like the Krait.

"No more," I was saying, and he was saying, "But you don't know anything else, you shitting?" Nobody in the big CA kids, they all shit; loose juice.

"Your contract goes another two and I get the option, I always get the option. And you love it, Gina, you know that, you're no good without it."

And then it was flashback time and I was in the pod with all my sockets plugged, rocking Man-O-War through the wires, giving him the meat and bone that made him Man-O-War and the machines picking it up, sound and vision, so all the tube babies all around the world could play it on their screens whenever they wanted. Forget the road, forget the shows, too much trouble, and it wasn't like the tapes, not as exciting, even with the biggest FX, lasers, spaceships, explosions, no good. And the tapes weren't as good as the stuff in the head, rock 'n' roll visions straight from the brain. No hours of setup and hours more doctoring in the lab. But you had to get everyone in the group dreaming the same way. You needed a synthesis, and for that you got a synthesizer, not the old kind, the musical instrument, but something — somebody — to channel your group through, to bump up their tube-fed little souls, to rock them and roll them the way they couldn't do themselves. And anyone could be a rock 'n' roll hero then. Anyone!

In the end, they didn't have to play instruments unless they really wanted to, and why bother? Let the synthesizer take their imaginings and boost them up to Mount Olympus.

Synthesizer. Synner. Sinner.

Not just anyone can do that, sin for rock 'n' roll. I can.

But it's not the same as jumping all night to some bar band nobody knows yet. . . . Man-O-War and his blown-out living room came back, and he said, "You rocked the walls right out of my house. I'll never let you go."

And I said, "I'm gone."

Then I was out, going fast at first because I thought he'd be hot behind me. But I must have lost him and then somebody grabbed my ankle.

Featherweight had a tray, he was Mr. Nursie-Angel-of-Mercy. Nudged the foot of the bed with his knee, and it sat me up slow. She rises from the grave, you can't keep a good sinner down.

"Here." He set the tray over my lap, pulled up a chair. Some kind of thick soup in a bowl he'd given me, with veg wafers to break up and put in. "Thought you'd want something soft and easy." He put his left foot up on his right leg and had a good look at it. "I *never* been rocked like that before."

"You don't have it, no matter who rocks you ever in this world. Cut and run, go into management. The *big* Big Money's in management."

He snacked on his thumbnail. "Can you always tell?"

"If the Stones came back tomorrow, you couldn't even tap your toes."

"What if you took my place?"

"I'm a sinner, not a clown. You can't sin and do the dance. It's been tried."

"*You* could do it. If anyone could."

"No."

His stringy cornsilk fell over his face and he tossed it back. "Eat your soup. They want to go again shortly."

"No." I touched my lower lip, thickened to sausage size. "I won't sin for Man-O-War and I won't sin for you. You want to pop me one again, go to. Shake a socket loose, give me aphasia."

So he left and came back with a whole bunch of them, techies and do-kids, and they poured the soup down my throat and gave me a poke and carried me out to the pod so I could make Misbegotten this year's firestorm.

I knew as soon as the first tape got out, Man-O-War would pick up the scent. They were already starting the machine to get me away from him. And they kept me good in the room—where their old sinner had done penance, the lady told me. Their sinner came to see me, too. I thought, poison dripping from his fangs, death threats. But he was just a guy about my age with a lot of hair to hide his sockets (I never bothered, didn't care if they showed). Just came to pay his respects, how'd I ever learn to rock the way I did?

Fool.

They kept me good in the room. Drunks when I wanted them and a poke to get sober again, a poke for vitamins, a poke to lose the bad dreams. Poke, poke, pig in a poke. I had tracks like the old B&O, and they didn't even know what I meant by that. They lost Featherweight, got themselves someone a little more righteous, someone who could go with it and work out, sixteen-year-old snip girl with a face like a praying mantis. But she rocked and they rocked and we all rocked until Man-O-War came to take me home.

Strutted into my room in full plumage with his hair all fanned out (hiding the sockets) and said, "Did you want to press charges, Gina darling?"

Well, they fought it out over my bed. When Misbegotten said I was theirs now, Man-O-War smiled and said, "Yeah, and I bought *you*. You're *all* mine now, you *and* your sinner. My sinner." That was truth. Man-O-War had his conglomerate start to buy Misbegotten right after the first tape came out. Deal all done by the time we'd finished the third one, and they never knew. Conglomerates buy and sell all the time. Everybody was in trouble but Man-O-War. And me, he said. He made them all leave and sat down on my bed to re-lay claim to me.

"Gina." Ever see honey poured over the edge of a sawtooth blade? Ever hear it? He couldn't sing without hurting someone bad and he couldn't dance, but inside, he rocked. If I rocked him.

"I don't want to be a sinner, not for you or anyone."

"It'll all look different when I get you back to Cee-Ay."

"I want to go to a cheesy bar and boogie my brains till they leak out the sockets."

"No more, darling. That was why you came here, wasn't it? But all the bars are gone and all the bands. Last call was years ago; it's all up here now. All up here." He tapped his temple. "You're an old lady, no matter how much I spend keeping your bod young. And don't I give you everything? And didn't you say I had it?"

"It's not the same. It wasn't meant to be put on a tube for people to *watch*."

"But it's not as though rock 'n' roll is dead, lover."

"You're killing it."

"Not me. You're trying to bury it alive. But I'll keep you going for a long, long time."

"I'll get away again. You'll either rock 'n' roll on your own or give it up, but you won't be taking it out of me any more. This ain't my way, it ain't my time. Like the man said, 'I don't live today.' "

Man-O-War grinned. "And like the other man said, 'Rock 'n' roll never forgets.' "

He called in his do-kids and took me home.

Commentary

Premise: Instead of musical synthesizers, rock and roll metamorphoses to use human synthesizers, "sinners," who amplify and coordinate the musical and rhythmic impulses of others by technological means.

This is a story in the relatively new subgenre generally called "cyberpunk," which features down-and-out characters who live most vividly as biological extensions of technology. They plug directly into computers. Often their realities are, in whole or in part, computer constructs—at least the parts that interest them most tend to be. The distinctive thing about these cyborgs is often the raunchy, nihilistic, and generally run-down nature of their social, physical, and mental landscape. It makes machine-life look clean and uncluttered by comparison. Plugged in, life becomes emotionally charged and intense.

Burn-out, down and dirty: hence, cyber*punk*.

This story, like several in this collection, begins with apparent normality and doesn't disclose its premise until near the middle. This has the effect of making the characters power the premise, rather than the other way around, although the premise may well have served as the writer's reason for inventing this particular set of characters to enact it.

In a lot of science fiction, the interest isn't primarily in the technology itself but in the impact of the technology on people. It's the "what if?" *What if* people could plug into their skulls an electrical jack that directly stimulated the pleasure centers of the brain—put a man in a chair, with a short extension cord, and would he starve and/or die of thirst rather than get up, unplug, and go to the sink or the refrigerator? That's the premise of Larry Niven's "Death by Ecstasy." That kind of *what if* story shows technology at the testing point—not a chronicle of how the gadget was invented or developed, but a dramatization of the crisis point when someone's life comes to depend on it or be changed by it in a very immediate way. What the technology has the potential of *doing to one specific person.*

Specifically, this story shows how Gina, a "sinner," runs from Man-O-War, the rock superstar who holds her contract, and is captured by a wanna-be group which she raises to prominence and which, in turn, is bought up by Man-O-War, so that Gina's attempted escape and rebellion fail. That's the plot. But the subtext is immersed in the nature of music, specifically rock and roll. The story presents, through Gina, the question whether music is something to be consumed, packaged, or something that rightfully has to be done, lived. That technological dilemma is a contemporary one, intensified but not begun with the advent of recorded sound. People currently argue whether recorded jazz *is* jazz, by definition. How live is "live on tape"?

As a result, for all its invented jargon ("sticky field"—an electronic tractor field to catch and hold would-be burglars; "pod"—a cross-connected sensory hookup via computer, controlled by the "sinner"; "sockets"—implanted connections for computer cables), the story has a surprisingly contemporary feel which is part of what makes the beginning so seductive. Dirty urban landscape—Boston—could be ours. Drunk woman, crude language—could be now. Cops rousting a vagrant—anywhere. Broken-hearted people trying not to admit their pain—everywhere. Not until we hear "they shot my retinas before they even brought my coffee," do we know that this blue lady, this "forty-year-old rock 'n' roll sinner" is a refugee from, and in, a world somewhere on down the timeline.

The story doesn't overpower us with its strangeness, especially not at first. It brings on Gina—her human misery, toughness, and characteristic musical preoccupations—and makes us care about her *first* before getting into the hardware of it all, or throwing at us such distinctive local color as a guy sporting a forked tongue with a zipper on the bottom.

This focus on the life lived rather than on the hardware, on perception rather than on the detailed mechanics of how that perception is achieved, has been the abiding concern of such writers as Theodore Sturgeon (*More Than Human*), Ursula LeGuin (*The Left Hand of Darkness*), and Anne McCaffrey (*The Ship Who Sang*). "Cyberpunk" differs from mainstream science fiction (if that's not a contradiction in terms) more in landscape and mood than in approach. This most techie of subgenres, premised on people plugging into and blending their being with machines, is paradoxically one of the least hardware-oriented; perhaps in compensation. It's the *punk*, not the *cyber*, that makes the stories in this subgenre memorable . . . although it helps to have done your homework and have your basic computerese at least straight enough not to embarrass the real techies among your readers.

This story, perhaps more than any other in this collection, emphasizes that the science in science fiction doesn't always come out of a physics or astrophysics text. Good psychology will do.

For the rest, improvise. That's what makes it rock 'n' roll.

Science fiction, like all other forms of literature, can deal primarily with adventure and action. Carried to an extreme as, for instance, in the novels of E. E. Smith, we have the "superscience story" which is considered passé and is rarely written these days.

At lesser extremes, though, we have adventure stories dealing with interplanetary or interstellar invasions and wars.

I have had trouble with such things. During my first few years as a science fiction writer, World War II was raging and I responded, very naturally, by writing stories in which wars were raging on a still larger scale as, for instance, in my early "Foundation" stories. However, once the atomic bomb fell on Hiroshima in 1945, I sobered suddenly. The war motif in my stories faded and finally stopped. I don't consider war a sane option any longer.

However, to each his own. Robert Heinlein's Starship Troopers, *published in 1959, was unbelievably warlike for it came at the height of America's apparent domination of the world by its unexampled military and economic strength, so that war seemed something we would surely win and therefore it was all fun and games.*

Relative American strength in the 1980s is far weaker than it once was, despite Reagan's "buildup" (or perhaps because of it) but war remains a popular motif in defiance of sanity. But if it must be done, let it be done well.

—Isaac Asimov

Transstar

Raymond E. Banks

The small group of Earth colonists stood on a hill, tense and expectant, as their leader advanced. He walked slowly away from the huddled mob, holding up his gun. You could hear the mother weep.

I stood at ease to one side, as was proper. I knew what would happen, because I was from Transstar. We have been taught to understand the inevitable.

The child came running out of the woods. I noted that they were not the woods of Earth, though they were brown. Nor was the grass the grass of Earth, though it was green.

The child cried, "Mother!" The leader raised his gun and shot it.

Even though I understood that the child was no longer a "him" and had become an "it" since falling into the hands of the aliens, I felt a tremor underneath my conditioning. In Transstar you are taught that the conditioning is a sheath, pliable but breakable; you do not put all faith in it.

Now the important thing was the reaction of the small group of Earth colonists.

They had seen the heartbreaking inevitable. They knew with the logic of their minds that the boy had to die. On this planet there were two races, two kinds of life: the eaber and the Earthmen. The eaber would lure a child away if they could and see to its infection, returning it to the Earth colony.

It was a good trick the first time or two, and for the love of their children three thousand lives had been lost, two starting colonies wiped out. This third colony had to succeed. I suspected that was why Transstar sent me here.

The leader turned sadly towards his colonists. A man advanced: "A burial! It is safe to bury!"

"It is not safe to bury," said the leader.

The man raised his arm. The leader hesitated and lost both his leadership and his life, because the half-maddened parent shot him in the chest . . .

Rackrill came to my Transstar ship. "You stood there," he said, eyes accusing. "You sit here now. You let the eaber do these things to us — yet you're from Transstar, representing the incredible power of the Sol system. Why?"

"Transstar was formed to handle star-sized situations," I replied. "So far this colony is meeting only the problems of a local situation."

"Local situation!" He laughed bitterly. "I'm the third mayor in three weeks."

"There'll be no more children lost to the eaber," I said.

"That's for certain sure," he said, "but Transstar might lose one of its representatives if it doesn't help us in our fight against the eaber. Our colony is sickened to watch you with your magnificent starship and your empire of power, standing by while we suffer."

"I am sorry."

He raised his hands and stepped towards me, but an orange light hummed from the walls. He looked surprised. He dropped his hands.

"Now that you've properly cursed me, tell me the real reason for your visit, Mr. Mayor," I said, flicking the protective button off.

He eased into his chair wearily. It was a great planet to take the starch out of the leaders.

"We had a visit from the eaber." He went on talking eagerly. The eaber had picked this planet, Point Everready, as an advance planet-city for their own culture. They would kill the Earth colony if it didn't leave. Rackrill had told them about Transstar, about me. That I represented the total war capacity of the solar system. That I was in instantaneous touch with Transstar Prime, near Mars, and that behind me stood a million space ships and countless prime fighting men with weapons of power and vigor that could pulverize the eaber to dust. That I was there to see that the Earth colony survived.

"This is only partly true," I said. "I am here to see *whether* an Earth colony can survive."

Anyway, Rackrill had gotten the eaber stirred up. They were coming to see me. Okay?

"I am Transstar," I said. "I can only observe, not interfere."

He got mad again, but there was really no more to say. He left, going from the marvelous machinery of my ship back to the crudeness of the village. I felt sorry for him and his people and wished I could reassure him.

I could not.

Yet somewhere back at Transstar Prime there was more than ordinary interest in Point Everready. I wondered, as every Transstar agent must, how far Transstar would go on this project. Few Transstar men have ordered Condition Prime Total Red. Condition Prime Total Red is the complete amassing and release of our total war-making capacity directed at one enemy in one place at one time. You don't get a CPTR more than once in decades; men in Transstar have served a lifetime and never directed one.

This is good, because CPTR is devastating in cost, machines, and men. It is the most jealously guarded prerogative of the Transstar system, which is in itself merely a check-and-report to keep track of all Earth colonies spread out among the stars.

I looked at my condition panel. It glowed an off-white on the neat starship wall. Condition white, nothing unusual; the same color I had stared at for five years as a full agent and fifteen years before that as both associate and assistant, learning the Transstar operation.

I thought about the dead boy, sleeping now on the grasses of Everready, as I made my daily report, pricking a card with three simple marks, feeding it to the transmitter which reported back to Prime. It seemed unfair, even with all my years of Transstar conditioning, that a boy would only deserve three pinpricks in a daily report. The human race had not been standing behind him.

It probably would not stand behind this colony.

For that matter, though I had the safety of this rather expensive starship, the human race would probably not stand behind *me*, if the eaber turned out to be tough aliens. Many an agent has died in local or regional situations.

I drank a cup of tea, but the warm drink didn't help. Somehow these last years I had become more emotional. It was hard to be a Transstar agent—for, by the time you learned how, you were too knowing in the ways of space to keep that prep school enthusiasm. I remembered the men who had lived and the men who had died as I drank my tea and felt sad.

Towards midnight the colonists sent scout ships up, as ordered by Rackrill. They were met by an equal number of eaber scout ships.

The patrol fight was dull, with drones being chopped off by both sides. Nothing decisive. The eaber were good. I wondered if they also had a Transstar somewhere back at their home planet, a totality of force that might match Condition Prime Total Red, and result in a stand-off fight. This had never happened in history. Someday we might even find somebody better than CPTR.

At that instant expansion to the stars would stop, I knew.

Whatever I thought about the eaber at long distance, I'd have a chance to learn more. A couple of them were now approaching my ship.

They were sentient life. They were neither monsters nor particularly Earthlike. It was this balance of like-unlike that gave me the beginnings of a shudder under my conditioning.

The reddish one advanced into my cabin. "Euben," he said. He made a motion of turning with his hands, tapered fingers spread. A surge of sickness tickled in me, rushed up to a nerve agony. I just had time to relax and let the raping power of his ray, or whatever it was, knock me out into a welcome darkness. A nonconditioned man would have screamed and writhed on the floor, fighting the overpowering darkness. I rushed with it, gave in to it.

Presently there was a gentle bird-twitter. I sat up; Euben's power turned off. He laughed down at me.

"Some Earth-power, some potency," he said, gesturing at my control panel. I had, indeed, pushed my orange safety button, which should have frozen him immobile as it had Rackrill. It had no effect on him or his friend.

I tried to get up but was as weak and shaking as an old man. So I sat there.

"You are the protector to the Earthians," he said.

"No, Euben. I am merely here to observe."

"You'll observe them made extinct, Watcher," he said. "This is the perimeter of eaber. We want this planet ourselves."

"That remains to be seen," I said, finally rising stiffly and plopping into my chair. I turned off the useless orange button.

Euben roamed his eyes around the ship. "Better than your colony has. You are special."

"I am special," I said.

"They say you represent great power," he said.

"That is true."

"We have waited a long time to see this power," said Euben. "We have exterminated two of your colonies, and have not seen it."

"If this is all of eaber, it isn't very large," I said. "This planet could hardly hold a hundred thousand."

"I said we were perimeter. Behind us, thousands of planets. Trillions of eaber. There is nothing like us in the universe."

"We've heard that before."

This time he brought up two hands, to begin his twirling. I reacted with a hypnosis block, which shunted off all my natural functions for a micro-second (with the help of the plate I was standing on). The pain was much less. He merely brought me to my knees.

"Ah, you are not totally feeble," he said. "Still I make you bow to me with the twisting of my bare hands in the air."

"Yes. But Earthmen do not greet new races with tricks and talk like two small boys bragging about how tough their older brothers are," I said. "I am not here to brag tough. I am here to observe."

"If you don't like what you observe?"

"Perhaps we will do something about it. Perhaps not."

He threw back his head and laughed. "You will die, die, die," he said. "Watch this." He nudged the other eaber who stepped forward and brought something out of his robe.

It was a boned, dehydrated human.

The thing—evidently a human survivor of an earlier colony—had the floppy, mindless manner of a puppy dog, mewling and whimpering on its long chain. Euben snapped his fingers. The former human ki-yied and scampered back under its owner's robe.

"Cute," said Euben. "De-skeletoned Earthmen bring a good price in the pet-shops of eaber, so you are not a total loss in the universe."

There came a sudden scream and convulsion from the eaber's robe. The eaber jumped back. The tragic, deboned human fell to the floor dead, spending a thin, too-bright red ebb of blood.

"Eh—how did you do that?" asked Euben, stepping back a little.

"I am Transstar," I said. "Certain things we do not permit with our life-form. I urge you not to continue this practice."

"So—" said Euben toeing at the dead man. "And he was so cute, too. Ah, well. There are more out there."

I controlled my voice and did not look down. "Can you establish your need for this planet?" I asked.

"Yes. We are eaber; that is enough anywhere in space."

I stepped to a wall chart and made a gesture. "This planet also falls along our perimeter. We occupy this space — so. We have well utilized the solar and alpha planet systems, and it is time that we move out once more. This planet is but one of a thousand Earth colonies moving out to new space."

Euben shook his head. "What a ridiculous civilization! All space in this arc is eaber. We close the door, so — "

He made a fast gesture with his hand that tore inside of me, like a hot knife, scraping the bottom of my lungs. I was pretty much riding on my conditioning now. I was sickened, angry with Euben and his race. But it was slightly different from dealing with an Earth neighbor you dislike. Bravery and caution! Always bravery — and caution.

"So you block us here," I said. "Perhaps we will go elsewhere for a hundred or a thousand years. It's no use to fight over space. There are millions of planets."

"Do you truly believe so?" smiled Euben. "Naive! The eaber do not like unknown life-forms prowling the universe. We will come to solar and alpha, as you call them, and put you on a chain like that one dead on the floor."

"We might resist that," I said.

"How?" said Euben, bringing a black box out from under his robe.

I have had my share of black boxes in my Transstar years. Before it was barely in sight, I had retreated to my all-purpose closet. He laughed, peering at me through the observation window and trying the various rays and whatnot in his weapon. Nothing much happened for a while — heat, radiation, gas, sonic vibrations, the standard stuff. Pretty soon I knew he could take me; but it would take him about three days. Fair enough.

The eaber were tough, but not unbeatable — at least on what he had shown me.

He put away his black box. I stepped through the door. Decontamination worked all right, but the heat-reducer was wheezing like an asthma victim in a grain field.

"So. You are junior good," said Euben. He turned and left the ship, whistling in a very Earthian way, not bothering to look back.

The other eaber remained. I offered him a cup of tea, which he drank greedily. He had something that looked a little like a serpent's tongue which he ran quickly over the control board panels. He sniff-tasted the instruments, the furnishings, the modest weapons and communications equipment I had. Then he stepped back.

"You will not survive eaber," he said. He left, not bothering to step over the deboned Earthman.

I picked up the soft, cooling mass and set it on the TV cradle. I didn't call through channels. I slapped the Transstar Central button and let them have a look at the creature on the plate.

Hennessy was on the monitor at Transstar Prime, near Mars. He gasped. "That's not good," he said. "Just a minute."

I sank into the chair and made more tea with shaking hands. The screen above me lighted and I was staring at Twelve. Thirteen is as high as you get in Transstar. "You've bought it," he said. "In your arc you have the only mind-contact with the eaber. Elsewhere they've only made patrol war."

"Anybody solved them?" I asked.

"Yes and no," said Twelve Jackson slowly. "They can hit us with a freeze-burn system they've got. Explodes you. We can reach them with most of our conventionals, but they don't die easily. Range and depth of their civilization, unknown."

I told him about their trillion — according to Euben. Then I asked, "What's my condition?"

Jackson hesitated and I saw his hands twiddle over his buttons. "Condition orange," he said, taking me off white. Power reached through space. In seventy-five seconds I could feel the sudden, subtle shift in the ship's power fields, as they built up.

"Don't get excited," he said. "I've got a dozen oranges on the board."

"What about the colony here?" I said.

"A colony is a local situation," said Jackson. "Unfortunately, if we squandered our life-power every time a few colonists died, we'd still be confined to the moon. They colonize of their own free will."

I touched the dead Earthman.

"Yeah," he said. "Nobody knew about that. It'll get your planet plenty of free space in the TV casts. We'll get a little blubbering from the League for Space Safety."

"It makes me want to blubber a little myself," I said.

Twelve Jackson gave me a long, hard look. "Stay Transstar or get out," he said.

I gave him the rest of my report-interview on the tape and tried to get some sleep. The eaber came over the colony about midnight and bombed it a little, and I groaned awake.

It must have been a half hour later that I heard a scratching on the ship's window. It was Rackrill, peering in at me.

When I joined him in the soft spring night he was excited.

"I've got something to show your high-falutin boys back at Mars," he said. "A real something."

We went in silence to his headquarters through the sweet night grasses of Everready. It was truly a planet of richness and beauty in a natural sense, and I thought again of the contrast of the poisoned boy and the monstrosities of human pets that the eaber had created under this moon, in their eaber cities, on this fine world.

My mood was shattered the instant we stepped into Rackrill's combination mayor's home and administration center. The Colony Correspondent had arrived.

There are simply too many Earth colonies for the space news services to cover them all. So they assign a Colony Correspondent to cover the whole arc, and you always find them where the most trouble is.

This one was a woman. She was of the young, peppy breed of females that start out life as a tomboy and remain in trouble all of their lives because they like to take chances. I was doubly disturbed. First, because it meant that wildly distorted stories would soon be muddying things back in solar and alpha; second, because this cute lady reminded me of my own Alicia, who had been a Transstar agent along with me, back a seeming thousand years ago when I was merely a Four. She had the same snapping black eyes, the same statuesque figure, the same light-humored air.

"Well, so Transstar is really here!" she said. "Hey, Chief, how about a Transstar quote?"

"Young lady, I am not Chief," I said drily. "My name is Webster, and I hold the Transstar rank of Seven, and you well know that all Transstar quotes must come from Transstar Prime."

"Those fossilized, dehumanized old men on Mars," she said. "Never mind. I'll find my own stories."

"Not here you won't," said Rackrill, with authority's natural fear of the tapes. "It's past midnight. Go to bed. Tomorrow my tape man will give you a tour."

She stuck out her tongue. "I've had the tour. They're all alike, full of lies and grease, signifying nothing. Only thing I ever learned on an official tour was how to defend myself against the passes of the tape men."

But she allowed herself to be pushed out. I guess it was the near-tragic urgency of our manner.

Rackrill led me into an inner room. On the bed rested a woman, but there was a strangeness to her. She was ancient in her skin, yet something about her bones told you she was hardly thirty. Her flesh was blue-splotched, the eyes animal-bright. Rackrill gestured at her; she whimpered and squirmed in her bed.

I laid a hand on his arm. "The eaber can hypnotize and make a hand gesture that tears you apart inside," I said. "Don't hold up your hands in front of her."

"We got her story," said Rackrill, low-voiced. "She's been a prisoner of the eaber for over a year. From Colony Two, I guess. The eaber used her for—breeding."

He led me to a smaller cot, where a blanket covered a figure. For a fleeting second I didn't want him to pull back the blanket. He pulled it back.

The creature on the bed was dead, shot with a Colony bullet. You could tell that it was a boy about three feet long. There was Earthman in him and eaber. The head and arms were Earthian, the rest eaber. It was shocking to see the hard-muscled, dwarf body under that placid, almost handsome head.

"Barely five months," whispered the hag on the bed. "Forced insemination. Always the hands twisting—always the pain."

"A friendly scientific experiment," said Rackrill. "They want drones for the slag jobs in their cities. Jobs eaber won't do. They've produced a hundred or so of those idiots from captive women colonists. Force-fed and raised—this one is barely five months old, yet look at his size!"

I said nothing, busy with taking my tape, holding on to my objectivity through a force of will and my conditioning.

Rackrill opened the dead mouth. It was an exaggerated eaber tongue, black and reptile shaped. "No speech, therefore no intellect. Nor does it have mind speech like true eaber. It begs for food and does crude tasks to get it. I showed it to the men. One of them shot it. Nobody blamed him. Tomorrow we're going out and take these rats, and rescue those poor women that are still over there. Does your highness condescend to ask for a little Transstar help?"

"Transstar won't like this life-form meddling," I said. "This is the second time."

Rackrill slumped into a chair, looking at the woman who whispered some private incantation against the evils she had come to know.

"I've got two thousand colonists, five hundred ships," he said. "With or without your help, we're going out tomorrow and take them."

"They've got a few more ships, Rackrill."

He appeared not to hear. He sat there staring at the woman while I gathered up the eaber drone's body to take back to my ship.

"For God's sake, get Transstar," he said, as I left, and it was a prayer.

Shortly before noon next day, Rackrill was back at my ship. He pointed to the sky over the colony, where his small fighting ships were rising. "What did your bosses say?" he asked.

"They said," I replied, "that Transstar has to look after the safety of the whole human race, and cannot match colonists man for man. There are safe places in alpha and solar to live — men are not obligated to seek danger. However, they are disturbed about the drone. I am to give an official protest and warning to Euben the eaber, which I have done."

"Is that *all!*"

I closed my eyes. "They also demoted me one rank, from a Seven to a Six, for having left my ship unattended in the middle of last night. During the time we examined the drone, a bumptious Colony Correspondent sneaked in to my ship and taped an eaber monstrosity I had on the TV plate. She flung her sensationalism to the planets and nations of alpha and solar. To put it mildly, this has rocked the galaxy, which is fine with our Colony Correspondent. She gets paid according to the number of TV stations that play her tape."

"The universe should know!" cried Rackrill.

"The universe has always known," I said. "Every history book tells of worse things in almost every Middlesex village and town. Transstar is not in show business or in policy making. It observes and objectively attends to the broad general welfare of the Earthian universe."

Rackrill's voice was hoarse. "I have one empty ship," he said bitterly. "I lack a pilot. Will Transstar at least do me the favor of helping to fill that?"

"It will," I said, reaching for my combat slacks.

This was a wild, foolish mission, and I knew it. But I wanted to get as close as I could to eaber-land, which I had only observed at a distance.

And I wanted to do something about the affronts to my system.

Sometimes it's good to fire a killing ray, even if it doesn't mean much.

We passed over three middle-sized eaber cities, the queerest cities I'd ever seen.

"Practically all landing fields," said a feminine voice in my ear. I looked to my left. The Colony Correspondent was riding a patrol ship on my right. I thanked her for achieving my embarrassment.

"Oh, that's all right, Doc," she said. "You're officialdom. Natural enemy. You'll get in your licks."

"I'd rather take mine in kicks. And I know where I'd like to plant my foot," I said.

I got a brash laugh. Foolish girl! Women do not have to be aggressive. There's the kind that makes a fetish of rushing in where brave men hesitate. On their maimed and dead persons the news tapes fatten and flourish.

Rackrill's group thought they were fighting the battle of the eon. They were trying to land at the most advanced city, where the captive Earthwomen were thought to be. The action was good. I was gloriously bashed around and managed to shoot down my eaber ship. It wasn't a difficult action for a Transstar-trained man. I was more interested in observing that the eaber had out an equal patrol of five hundred to oppose us. But, with all the noise and banging that a thousand-ship fight makes, I could observe that there were easily ten or fifteen thousand more eaber military ships on the ground we ranged over.

So the cities were not colonies. They were military bases for a large operation.

More interesting than the ships at hand were the extremely large areas being cleared and laid out for additional ship concentrations. I estimated that they could eventually base over a hundred thousand ships.

That would interest Transstar immensely.

Rackrill broke off the action when he had a mere hundred ships left. We limped back to the colony without being able to land in eaber territory. In fact, I doubted if the eaber chiefs regarded this as more than a quiet afternoon's patrol action. With their layout I couldn't blame them.

We almost missed the colony and had to sweep back once more. Yes, there was my Transstar ship, glowing orangely on the ground. But what a changed ground! It was brown and bare, a desert as far as the horizon.

During Rackrill's attack a secret eaber counterattack had swept the colony's transport ships, its buildings, and Rackrill's fifteen hundred colonists into oblivion.

In times of shock men do drastic — or foolish — things. Rackrill's group of survivors began to bring down the cooking equipment and bedding from their ships, preparing a camp for the night on the blighted cemetery of their colony, dazed and tearful.

"Ada, Ada," Rackrill moaned softly, his thick fingers picking at a gleaming aluminum pot. "Ada gone, Johnny gone — "

I noticed that Martha Stoner, the tape girl, had at last lost some of her high gloss. She stared at the scene, stunned. I could almost calibrate the change in her, from a high-spirited girl to a shocked and understanding woman.

I couldn't hold back comment. "Now you see the frontier," I said to her. "Now you've got a real tape that all the stations can use." She shook her head dumbly. "Go home, Rackrill," I advised the benumbed leader. "Take your men and go home."

He turned on me with teeth bared and lip trembling. "You — and that Transstar fraud. You let this happen! Tell your piddling button-pushers we will never go home!"

The words rang bravely on the scorched ground, while an eaber patrol, high up, gently wafted over us on an observation mission.

I shook my head. "At least go off in the forest where you have some protection — and some wood for your fires!"

I turned to go. A clod of soil struck my back, then a small stone.

"Go, Transstar filth, go!" They were all picking up the chant now.

"I'll file a tape all right!" cried Martha. "I can still get through to the world. The people will act, even if Transstar won't."

I didn't want to run.

I swear, this was my worst moment, because I had seen this distress many times. I understood their monumental shock. But if I did not run I could be seriously disabled by their attack. At any moment one might pull a gun. My job was to remain in good health so I could observe.

So I ran towards my ship.

They followed in a ragged company, shouting, cursing, and at last pulling guns. I barely escaped into the orange-hued safety of the

Transstar ship before the rays flew. The colonists danced and pranced around the ship, shooting at it and beating on it, like nothing so much as forest natives attacking an interloper. I understood and discreetly closed the portholes.

"Order them home," I begged Twelve Jackson. "They are doomed here."

"We don't have the power," said Jackson. "We can only help them home if they want to go."

I rang up Euben on the eaber channel which I used for official communications — so far, mostly for protests. Euben made his innocent, bird-twitter laugh. "Thank you for your protest about the colony extinction," he said. "This keeps my clerks busy. Your colony may leave at any time. In fact, I recommend this. We will need all the space on this planet very soon."

Three days passed.

I found the remnant of Rackrill's tattered colony in a sort of forest stockade. They were stiff with me, embarrassed about the stoning incident. They were ghost men, and a few women, going through the motions of building crude houses and planting their food.

Martha was an exception.

"They will stay," she said proudly, her eyes glowing. "They will be buttressed by the great crusade our space tapes have started. First the story of the miserable pet-human, then the eaber drone thing, then the mass attack on the unguarded colony. Back home men are leaving their jobs, pouring their savings into fighting ships. Institutions are subscribing money. Governments are amassing new fighters. We've got the backing of all the thinking men in solar and alpha!"

"It is too late in civilization for an emotion-powered, unorganized mass movement to succeed," I said. "Only Transstar is properly equipped for space war."

"Even Transstar men are quitting to join us!" she cried.

"Possibly a few at the lower levels. Not the agents."

"No — not the dehumanized agents! Nor the feeble old men of Transstar Prime who stole their power from the governments of men, who drool over buttons they never dare push!"

"The eaber do this to provoke us," I said, "to show our power at their command, at their site of battle, at a time they control. That's why Transstar Prime won't be sucked into the trap."

"They want to fight us. The time is now!" she said.

"The time is not yet," I said.

I went back to my lonely ship, haunted by the faces of Rackrill and his men as they glowed on my report tapes. I hunted the news broadcasts of solar and alpha and watched the revulsion and convulsion of men back home — the enormous waste of the emotional jag. I saw ships starting from Earth to reach us, ill-prepared even to reach the Moon, hurling across space vastnesses to become derelicts. I saw men throwing their pocket money at passing paraders of the anti-eaber crusade, normal shipping woefully hampered by the ridiculous items being sent to Rackrill's defenders. Government leaders, sensing the temper of the voters, threw their weight at Transstar Prime, calling for action. They got nowhere. Transstar resists temporary popular politics just as it does local situations.

"You certainly can't call this a local situation!" I told Twelve Jackson.

He sighed. "No, not any more. But the principle is missing. Everybody's mad, but the eaber haven't yet posed a major threat to the human race."

"They've got a couple hundred thousand fighting ships at our perimeter," I said.

"They haven't invaded territory we call our own. All the fighting is in no man's land. We're trained to determine a real danger from a false one, and so far they don't seem to be a real danger."

"It can get late fast," I said.

"Are you ready to ask for Condition Prime Total Red?"

There was a silence while I tried to separate my sympathetic feelings from the intelligence of the military situation. "No, sir," I said.

"Thirteen Mayberry agrees with you," said Twelve, looking over his shoulder, and then I saw the shadow of a sleeve of the top man. Transstar's Prime Prime, as the agents half-jokingly called him.

At least the desiccated old men near Mars were getting more interested.

On the day the first Earth-crusade task force arrived, both Martha and Rackrill came to the ship.

"You know it's the end of Transstar," Martha told me. She was more subdued and serious, but she still had the high-school glow of mysticism in her eyes. "The people have been sold out for the last time."

"No one's been sold out," I said. "We are in a painful contact with a race that is both powerful and primitive. They can't be reasoned with, yet we can't blow them up until, at least, they give evidence that they intend to blow us up. So far it's only a border incident, as they used to be called in one-world days."

"We aren't waiting," said Martha. "Five thousand ships! The first wave of the anti-eaber crusade will attack soon."

Martha put me so much in mind of Alicia—the way she held her head, the way she moved her hands. Once both Alicia and I had been at a point of resigning from Transstar and leading normal lives. But something in the blood and bone had made our marriage to Transstar stronger—until she was killed on a mission, and it was forever too late for me to quit. I was aware that I was too loyal to the organization, which was, after all, merely another society of men.

Yet, right now, I found myself questioning Prime's judgment.

Certainly they could have given me power to negotiate for the colony with Euben. Certainly there were some potent weapons, short of total war, which we could have used on these vain primitives as easily as the ones they used on us. Nor need I have been brought to my knees in front of Euben.

Yet my orders were to observe—report—take no action.

We went aloft to watch the Earthmen's attack. Both Martha and Rackrill were set for an initial penetration to the first eaber city. As the massive fleet from Earth wheeled in from space and went directly to the attack, they cheered like students in a rooting section. I cautioned them that five thousand ships, strained from a long flight from alpha, could hardly upset the eaber.

"It's only the first group!" cried Martha. "This is only the glorious beginning!"

The eaber took no chances. They lofted fifteen thousand ships and pulled the Earthmen into a box.

It took them about four hours to defeat the Earth attack. When the four hours passed, only about three hundred of the Earth fleet remained to sink to the oblivion of Rackrill's colony and lick their wounds.

"No matter," said Martha as we landed. "There will be more tomorrow and the day after that and after that. We'll blacken the skies with ships."

But she went quickly, avoiding my eyes.

"You'll always have sanctuary on my ship," I told Rackrill as he went.

"Your ship!" he snorted. "After today I'd rather trust my own stockade when Euben comes around. Incidentally, he has been kidnaping my work parties. Tell him we don't like that. Tell him we've been able to catch a few eaber, and when we do we cut them into four equal parts while they're still alive."

"Please don't," I said.

Euben came along as I was having my evening tea. "Ah, my scholarly friend with the glasses and the tea-drinking, the big words and the scoldings. I must thank you for keeping at least a part of our fleet in practice. A rather nice patrol action today, Webster. Is that your Transstar?"

"No. I ask you now what your intentions are as to this planet and our future relations," I said, aware that Transstar Prime, through this ship, had been watching the long day's affairs.

Euben had brought his friend with him. They both lolled at their ease in my cabin.

"It has been hard to determine," said Euben. "We have finally decided that, rather than waste rays killing off all Earthmen, we shall simply turn them into eaber. An inferior eaber, but still eaber. We have taken a few samples from Rackrill's post as prototypes."

"This is forbidden!" I snapped.

"You will declare war?" asked Euben eagerly. I thought his eagerness had grown.

"We don't know whom we deal with," I said. "You may be only a patrol captain, with a small command."

"I could also be commander-in-chief of all the eaber in space," said Euben. "Which I happen to be."

He said it too offhandedly for it to be a lie, although I suspected he was really deputy commander to the silent eaber who stood behind him.

"Then I formally demand that you cease and desist all harassments, mutilations, and hostilities against humans," I said.

Euben looked at me a long time. Then he held out what could reasonably be called an arm, which his companion grasped.

My ship seemed to whirl about me. It was no such thing. Instead I was suspended upside down in the air over my desk, and Euben and the other left the ship. "Farewell, brave-foolish," called Euben mockingly. "Next time I come it is to collect you for eaberization!"

His laugh was proud and full of confidence.

When I finally managed to right myself and get back behind my desk, I called Transstar Prime and got Twelve Jackson. I feared I saw a flick of amusement in his eyes. "They are determined now for war," I said. "How do we stand?"

"You continue to observe," said Jackson. "Point Everready is not necessary to Earth. And you have not convinced us that a battle needs to be fought."

I had not convinced them. But what did *I*—a mere agent—have to do with it?

I rang off and closed the ship, in sorrow and anger. I had been aloof from the situation, to the point where Euben had stood me on my head and threatened to capture me bodily.

I put on my combat slacks and broke out my weapons. Transstar could remain uninvolved, but I wasn't going to sit at my desk, be stood on my ear, and blithely be turned into an eaber all for the glory of the organization.

I rode over to Rackrill's stockade full of cold purpose.

I was no rugged primitive colonist. I was a trained agent, with quite a few good weapons and considerable experience in hostilities, especially against alien life-forms. Euben would have no easy time taking me.

I found Rackrill in more trouble. "Look," he fumed, pointing to a dead eaber at the wall of the stockade. "We shot this fellow. Look closely."

It was easy to see that it was one of his own colonists, upon whom extensive biology had been used to turn him into something eaberlike.

"It's going to happen to us all," shuddered Martha. "The crusade has collapsed. There'll be no more Earth ships. Distances are too great—governments are too busy with their home affairs. We have been outlawed in all major planets."

I stared at the white-faced colonial leaders in distaste.

"For God's sake, quit sniveling and feeling sorry for yourselves," I said. "We're going to fight these beasts and do it right. First, I want an antenna. I can draw power from my ship that the eaber can't crack. Second, I want to fight an eaber-type war. Get your colonists together for indoctrination. These eaber have primitive mind-reading abilities; I want to start training our men to set up mind guards against that. Last, we're going to dig some tunnels in this ground and blow the eaber into orbit. They don't like things underground. They have no defense for it. So let's get organized!"

"Thank God!" cried Martha. "Transstar is coming in at last."

"No," I said. "Just Charles Webster."

We fought the eaber for twenty days.

They couldn't penetrate the power wall I set up with the help of the ship, using Transstar power. They couldn't waylay our work parties in the woods after I taught them how to use mind-blocks which were meaningless to the eaber.

We got our tunnel through and blew up one third of an eaber city with one of my strontium 90 pills. We were also able to capture a few eaber patrol ships and send them right back, with fair-sized atomic blasts. The rest we manned and used against the eaber. They were totally confused with being attacked by their own ships. It wasn't enough to destroy a twentieth of their operation. But it kept them busy.

I was never once outside my combat slacks.

I got little sleep. I lived for the present moment, working hand and shoulder with Rackrill's men. When disaster came, it came all at once.

I led a night patrol to place the next strontium 90 pill overland — tunneling was too slow. I caught an eaber freeze-ray that shattered my leg. In the confusion we lost Martha to the eaber, which I only learned when I'd been carried back to the stockade.

When dawn broke, Rackrill shook me out of a dazed sleep.

"Look," he said.

"Ten thousand ships to destroy two dozen men," I laughed. "It's all right, Alicia."

Rackrill slapped my face. "Better come out of it, Webster. Can we stand an attack like that?"

I gulped a wake-up pill and brought myself alert. "No, we cannot. This is our day for extinction. Our only decision now is to pick the time and place of our going. Let's get over to the Transstar ship as fast as possible."

"I'm not leaving Point Everready," growled Rackrill.

"Nor am I," I said. "Let's move, man."

It was a sticky hour getting back to my ship. By that time our stockade, power block and all, had been pulverized to dust behind us by the attacking weight of the eaber ships.

"Take me up, Rackrill," I said as we reached the bottom of the ship. "I can't climb any more."

He pointed up dumbly. The fox faces of Euben and his eternal companion grinned down at us. I shifted out a gun and took off the safety. "Take me up, Rackrill."

It was almost ceremonial as Rackrill and the bare half-dozen who had made it through gathered about me in the cabin. I eased painfully into my chair. Euben saw my leg and grinned. "Looks like an amputation before we can make you a useful eaber," he said.

My bullet skipped across his shoulder. "Stand over by that wall, you," I said. "You, Euben! I'm talking to you."

"You cannot order me," he said, but he moved back sprightly enough. "I humor you, you see," he said. "Your stockade is gone. You have nothing but this ship. I have decided to have it gently blasted into space as worthless junk."

He gestured out of the window, where his ships were making passes now. My Transstar ship shuddered. "We can bounce it off the planet like a harmless rubber ball," he said. He gestured in back of me. "I have also returned your woman, of whom you think so much. She is worthless to become an eaber."

I turned and saw the thin shape of what had once been Martha, huddled on my navigator's bench. It was obvious that they had treated her roughly. From the trickle of blood at her mouth, she was badly hemorrhaged. She could not live.

I stared down at her. It was hard to tell if she still recognized me. She opened her mouth slightly, and I saw the black familiar shape of the eaber reptile tongue.

I turned away, light-headed with sorrow and anger.

I jabbed a button and looked up at the tall TV. It wasn't Twelve Jackson. It was Thirteen Mayberry, Mr. Prime himself.

"What are you staring at, you old goat?" I cried, a little hysterically. "Sore because I took action to save my own hide?"

"No, you young fool. I was just wondering how long you'd permit this minor outrage to go on."

"It ends now!" I said. "Listen, Prime, I have Earth people here who demand sanctuary of Transstar."

"You have it," he said. "We will up that ship, son. No power in the universe will keep it on the ground."

"The eaber are upping it quite nicely, thanks," I said. "But we don't want it upped!"

I had to stop talking while the thudding blows of the gentle eaber rays buffeted the ship.

"Not upped?" asked Mayberry.

"No, sir, not upped. We're staying! We hold the ground that this

Transstar ship rests on, in the name of Earth. It isn't much, only about fifty feet long and twenty-five wide, but it's Earth territory. No race or force may deprive us of our real estate."

"You tell him!" cried Rackrill.

I turned to Euben. "Now, friend," I said, "just ease this ship back to our ground. It's Earth ground. We intend to hold it!"

"Your leg wound has made you mad," said Euben, with a shrug. "We have decided that you are not even worthy to be eaber pets."

"Last warning, Euben! You've got yourself a Transstar situation."

Euben didn't hesitate.

He turned his hands in the air. I rolled in pain, but I kept seated. When I could see again from the pain, I looked up. Mayberry and Jackson and Hennessy and the forty-one division commanders of Transstar were blazing from the wall. The TV looked like a Christmas tree.

"Transstar orders this ship down and that ground preserved in the name of the Earth-alpha!" said Mayberry shortly to Euben.

Euben looked at the old man and shook his head. "Madmen," he said. "I spit on you." He spit on the screen at Mayberry. He had learned Earth insults well.

"My condition is Prime Total Red," I told Mayberry.

He leaned forward and closed the seldom-closed circuit at Transstar Prime.

"Your condition is Prime Total Red, and your ship is now command post for all Earth-alpha star power."

I leaned over and tapped a button. We left Point Everready in the beautiful swoop that only a Transstar ship could perform. I held us high in the atmosphere over the planet and looked sadly down. It had been a beautiful planet.

I hit another button and looked up at the forty-one division commanders of Transstar. "Your orders are to destroy the eaber," I said.

I sat back. For a few seconds it was deathly silent, while Euben sputtered and fussed about his quick ride up over the planet. Then there was the faintest whisper of—something—back and out and behind us.

"Brace yourselves, folks," I told the Earthmen. "It's going to be loud and crowded around here!"

Euben jabbered at some kind of communicator he held in his hands. His partner likewise gabbled.

"We have a hundred and fifty thousand ships," he told me. "We'll tear you to shreds!"

I kicked a chair over at him. "Sit down. You're going to want to sit in a minute."

"Something's wrong with the ship!" cried Rackrill. "It's heavy and dead!"

"We're drawing most of the broadcast power this side of Mars," I said. "In a minute you'll be glad we have that protection!"

Transstar came then. The fast patrols whisked out of black space and leaped into our atmosphere like gleaming fish, fired a rocking blast of weaponry, and were gone to rendezvous, reform, and pass again. They were like nothing the eaber had ever seen. They were made for a star-go like this, a burst of light, a dazzle, and a thunder that came and came and came. Behind them came the light patrols and then the medium patrols and then the heavy patrols and then the fast light shock ships and then the medium shock ships and then the heavy shocks, wave upon wave upon wave.

Even wrapped in our thick blanket of power we were stunned.

The planet came alight like a pearl below us. The air was jammed with sound shocks, the dazzle was like a spreading, thickening bomb of light that transfixed the eyeballs even through the dark screens I had set up.

"This is early stuff," I told Euben conversationally. "They just do a little holding till the important ships arrive. Patrols and first shocks — the usual things, you know."

Euben's mouth was open. He took time to swallow before he screamed orders to his ships below.

The patrols and shocks were suddenly past firing range. For a moment you could see the planet through the haze. Its shore lines and rivers had sickened and wavered. The eaber ships, which had been a blanket, were a tattered rag.

Hennessy, the headquarters jokester, couldn't resist a comment that probably earned him a fine. "Here comes the cavalry," he said over the TV.

And they came.

It was good professional stuff, geared to star action. Now we had the regulars. They came in waves of ten thousand, which was a wee bit impressive, I thought. There were the ground regulars, the medium regulars, and the high regulars, each division with thirty categories, each category with its subdivisions of missiles, rockets, and drones. The atmosphere screamed at us. The density of the light assumed sun proportions, and our poor little ship was like a chip on an angry ocean. Rackrill had his mouth wide open. He was yelling to relieve his tension at the awesome sight; the others were lost in the overwhelming cataclysm of it. I had seen it in movies.

I poured myself a cup of tea.

"These are just the on-call regulars," I told Euben. "Of course, you realize that in a Prime Red we're getting total mobilization. We'll get slightly less than a million ships in the first hour. The rest will come later."

Euben had stopped shouting orders. He stared at me. He said something that I couldn't hear. The pounding went on for fifteen minutes; then the planet cleared. There weren't any shore lines or rivers any more. There weren't very many eaber ships.

"Stop it," he said.

I shook my head. "Sorry. A Prime Red can't be stopped easily. Once the momentum starts it has to run its course. Get set now. Here come your specials."

As the specials started to arrive, I taunted the division commanders. "Transstar is getting rusty. You've hardly nicked the planet. Can't your boys shoot properly any more?"

They came in fat and sleek. Far off they waddled and wallowed, like a bunch of old ladies hitting a bargain counter. But suddenly they were serious, close up, and I had to close the portholes against the awesome roar and light of their work. You name the ray, bullet, bomb, gas—it was there.

A half hour later the din eased off and we looked. A large fragment of seared rock floated in space. The entire eaber fleet had long ago disappeared. So had everything else except that radioactive rock.

The last wave was the massive attack unit, very slow and lumbering compared to the others, but packed with power. The first five thousand took eager bites of the rock—and there was nothing left for the other twenty-five thousand. There was nothing left at all of Point Everready except some haze hanging below us in space. But it was too late to stop the attack.

To one side of us the returning waves began to streak by—the patrols, fast, light, medium, and heavy, the shocks, first, second, and third, the regulars in their streaming divisions and then the specials. Meanwhile, closer by, the second wave was coming in, first patrols and first shocks, darting a few shots to keep their hand in, at the floating dust patches.

Euben looked out and saw ships to his left and to his right and behind him and below him and above him and in all positions in between. It was such a heavy concentration that the stars were blocked out and, though no atmosphere existed for a nonexistent planet, we were a planet of moving ships, ourselves creating a gravity and a stinking jet-flame atmosphere. It was a moving dream of hell, enough to make your mind crack open with the motion of it. It was the phantom action of a near-million starships — and another million on the way.

This was the total war capacity delivered to order.

What it cost in disruption and money and waste was incredible to contemplate. But that was Prime Total Red — everything we had. And it wasn't at all pointless.

"The eaber surrender," said Euben.

He stood respectfully now, his commander behind him. I guess he was thinking of the remaining eaber colonies on other planets, as there was nothing left to surrender here.

I handed him a rag. "You may now wipe the spit off my TV plate receiver," I said. He did it with alacrity.

"We will go elsewhere," said Euben's companion. "After all, space is big. There is plenty of room for two great races."

"One great race," I said.

"Of course," he said affably. "May we have our lives spared?"

"We want you to have them — so you can take the word home."

The action outside had stilled. I opened the ports and began to move slowly towards another planet where the eaber had dwellings, as requested by the shaken Euben. Rackrill patted my shoulder. "Boy, that Transstar!" he exulted.

"It's quite a lot," I admitted. I painfully inched over to the stricken Martha and squeezed her hand. I thought she squeezed back. I thought I saw a flicker of joy at our success — but there was so much eaber and so much death in her eyes it was hard to know. I had to leave her then, for the medics came aboard for her.

I began to glide down on the new planet to discharge Euben and the other eaber. "Look," I said gesturing over my shoulder. Behind us the Transstar fleet followed docilely, the mass and weight of them, guns racked and quiet, the great beast behind my tiny patrol dot.

"We'll stay around a few days in case you want to argue some more," I told Euben.

He shook his head. "That will not be necessary, my good friend. We are not stupid. In the future you'll see very little of the eaber."

The ship settled. I opened the door and put down the ladder and Euben's companion descended, then Euben. "I am sorry—" he began.

But I thought of Martha and the dead boy who had died on Everready and the pet human and the drone eaber and the others who had suffered and died to make this creature sorry. So I planted my good foot on his rear. He crashed into his master and they both fell in the mud at the bottom of the ladder. They got up, mud-splattered, and ran like the wind towards eaberdom, capes flying out behind them.

Rackrill laughed. It was the first relaxed laugh I'd heard in all that assignment. It pulled things back to normal.

I turned back to my blazing board and hit a button. "Condition White," I said, "and don't kid me that you got up all these starships on seventy-five seconds' notice. They left Earth-alpha weeks ago. You knew from the first we were in for a Condition Prime Total Red with the eaber."

The old man grinned. "It's the agents who louse us up. We were afraid you'd observe so long that you'd start the action on an orange and build a whole new tradition—Ten."

Ten! I remembered then that anybody who ordered a CPTR was automatically up for Ten rank and sent to a nice, soft job at Prime.

"Save me a wide, plump chair at the TV console at Prime," I said. "Get me a desk-sized teapot, and a soft cushion for a bum leg."

I turned the ship around and started to lead the massive fleet home.

I stared at the far-flung stars of space as I drank my tea, eyes blurred a little with tears. I was an organization man. The organization was all I had, or would ever have. It didn't seem enough. Even the playing of the Transstar victory song left me depressed.

Then suddenly the light broke.

A Transstar agent is both the most and the least important of men. He is a fireman who puts out fires—a hero, but a shadow. A master sometimes, but mostly a servant. I winked at Mayberry on the screen. They saw I knew and winked back. They had finally lost a pompous, Transstar-impressed agent and gained a useful career man.

They were satisfied.

So was I.

Commentary

Premise: After repeated, brutal provocations by militaristic aliens who refuse all reasonable compromise, the overwhelming might of distant Earth's imperial armada is put under the control of the lone agent in the field to teach that low-life slime not to mess with Earthmen.

This is the kind of story for which the term "space opera" was coined, on the analogy to the earlier term "horse opera" for westerns. Slam-bang adventure in Outer Space, with lots of action and simplified, broadly drawn characters including heroic, stalwart protagonists not inclined to introspection; vile, leering villains (usually after our women for who knows what unspeakable purpose); and dimwitted and pneumatic bimbos in need of rescuing but kept decently out of the way most of the time while the "boys" do the real work of making the spacelanes safe for the good ol' Terran Federation/Empire/Instrumentality.

No moral ambiguity, no shades of grey. Just a general good time bashing the opposition after all seems lost. Rambo (or John Wayne) in space, occasionally with a touch of *High Noon*.

From E. E. "Doc" Smith's *Lensman* series to the serial adventures of Buck Rogers and George Lucas' *Star Wars* trilogy, this subgenre has probably had the most widespread and enduring appeal of any in science fiction. It has great verve and abundant energy, racing at breakneck speed from crisis to crisis to climax, with virtually no exposition or nuanced exploration of the characters' psychology. Aliens are either colorful, comical sidekicks (like Wookies) or else horrible monsters (Jabba the Hutt; the Rancor) with the moral sense of piranhas. There's action on every page, or things start to sag—and in a space opera, the least trace of sag is deadly. The good guy(s) may be losing, may be taking a beating, but there's never the least doubt in anyone's mind that *there's a fight going on*.

The fight, in this story, is between the dastardly eaber and the lone sheriff (oops, agent) Charles Webster. Webster abides by the stoical code of the west (oops, Transstar) which dictates he take no action and merely report on the eaber's methodical decimation of the Earth colony. The story's progression is one of escalating provocation and violence toward the Earth colonists by the eaber, represented by

Euben, who gloats, sneers, and is given bombastic lines like "Still I make you bow to me with the twisting of my bare hands in the air," and "You will die, die, die." In acting, this is known as "chewing the scenery," and Euben does it with great flair, so that no reader is in any doubt whatsoever that Euben deserves to be squashed like a bug at the first available opportunity. We're waiting for it to happen. The story makes us wait, building Euben and the eaber's villainy up and up, delaying Webster's justified retribution until the last possible second so that it will have the maximum emotional impact when it happens.

Let's look at how this story earns and builds toward its wowie climax.

We're limited to Webster's viewpoint so that, like him, we're supposedly neutral to start with: siding with neither the colonists (a feckless bunch) nor the eaber. But author Banks has stacked the deck against neutrality from the very beginning. The first scene shows an innocent child (yelling for its mother, no less!) that has to be murdered because the eaber have infected it with a disease in hope that the child will spread the disease among the colonists. Even the battle-hardened Webster finds the event sickening. Not only are the eaber vile; they're devious, making the colonists kill their own. Because of this opening scene, we're pretty sure that the eaber are going to have no redeeming qualities whatsoever and that retribution can't be far away.

But Webster does nothing. He's still observing. And the tension and suspense mount.

Next, we actually see some eaber. Euben shows up, torments and humiliates Webster without provocation, and proudly displays a de-boned and desiccated former human which the eaber apparently peddle as pets. Webster kills this pathetic object but otherwise swallows all the abuse. Now, we not only know that the eaber are beyond mercy as a race: we're given a particular person to hate and know that eaber individuals are also scum, without exception. So we can justly hate them as hard as we want, without any misgivings or ambiguities. And we know: they're going to *get* it . . . but not yet. Webster still waits, and so do we. And the suspense mounts some more.

For further provocation, we find out that the eaber are breeding monsters on helpless human women prisoners (aha! we *knew* they had unspeakable designs on our women!) and building military bases for an attack on Earth. They slaughter all but a fraction of the colonists in a sneak attack, then utterly defeat the ill-considered and emotional retaliation by ships from the indignant Earth. Surely Webster will have to do something now, we think!

And, finally, he does—leads a Rambo-style attack on the eaber cities. Though effective, the attacks are doomed by the greater numbers and firepower that the eaber command. Even personal gallantry isn't enough to give the eaber their deserved comeuppance.

Things look black. Webster admits, in fine, melodramatic space opera style, "This is our day for extinction. Our only decision now is to pick the time and place of our going."

Then, when absolutely everything seems lost, Webster finally gets really mad and refuses Transstar's offer to evacuate him and the few surviving colonists. They're going to fight to the end for the honor of Earth. When Euben commits the ultimate insult, spitting at the televised image of the director of Transstar, that's the last straw. Webster demands, and gets, Transstar's designation of the situation as "Prime Total Red"—total war.

As the story puts it, perfectly aptly, "Here comes the cavalry."

And the eaber are totally unable to stand against the overwhelming power of the weaponry of Man. It's more than "a wee bit impressive": it's awesome. We have the biggest stick in the known universe, and we're not afraid to use it when galactic bullies leave us no choice.

The bullies satisfactorily defeated and Euben personally humiliated (Webster, a subtle fellow, kicks him down a ladder), the spacelanes are again safe for innocent, foolish people like colonists (who earlier stoned Webster, not appreciating the Transstar code of nonintervention) and the depressingly "peppy," tomboyish, and unrealistic newswoman, Martha (who insists on going where the action is, where women don't belong, and whose rashness is rewarded by her being banged up so badly she's reduced to feeble hand-squeezes with the hero by the story's end).

Ninety percent of the story is push, push, push: squeezing down the spring, creating tension and suspense because we know that so much action *must* provoke a proportionate reaction. So unlike the colonists, we're not impatient with Webster's inaction. We know the stakes have simply gone up again with each new provocation. Therefore when the moment comes for the cavalry to arrive, with Webster in personal command of the battle, wielding the total might of Transstar, we'll be whooping and cheering to watch those suckers *die*, as do the Ewoks when the Death Star is finally destroyed at the end of *Return of the Jedi.* The final explosion of brute force and righteous indignation is made satisfying and appropriate by the escalating and outrageous provocations throughout the story, building momentum, speed, and pressure to the point where some explosion simply has to happen.

The itch has gotten bad enough, the tension unbearable. So we can just *swat* the unprintable mosquito without a second's guilt or misgiving.

Life is simpler and success is sweeter in space opera. But sometimes, that's precisely the way lots of us readers want it.

Social satire is a natural concomitant of science fiction. Indeed, before science fiction might truly be said to exist (in the sense of stories appearing that deal with the consequences of scientific and technological advances) there were social satires set in imaginary societies that might be considered "proto-science-fiction." The best example of this would be Jonathan Swift's Gulliver's Travels, *which was first published in 1726.*

Social satire doesn't always have to be realistic and convincing (though it can be). Ideally, it takes a social trend and carries it to an extreme. If the trend is (in the opinion of the author) a bad one, its viciousness can be more clearly demonstrated if one puts it under the microscope, so to speak, by imagining it to continue to a point well beyond reason.

Generally, the result is an "anti-Utopia" or a "dystopia," a society which is a nightmare. It is made all the more nightmarish if it is told with a straight face, dealing with people who accept their surroundings and are unaware of its nightmarish qualities.

J. G. Ballard's "Billenium" is a way of discussing the problem of overpopulation in the world today, and it is more effective on the subject than any number of sober essays, filled with statistics, could be.

— Isaac Asimov

Billenium

J. G. Ballard

All day long, and often into the early hours of the morning, the tramp of feet sounded up and down the stairs outside Ward's cubicle. Built into a narrow alcove in a bend of the staircase between the fourth and fifth floors, its plywood walls flexed and creaked with every footstep like the timbers of a rotting windmill. Over a hundred people lived in the top three floors of the old rooming house, and sometimes Ward would lie awake on his narrow bunk until 2 or 3 A.M., mechanically counting the last residents returning from the all-night movies in the stadium half a mile away. Through the window he could hear giant fragments of the amplified dialogue booming among the rooftops. The stadium was never empty. During the day the huge four-sided screen was raised on its davit and athletics meetings or football matches ran continuously. For the people in the houses abutting the stadium the noise must have been unbearable.

Ward, at least, had a certain degree of privacy. Two months earlier, before he came to live on the staircase, he had shared a room with seven others on the ground floor of a house in 755th Street, and the ceaseless press of people jostling past the window had reduced him to a state of chronic exhaustion. The street was always full, an endless clamour of voices and shuffling feet. By 6:30, when he woke, hurrying to take his place in the bathroom queue, the crowds already jammed it from sidewalk to sidewalk, the din punctuated every half minute by the roar of the elevated trains running over the shops on the opposite side of the road. As soon as he saw the advertisement describing the staircase cubicle he had left (like everyone else, he spent most of his spare time scanning the classifieds in the newspapers, moving his lodgings an average of once every two months) despite the higher rental. A cubicle on a staircase would almost certainly be on its own.

However, this had its drawbacks. Most evenings his friends from the library would call in, eager to rest their elbows after the bruising crush of the public reading room. The cubicle was slightly more than four and a half square metres in floor area, half a square over the statutory maximum for a single person, the carpenters having taken advantage, illegally, of a recess beside a nearby chimney breast. Consequently Ward had been able to fit a small straight-backed chair into the interval between the bed and the door, so that only one person at a time need to sit on the bed — in most single cubicles host and guest had to sit side by side on the bed, conversing over their shoulders and changing places periodically to avoid neckstrain.

"You were lucky to find this place," Rossiter, the most regular visitor, never tired of telling him. He reclined back on the bed, gesturing at the cubicle. "It's enormous, the perspectives really zoom. I'd be surprised if you hadn't got at least five metres here, perhaps even six."

Ward shook his head categorically. Rossiter was his closest friend, but the quest for living space had forged powerful reflexes. "Just over four and a half, I've measured it carefully. There's no doubt about it."

Rossiter lifted one eyebrow. "I'm amazed. It must be the ceiling then."

Manipulating the ceiling was a favourite trick of unscrupulous landlords — most assessments of area were made upon the ceiling, out of convenience, and by tilting back the plywood partitions the rated area of cubicle could be either increased, for the benefit of a prospective tenant (many married couples were thus bamboozled into taking a single cubicle), or decreased temporarily on the visits of the housing inspectors. Ceilings were criss-crossed with pencil marks staking out the rival claims of tenants on opposite sides of a party wall. Someone timid of his rights could be literally squeezed out of existence — in fact, the advertisement "quiet clientele" was usually a tacit invitation to this sort of piracy.

"The wall does tilt a little," Ward admitted. "Actually, it's about four degrees out — I used a plumb-line. But there's still plenty of room on the stairs for people to get by."

Rossiter grinned. "Of course, John. I'm just envious, that's all. My room's driving me crazy." Like everyone, he used the term "room" to describe his tiny cubicle, a hangover from the days fifty years earlier when people had indeed lived one to a room, sometimes, unbelievably, one to an apartment or house. The microfilms in the architecture catalogues at the library showed scenes of museums, concert halls and other public buildings in what appeared to be everyday settings, often virtually empty, two or three people wandering down an enormous gallery or staircase. Traffic moved freely along the centre of streets, and in the quieter districts sections of sidewalk would be deserted for fifty yards or more.

Now, of course, the older buildings had been torn down and replaced by housing batteries, or converted into apartment blocks. The great banqueting room in the former City Hall had been split horizontally into four decks, each of these cut up into hundreds of cubicles.

As for the streets, traffic had long since ceased to move about them. Apart from a few hours before dawn when only the sidewalks were crowded, every thoroughfare was always packed with a shuffling mob of pedestrians, perforce ignoring the countless "Keep Left" signs suspended over their heads, wrestling past each other on their way to home and office, their clothes dusty and shapeless. Often "locks" would occur when a huge crowd at a street junction became immovably jammed. Sometimes these locks would last for days. Two years earlier Ward had been caught in one outside the stadium, for over forty-eight hours was trapped in a gigantic pedestrian jam containing over 20,000 people, fed by the crowds leaving the stadium on one side and those approaching it on the other. An entire square mile of the local neighbourhood had been paralysed, and he vividly remembered the nightmare of swaying helplessly on his feet as the jam shifted and heaved, terrified of losing his balance and being trampled underfoot. When the police had finally sealed off the stadium and dispersed the jam he had gone back to his cubicle and slept for a week, his body blue with bruises.

"I hear they may reduce the allocation to three and a half metres," Rossiter remarked.

Ward paused to allow a party of tenants from the sixth floor to pass down the staircase, holding the door to prevent it jumping off its latch. "So they're always saying," he commented. "I can remember that rumour ten years ago."

"It's no rumour," Rossiter warned him. "It may well be necessary soon. Thirty million people packed into this city now, a million increase in just one year. There's been some pretty serious talk at the Housing Department."

Ward shook his head. "A drastic revaluation like that is almost impossible to carry out. Every single partition would have to be dismantled and nailed up again, the administrative job alone is so vast it's difficult to visualise. Millions of cubicles to be redesigned and certified, licences to be issued, plus the complete resettlement of every tenant.

Most of the buildings put up since the last revaluation are designed around a four-metre modulus — you can't simply take half a metre off the end of each cubicle and then say that makes so many new cubicles. They may be only six inches wide." He laughed. "Besides, how can you live in just three and a half metres?"

Rossiter smiled. "That's the ultimate argument, isn't it? They used it twenty-five years ago at the last revaluation, when the minimum was cut from five to four. It couldn't be done they all said, no one could stand living in only four square metres, it was enough room for a bed and a suitcase, but you couldn't open the door to get in." Rossiter chuckled softly. "They were all wrong. It was merely decided that from then on all doors would open outwards. Four square metres was here to stay."

Ward looked at his watch. It was 7:30. "Time to eat. Let's see if we can get into the food bar across the road."

Grumbling at the prospect, Rossiter pulled himself off the bed. They left the cubicle and made their way down the staircase. This was crammed with luggage and packing cases so that only a narrow interval remained around the bannister. On the floors below the congestion was worse. Corridors were wide enough to be chopped up into single cubicles, and the air was stale and dead, cardboard walls hung with damp laundry and makeshift larders. Each of the five rooms on the floors contained a dozen tenants, their voices reverberating through the partitions.

People were sitting on the steps above the second floor, using the staircase as an informal lounge, although this was against the fire regulations, women chatting with the men queueing in their shirtsleeves outside the washroom, children diving around them. By the time they reached the entrance Ward and Rossiter were having to force their way through the tenants packed together on every landing, loitering around the notice boards or pushing in from the street below.

Taking a breath at the top of the steps, Ward pointed to the food bar on the other side of the road. It was only thirty yards away, but the throng moving down the street swept past like a river at full tide, crossing them from right to left. The first picture show at the stadium started at 9 o'clock, and people were setting off already to make sure of getting in.

"Can't we go somewhere else?" Rossiter asked, screwing his face up at the prospect of the food bar. Not only would it be packed and take them half an hour to be served, but the food was flat and unappetising.

The journey from the library four blocks away had given him an appetite.

Ward shrugged. "There's a place on the corner, but I doubt if we can make it." This was two hundred yards upstream; they would be fighting the crowd all the way.

"Maybe you're right." Rossiter put his hand on Ward's shoulder. "You know, John, your trouble is that you never go anywhere, you're too disengaged, you just don't realise how bad everything is getting."

Ward nodded. Rossiter was right. In the morning, when he set off for the library, the pedestrian traffic was moving with him towards the down town offices; in the evening, when he came back, it was flowing in the opposite direction. By and large he never altered his routine. Brought up from the age of ten in a municipal hostel, he had gradually lost touch with his father and mother, who lived on the east side of the city and had been unable, or unwilling, to make the journey to see him. Having surrendered his initiative to the dynamics of the city he was reluctant to try to win it back merely for a better cup of coffee. Fortunately his job at the library brought him into contact with a wide range of young people of similar interests. Sooner or later he would marry, find a double cubicle near the library and settle down. If they had enough children (three was the required minimum) they might even one day own a small room of their own.

They stepped out into the pedestrian stream, carried along by it for ten or twenty yards, then quickened their pace and side-stepped through the crowd, slowly tacking across to the other side of the road. There they found the shelter of the shop-fronts, slowly worked their way back to the food bar, shoulders braced against the countless minor collisions.

"What are the latest population estimates?" Ward asked as they circled a cigarette kiosk, stepping forward whenever a gap presented itself.

Rossiter smiled. "Sorry, John, I'd like to tell you but you might start a stampede. Besides, you wouldn't believe me."

Rossiter worked in the Insurance Department at the City Hall, had informal access to the census statistics. For the last ten years these had been classified information, partly because they were felt to be inaccurate, but chiefly because it was feared they might set off a mass attack of claustrophobia. Minor outbreaks had taken place already, and the official line was that world population had reached a plateau, levelling off at 20,000 million. No one believed this for a moment, and Ward assumed that the 3 percent annual increase maintained since the 1960's was continuing.

How long it could continue was impossible to estimate. Despite the gloomiest prophecies of the Neo-Malthusians, world agriculture had managed to keep pace with the population growth, although intensive cultivation meant that 95 percent of the population was permanently trapped in vast urban conurbations. The outward growth of cities had at last been checked; in fact, all over the world former suburban areas were being reclaimed for agriculture and population additions were confined within the existing urban ghettos. The countryside, as such, no longer existed. Every single square foot of ground sprouted a crop of one type or other. The one-time fields and meadows of the world were now, in effect, factory floors, as highly mechanised and closed to the public as any industrial area. Economic and ideological rivalries had long since faded before one overriding quest — the internal colonisation of the city.

Reaching the food bar, they pushed themselves into the entrance and joined the scrum of customers pressing six deep against the counter.

"What is really wrong with the population problem," Ward confided to Rossiter, "is that no one has ever tried to tackle it. Fifty years ago short-sighted nationalism and industrial expansion put a premium on a rising population curve, and even now the hidden incentive is to have a large family so that you can gain a little privacy. Single people are penalised simply because there are more of them and they don't fit conveniently into double or triple cubicles. But it's the large family with its compact, space-saving logistic that is the real villain."

Rossiter nodded, edging nearer the counter, ready to shout his order. "Too true. We all look forward to getting married just so that we can have our six metres."

Directly in front of them, two girls turned around and smiled, "Six square metres," one of them, a dark-haired girl with a pretty oval face, repeated. "You sound like the sort of young man I ought to get to know. Going into the real-estate business, Peter?"

Rossiter grinned and squeezed her arm. "Hello, Judith. I'm thinking about it actively. Like to join me in a private venture?"

The girl leaned against him as they reached the counter. "Well, I might. It would have to be legal, though."

The other girl, Helen Waring, an assistant at the library, pulled Ward's sleeve. "Have you heard the latest, John? Judith and I have been kicked out of our room. We're on the street right at this minute."

"What?" Rossiter cried. They collected their soups and coffee and edged back to the rear of the bar. "What on earth happened?"

Helen explained: "You know that little broom cupboard outside our cubicle? Judith and I have been using it as a sort of study hole, going in there to read. It's quiet and restful, if you can get used to not breathing. Well, the old girl found out and kicked up a big fuss, said we were breaking the law and so on. In short, out." Helen paused. "Now we've heard she's going to let it as a single."

Rossiter pounded the counter ledge. "A broom cupboard? Someone's going to live there? But she'll never get a licence."

Judith shook her head. "She's got it already. Her brother works in the Housing Department."

Ward laughed into his soup. "But how can she let it? No one will live in a broom cupboard."

Judith stared at him sombrely. "You really believe that, John?"

Ward dropped his spoon. "No, I guess you're right. People will live anywhere. God, I don't know who I feel more sorry for—you two, or the poor devil who'll be living in that cupboard. What are you going to do?"

"A couple in a place two blocks west are subletting half their cubicle to us. They've hung a sheet down the middle and Helen and I'll take turns sleeping on a camp bed. I'm not joking, our room's about two feet wide. I said to Helen that we ought to split up again and sublet one half at twice our rent."

They had a good laugh over all this and Ward said goodnight to the others and went back to his rooming house.

There he found himself with similar problems.

The manager leaned against the flimsy door, a damp cigar butt revolving around his mouth, an expression of morose boredom on his unshaven face.

"You got four point seven two metres," he told Ward, who was standing out on the staircase, unable to get into his room. Other tenants milled, passed onto the landing, where two women in curlers and dressing gowns were arguing with each other, tugging angrily at the wall of trunks and cases. Occasionally the manager glanced at them irritably. "Four seven two. I worked it out twice." He said this as if it ended all possibility of argument.

"Ceiling or floor?" Ward asked.

"Ceiling, whaddya think? How can I measure the floor with all this junk?" He kicked at a crate of books protruding from under the bed.

Ward let this pass. "There's quite a tilt on the wall," he pointed out. "As much as three or four degrees."

The manager nodded vaguely. "You're definitely over the four. Way over." He turned to Ward, who had moved down several steps to allow a man and woman to get past. "I can rent this as a double."

"What, only four and a half?" Ward said incredulously. "How?"

The man who had just passed him leaned over the manager's shoulder and sniffed at the room, taking in every detail in a one-second glance. "You renting a double here, Louie?"

The manager waved him away and then beckoned Ward into the room, closing the door after him.

"It's a nominal five," he told Ward. "New regulation, just came out. Anything over four five is a double now." He eyed Ward shrewdly. "Well, whaddya want? It's a good room, there's a lot of space here, feels more like a triple. You got access to the staircase, window slit —" He broke off as Ward slumped down on the bed and started to laugh. "Whatsa matter? Look, if you want a big room like this you gotta pay for it. I want an extra half rental or you get out."

Ward wiped his eyes, then stood up wearily and reached for the shelves. "Relax, I'm on my way. I'm going to live in a broom cupboard. 'Access to the staircase —' that's really rich. Tell me, Louis, is there life on Uranus?"

Temporarily, he and Rossiter teamed up to rent a double cubicle in a semi-derelict house a hundred yards from the library. The neighbourhood was seedy and faded, the rooming houses crammed with tenants. Most of them were owned by absentee landlords or by the city corporation, and the managers employed were of the lowest type, mere rent-collectors who cared nothing about the way their tenants divided up the living space, and never ventured beyond the first floors. Bottles and empty cans littered the corridors, and the washrooms looked like sumps. Many of the tenants were old and infirm, sitting about listlessly in their narrow cubicles, wheedling at each other back to back through the thin partitions.

Their double cubicle was on the third floor, at the end of a corridor that ringed the building. Its architecture was impossible to follow, rooms letting off at all angles, and luckily the corridor was a cul-de-sac. The mounds of cases ended four feet from the end wall and a partition divided off the cubicle, just wide enough for two beds. A high window overlooked the area ways of the building opposite.

Possessions loaded onto the shelf above his head, Ward lay back on his bed and moodily surveyed the roof of the library through the afternoon haze.

"It's not bad here," Rossiter told him, unpacking his case. "I know there's no real privacy and we'll drive each other insane within a week, but at least we haven't got six other people breathing into our ears two feet away."

The nearest cubicle, a single, was built into the banks of cases half a dozen steps along the corridor, but the occupant, a man of seventy, was deaf and bedridden.

"It's not bad," Ward echoed reluctantly. "Now tell me what the latest growth figures are. They might console me."

Rossiter paused, lowering his voice. "Four percent. *Eight hundred million extra people in one year* — just less than half the earth's total population in 1950."

Ward whistled slowly. "So they will revalue. What to? Three and a half?"

"Three. From the first of next year."

"Three square metres!" Ward sat up and looked around him. "It's unbelievable! The world's going insane, Rossiter. For God's sake, when are they going to do something about it? Do you realise there soon won't be room enough to sit down, let alone lie down?"

Exasperated, he punched the wall beside him, on the second blow knocked in one of the small wooden panels that had been lightly papered over.

"Hey!" Rossiter yelled. "You're breaking the place down." He dived across the bed to retrieve the panel, which hung downwards supported by a strip of paper. Ward slipped his hand into the dark interval, carefully drew the panel back on to the bed.

"Who's on the other side?" Rossiter whispered. "Did they hear?"

Ward peered through the interval, eyes searching the dim light. Suddenly he dropped the panel and seized Rossiter's shoulder, pulled him down on to the bed.

"Henry! Look!"

Rossiter freed himself and pressed his face to the opening, focussed slowly and then gasped.

Directly in front of them, faintly illuminated by a grimy skylight, was a medium-sized room, some fifteen feet square, empty except for the dust silted up against the skirting boards. The floor was bare, a few strips of frayed linoleum running across it, the walls covered with a drab floral design. Here and there patches of the paper peeled off and segments of the picture rail had rotted away, but otherwise the room was in habitable condition.

Breathing slowly, Ward closed the open door of the cubicle with his foot, then turned to Rossiter.

"Henry, do you realise what we've found? Do you realise it, man?"

"Shut up. For Pete's sake keep your voice down." Rossiter examined the room carefully. "It's fantastic. I'm trying to see whether anyone's used it recently."

"Of course they haven't," Ward pointed out. "It's obvious. There's no door into the room. We're looking through it now. They must have panelled over this door years ago and forgotten about it. Look at that filth everywhere."

Rossiter was staring into the room, his mind staggered by its vastness.

"You're right," he murmured. "Now, when do we move in?"

Panel by panel, they pried away the lower half of the door, nailed it on to a wooden frame so that the dummy section could be replaced instantly.

Then, picking an afternoon when the house was half empty and the manager asleep in his basement office, they made their first foray into the room, Ward going in alone while Rossiter kept guard in the cubicle.

For an hour they exchanged places, wandering silently around the dusty room, stretching their arms out to feel its unconfined emptiness, grasping at the sensation of absolute spatial freedom. Although smaller than many of the sub-divided rooms in which they had lived, this room seemed infinitely larger, its walls huge cliffs that soared upward to the skylight.

Finally, two or three days later, they moved in.

For the first week Rossiter slept alone in the room, Ward in the cubicle outside, both there together during the day. Gradually they smuggled in a few items of furniture: two armchairs, a table, a lamp fed from the socket in the cubicle. The furniture was heavy and Victorian; the cheapest available, its size emphasized the emptiness of the room. Pride of place was taken by an enormous mahogany wardrobe, fitted with carved angels and castellated mirrors, which they were forced to dismantle and carry into the house in their suitcases. Towering over them, it reminded Ward of the microfilms of gothic cathedrals, with their massive organ lofts crossing vast naves.

After three weeks they both slept in the room, finding the cubicle unbearably cramped. An imitation Japanese screen divided the room adequately and did nothing to diminish its size. Sitting there in the evenings, surrounded by his books and albums, Ward steadily forgot the city outside. Luckily he reached the library by a back alley and avoided the crowded streets. Rossiter and himself began to seem the only real inhabitants of the world, everyone else a meaningless byproduct of their own existence, a random replication of identity which had run out of control.

It was Rossiter who suggested that they ask the two girls to share the room with them.

"They've been kicked out again and may have to split up," he told Ward, obviously worried that Judith might fall into bad company. "There's always a rent freeze after a revaluation but all the landlords know about it so they're not re-letting. It's getting damned difficult to find anywhere."

Ward nodded, relaxing back around the circular red wood table. He played with a tassel of the arsenic green lamp shade, for a moment felt like a Victorian man of letters, leading a spacious, leisurely life among overstuffed furnishings.

"I'm all for it," he agreed, indicating the empty corners. "There's plenty of room here. But we'll have to make damn sure they don't gossip about it."

After due precautions, they let the two girls into the secret, enjoying their astonishment at finding this private universe.

"We'll put a partition across the middle," Rossiter explained, "then take it down each morning. You'll be able to move in within a couple of days. How do you feel?"

"Wonderful!" They goggled at the wardrobe, squinting at the endless relections in the mirrors.

There was no difficulty getting them in and out of the house. The turnover of tenants was continuous and bills were placed in the mail rack. No one cared who the girls were or noticed their regular calls at the cubicle.

However, half an hour after they arrived neither of them had unpacked her suitcase.

"What's up, Judith?" Ward asked, edging past the girls' beds into the narrow interval between the table and wardrobe.

Judith hesitated, looking from Ward to Rossiter, who sat on his bed, finishing off the plywood partition. "John, it's just that . . ."

Helen Waring, more matter-of-fact, took over, her fingers straightening the bedspread. "What Judith's trying to say is that our position here is a little embarrassing. The partition is—"

Rossiter stood up. "For heaven's sake, don't worry, Helen," he assured her, speaking in the loud whisper they had all involuntarily cultivated. "No funny business, you can trust us. This partition is as solid as a rock."

The two girls nodded. "It's not that," Helen explained, "but it isn't up all the time. We thought that if an older person were here, say Judith's aunt—she wouldn't take up much room and be no trouble, she's really awfully sweet—we wouldn't need to bother about the partition—except at night," she added quickly.

Ward glanced at Rossiter, who shrugged and began to scan to the floor.

"Well, it's an idea," Rossiter said. "John and I know how you feel. Why not?"

"Sure," Ward agreed. He pointed to the space between the girls' beds and the table. "One more won't make any difference."

The girls broke into whoops. Judith went over to Rossiter and kissed him on the cheek. "Sorry to be a nuisance, Henry." She smiled at him. "That's a wonderful partition you've made. You couldn't do another one for Auntie—just a little one? She's very sweet but she is getting on."

"Of course," Rossiter said. "I understand. I've got plenty of wood left over."

Ward looked at his watch. "It's seven-thirty, Judith. You'd better get in touch with your aunt. She may not be able to make it tonight."

Judith buttoned her coat. "Oh, she will," she assured Ward. "I'll be back in a jiffy."

The aunt arrived within five minutes, three heavy suitcases soundly packed.

"It's amazing," Ward remarked to Rossiter three months later. "The size of this room still staggers me. It almost gets larger every day."

Rossiter agreed readily, averting his eyes from one of the girls changing behind the central partition. This they now left in place as dismantling it daily had become tiresome. Besides, the aunt's subsidiary partition was attached to it and she resented the continuous upsets. Insuring she followed the entrance and exit drills through the camouflaged door and cubicle was difficult enough.

Despite this, detection seemed unlikely. The room had obviously been built as an afterthought into the central well of the house and any noise was masked by the luggage stacked in the surrounding corridor. Directly below was a small dormitory occupied by several elderly women, and Judith's aunt, who visited them socially, swore that no sounds came through the heavy ceiling. Above, the fanlight let out through a dormer window, its lights indistinguishable from the hundred other bulbs burning in the windows of the house.

Rossiter finished off the new partition he was building and held it upright, fitting it into the slots nailed to the wall between his bed and Ward's. They had agreed that this would provide a little extra privacy.

"No doubt I'll have to do one for Judith and Helen," he confided to Ward.

Ward adjusted his pillow. They had smuggled the two armchairs back to the furniture shop as they took up too much space. The bed, anyway, was more comfortable. He had never got completely used to the soft upholstery.

"Not a bad idea. What about some shelving around the wall? I've got nowhere to put anything."

The shelving tidied the room considerably, freeing large areas of the floor. Divided by their partitions, the five beds were in line along the rear wall, facing the mahogany wardrobe. In between was an open space of three or four feet, a further six feet on either side of the wardrobe.

The sight of so much space fascinated Ward. When Rossiter mentioned that Helen's mother was ill and badly needed personal care he immediately knew where her cubicle could be placed — at the foot of his bed, between the wardrobe and the side wall.

Helen was overjoyed. "It's awfully good of you, John," she told him, "but would you mind if Mother slept beside me? There's enough space to fit an extra bed in."

So Rossiter dismantled the partitions and moved them closer together, six beds now in line along the wall. This gave each of them an interval two and a half feet wide, just enough room to squeeze down the side of their beds. Lying back on the extreme right, the shelves two feet above his head, Ward could barely see the wardrobe, but the space in front of him, a clear six feet to the wall ahead, was uninterrupted.

Then Helen's father arrived.

Knocking on the door of the cubicle, Ward smiled at Judith's aunt as she let him in. He helped her swing out the made-up bed which guarded the entrance, then rapped on the wooden panel. A moment later Helen's father, a small, grey-haired man in an undershirt, braces tied to his trousers with string, pulled back the panel.

Ward nodded to him and stepped over the luggage piled around the floor at the foot of the beds. Helen was in her mother's cubicle, helping the old woman to drink her evening broth. Rossiter, perspiring heavily, was on his knees by the mahogany wardrobe, wrenching apart the frame of the central mirror with a jimmy. Pieces of the wardrobe lay on his bed and across the floor.

"We'll have to start taking these out tomorrow," Rossiter told him. Ward waited for Helen's father to shuffle past and enter his cubicle. He had rigged up a small cardboard door, and locked it behind him with a crude hook of bent wire.

Rossiter watched him, frowning irritably. "Some people are happy. This wardrobe's a hell of a job. How did we ever decide to buy it?"

Ward sat down on his bed. The partition pressed against his knees and he could hardly move. He looked up when Rossiter was engaged and saw that the dividing line he had marked in pencil was hidden by the encroaching position. Leaning against the wall, he tried to ease it back again, but Rossiter had apparently nailed the lower edge to the floor.

There was a sharp tap on the outside cubicle door—Judith returning from her office. Ward started to get up and then sat back. "Mr. Waring," he called softly. It was the old man's duty night.

Waring shuffled to the door of his cubicle and unlocked it fussily, clucking to himself.

"Up and down, up and down," he muttered. He stumbled over Rossiter's tool bag and swore loudly, then added meaningly over his shoulder: "If you ask me there's too many people in here. Down below they've only got six to our seven, and it's the same size room."

Ward nodded vaguely and stretched back on his narrow bed, trying not to bang his head on the shelving. Waring was not the first to hint that he move out. Judith's aunt had made a similar suggestion two days earlier. Since he left his job at the library (the small rental he charged the others paid for the little food he needed) he spent most of his time in the room, seeing rather more of the old man than he wanted to, but he had learned to tolerate him.

Settling himself, he noticed that the right-hand spire of the wardrobe, all he had been able to see for the past two months, was now dismantled.

It had been a beautiful piece of furniture, in a way symbolising this whole private world, and the salesman at the store told him there were few like it left. For a moment Ward felt a sudden pang of regret, as he had done as a child when his father, in a mood of exasperation, had taken something away from him and he knew he would never see it again.

Then he pulled himself together. It was a beautiful wardrobe, without doubt, but when it was gone it would make the room seem even larger.

Commentary

Premise: World population continues unchecked but food supplies remain adequate, so that people are allocated decreasing amounts of space for living quarters.

Take a current problem or trend, assume it gets even more so as time passes, and show the result in human terms. This is the basis of "If this goes on . . ." stories.

Most science fiction stories have a premise, an idea which is both spun out, extrapolated, and put into action so that the reader can watch it operating. So although science fiction has been called "the fiction of ideas," authors use their imaginations, not to invent stranger and stranger concepts, but to find ways to make the abstract premises concrete, particular. *This* time, *this* person, *this* problem, to make the reader *care*. If the premise remains theoretical, stories become intellectual exercises about as gripping as thumbing through a statistical table of average rainfall in the Faroe Islands.

In this story, we see both sides of the process—the concept, and the way that concept has been made specific, given flesh, immediacy, and poignance.

Using the concept of decreasing living space, one author might envision epidemic claustrophobia and riots, and choose to dramatize that set of possibilities. Another might have focused on scientists coping with more and more unmanageable population statistics and the dangers of worldwide pandemics. A third might have dealt with the logistics of simply *delivering* food to so huge a population. A fourth might have hypothesized a religion which would make suicide a sacrament — the ultimate self-denial for the greater good.

There are dozens of other ways the same basic concept might have been approached and rendered. For a writer, having an interesting concept is only the beginning. The effectiveness of the resulting story depends on how compelling the situation can be made to readers — how fully that abstract premise is given a human face we can imagine and want to care about.

In this story, Ballard has chosen to show the premise by demonstrating the impact of crowding one man: a meek, inoffensive Average Guy, Ward. Mr. Everyman: neither very good nor very bad, simply very crowded. Not so individualized that we can't imagine ourselves in his situation. Not so generalized we don't care what becomes of him. A librarian, to give Ward some perspective on how things got to be the way they are; but not a vast intellect. Neither a scientist nor a man of action.

Ward has no answers to the problem of overcrowding, except to try to make a separate peace when he discovers a hidden door that opens on a vast treasure of space: a lost and forgotten room maybe fifteen feet square. And then his problem, in inhabiting that space, recapitulates the problems of the world at large. Ward is too humane, civilized, and passively unaggressive ever to say enough is enough or set and enforce limits to acceptable crowding, just as the outside world has apparently failed to do. As successive friends and acquaintances want to move in, he accepts the diminution of his own space without ever putting up an argument, much less a fight. The story's end suggests that this once-generous space has now become as intolerable as any other overstuffed cubicle and that Ward himself is about to be forced out altogether by his space-hungry "tenants."

So the story's question isn't "How will Earth cope with a population exceeding 20,000 million?" It's "Will Ward manage to find happiness in his secret hideaway?" And it's the latter question, pinning the problem down to a particular character's fate, which makes the story live in our imaginations.

And just as Ward's experience is a microcosm of the world's, what's being lost with overcrowding is also given a specific, concrete form: the Victorian wardrobe. "It had been a beautiful piece of furniture, in a way symbolizing this whole private world, and the salesman at the store told [Ward] there were few like it left." The wardrobe is also a status symbol: its value is in being able to afford the space to keep it. It's an emblem of wealth as measured in space rather than in money.

As the space afforded the wardrobe is gradually whittled away, as the wardrobe itself is gradually dismantled, the action parallels and exemplifies what's happening to the room and to civilization itself. Whatever kind of life comes next, it won't include the gentle generosities of spirit or of surroundings that Ward and his wardrobe stand for.

The abstract made particular, made human and involving, brought down to a single set of human circumstances, rendered in terms of the impact on a single human life. That's what renders this low-key, understated and rather literary story so memorable.

Science fiction gives you chances of doing many things you can't really do in other forms of fiction. That's one of its chief attractions. For instance, you can, in science fiction, go into detail on alien forms of life drawn out of your fancy. This enables you to develop adventures of a new type, to say nothing of indulging in biological novelties.

Alien life is as old as fantasy. We have always had demons and spirits and ogres and dragons and fearful monsters of all sorts. Early science fiction borrowed such things from earlier fantasy, and in later decades, Hollywood remained stuck with them, giving us menaces in the form of giant spiders, giant amoebae, giant insects, giant apes, giant dinosaurs and so on. Such things, unless done very well, are simply childish and unimaginative extrapolations.

The first person I know of to try to work out an intelligent consideration of alien lifeforms on another world was Stanley G. Weinbaum in his "A Martian Odyssey" published in 1934. Since then, others have tried the same. It is good exercise for the imagination and requires a certain knowledge of biology and natural history.

James H. Schmitz's "Grandpa" is a contemporary example of what can be done in that direction, and how absorbing one can make a consideration of lifeforms that exist only in the writer's imagination.

— Isaac Asimov

Grandpa

James H. Schmitz

A green-winged, downy thing as big as a hen fluttered along the hill-side to a point directly above Cord's head and hovered there, twenty feet above him. Cord, a fifteen-year-old human being, leaned back against a skipboat parked on the equator of a world that had known human beings for only the past four Earth years, and eyed the thing speculatively. The thing was, in the free and easy terminology of the Sutang Colonial Team, a swamp bug. Concealed in the downy fur back of the bug's head was a second, smaller, semiparasitical thing, classed as a bug rider.

The bug itself looked like a new species to Cord. Its parasite might or might not turn out to be another unknown. Cord was a natural research man; his first glimpse of the odd flying team had sent endless curiosities thrilling through him. How did that particular phenomenon tick, and why? What fascinating things, once you'd learned about it, could you get it to *do*?

Normally, he was hampered by circumstances in carrying out any such investigation. The Colonial Team was a practical, hardworking outfit—two thousand people who'd been given twenty years to size up and tame down the brand-new world of Sutang to the point where a hundred thousand colonists could be settled on it, in reasonable safety and comfort. Even junior colonial students like Cord were expected to confine their curiosity to the pattern of research set up by the station to which they were attached. Cord's inclination toward independent experiments had got him into disfavor with his immediate superiors before this.

He sent a casual glance in the direction of the Yoger Bay Colonial Station behind him. No signs of human activity about that low, fortress-like bulk in the hill. Its central lock was still closed. In fifteen minutes, it was scheduled to be opened to let out the Planetary Regent, who was inspecting the Yoger Bay Station and its principal activities today.

Fifteen minutes was time enough to find out something about the new bug, Cord decided.

But he'd have to collect it first.

He slid out one of the two handguns holstered at his side. This one was his own property: a Vanadian projectile weapon. Cord thumbed it to position for anesthetic small-game missiles and brought the hovering swamp bug down, drilled neatly and microscopically through the head.

As the bug hit the ground, the rider left its back. A tiny scarlet demon, round and bouncy as a rubber ball, it shot toward Cord in three long hops, mouth wide to sink home inch-long, venom-dripping fangs. Rather breathlessly, Cord triggered the gun again and knocked it out in mid-leap. A new species, all right! Most bug riders were harmless plant-eaters, mere suckers of vegetable juice —

"*Cord!*" A feminine voice.

Cord swore softly. He hadn't heard the central lock click open. She must have come around from the other side of the station.

"Hi, Grayan!" he shouted innocently without looking around. "Come see what I got! New species!"

Grayan Mahoney, a slender, black-haired girl two years older than himself, came trotting down the hillside toward him. She was Sutang's star colonial student, and the station manager, Nirmond, indicated from time to time that she was a fine example for Cord to pattern his own behavior on. In spite of that, she and Cord were good friends, but she bossed him around considerably.

"Cord, you dope!" she scowled as she came up. "Quit acting like a collector! If the Regent came out now, you'd be sunk. Nirmond's been telling her about you!"

"Telling her what?" Cord asked, startled.

"For one," Grayan reported, "that you don't keep up on your assigned work. Two, that you sneak off on one-man expeditions of your own at least once a month and have to be rescued — "

"Nobody," Cord interrupted hotly, "has had to rescue me yet!"

"How's Nirmond to know you're alive and healthy when you just drop out of sight for a week?" Grayan countered. "Three," she resumed checking the items off on slim fingertips, "he complained that you keep private zoological gardens of unidentified and possibly deadly vermin in the woods back of the station. And four . . . well, Nirmond simply doesn't want the responsibility for you any more!" She held up the four fingers significantly.

"Golly!" gulped Cord, dismayed. Summed up tersely like that, his record *didn't* look too good.

"Golly is right! I keep warning you! Now Nirmond wants the Regent to send you back to Vanadia—and there's a starship coming in to New Venus forty-eight hours from now!" New Venus was the Colonial Team's main settlement on the opposite side of Sutang.

"What'll I do?"

"Start acting like you had good sense mainly." Grayan grinned suddenly. "I talked to the Regent, too—Nirmond isn't rid of you yet! But if you louse up on our tour of the Bay Farms today, you'll be off the Team for good!"

She turned to go. "You might as well put the skipboat back; we're not using it. Nirmond's driving us down to the edge of the Bay in a treadcar, and we'll take a raft from there. Don't let them know I warned you!"

Cord looked after her, slightly stunned. He hadn't realized his reputation had become as bad as all that! To Grayan, whose family had served on Colonial Teams for the past four generations, nothing worse was imaginable than to be dismissed and sent back ignominiously to one's own homeworld. Much to his surprise, Cord was discovering now that he felt exactly the same way about it!

Leaving his newly bagged specimens to revive by themselves and flutter off again, he hurriedly flew the skipboat around the station and rolled it back into its stall.

Three rafts lay moored just offshore in the marshy cove, at the edge of which Nirmond had stopped the treadcar. They looked somewhat like exceptionally broad-brimmed, well-worn sugarloaf hats floating out there, green and leathery. Or like lily pads twenty-five feet across, with the upper section of a big, gray-green pineapple growing from the center of each. Plant animals of some sort. Sutang was too new to have had its phyla sorted out into anything remotely like an orderly classification. The rafts were a local oddity which had been investigated and could be regarded as harmless and moderately useful. Their usefulness lay in the fact that they were employed as a rather slow means of transportation about the shallow, swampy waters of the Yoger Bay. That was as far as the Team's interest in them went at present.

The Regent had stood up from the back seat of the car, where she was sitting next to Cord. There were only four in the party; Grayan was up front with Nirmond.

"Are those our vehicles?" The Regent sounded amused.

Nirmond grinned, a little sourly. "Don't underestimate them, Dane! They could become an important economic factor in this region in time. But, as a matter of fact, these three are smaller than I like to use." He was peering about the reedy edges of the cove. "There's a regular monster parked here usually—"

Grayan turned to Cord. "Maybe Cord knows where Grandpa is hiding."

It was well-meant, but Cord had been hoping nobody would ask him about Grandpa. Now they all looked at him.

"Oh, you want Grandpa?" he said, somewhat flustered. "Well, I left him . . . I mean I saw him a couple of weeks ago about a mile south from here—"

Grayan sighed. Nirmond grunted and told the Regent, "The rafts tend to stay wherever they're left, providing it's shallow and muddy. They use a hair-root system to draw chemicals and microscopic nourishment directly from the bottom of the bay. Well— Grayan, would you like to drive us there?"

Cord settled back unhappily as the treadcar lurched into motion. Nirmond suspected he'd used Grandpa for one of his unauthorized tours of the area, and Nirmond was quite right.

"I understand you're an expert with these rafts, Cord," Dane said from beside him. "Grayan told me we couldn't find a better steersman, or pilot, or whatever you call it, for our trip today."

"I can handle them," Cord said, perspiring. "They don't give you any trouble!" He didn't feel he'd made a good impression on the Regent so far. Dane was a young, handsome-looking woman with an easy way of talking and laughing, but she wasn't the head of the Sutang Colonial Team for nothing. She looked quite capable of shipping out anybody whose record wasn't up to par.

"There's one big advantage our beasties have over a skipboat, too," Nirmond remarked from the front seat. "You don't have to worry about a snapper trying to climb on board with you!" He went on to describe the stinging ribbon-tentacles the rafts spread around them under water to discourage creatures that might make a meal off their tender underparts. The snappers and two or three other active and aggressive species of the Bay hadn't yet learned it was foolish to attack armed human beings in a boat, but they would skitter hurriedly out of the path of a leisurely perambulating raft.

Cord was happy to be ignored for the moment. The Regent,

Nirmond and Grayan were all Earth people, which was true of most of the members of the Team; and Earth people made him uncomfortable, particularly in groups. Vanadia, his own homeworld, had barely graduated from the status of Earth colony itself, which might explain the difference. All the Earth people he'd met so far seemed dedicated to what Grayan Mahoney called the Big Picture, while Nirmond usually spoke of it as "Our Purpose Here." They acted strictly in accordance with their Team Regulations—sometimes, in Cord's opinion, quite insanely. Because now and then the Regulations didn't quite cover a new situation and then somebody was likely to get killed. In which case, the Regulations would be modified promptly, but Earth people didn't seem otherwise disturbed by such events.

Grayan had tried to explain it to Cord:

"We can't really ever *know* in advance what a new world is going to be like! And once we're there, there's too much to do, in the time we've got, to study it inch by inch. You get your job done, and you take a chance. But if you stick by the Regulations you've got the best chances of surviving anybody's been able to figure out for you—"

Cord felt he preferred to just use good sense and not let Regulations or the job get him into a situation he couldn't figure out for himself.

To which Grayan replied impatiently that he hadn't yet got the Big Picture—

The treadcar swung around and stopped, and Grayan stood up in the front seat, pointing. "That's Grandpa, over there!"

Dane also stood up and whistled softly, apparently impressed by Grandpa's fifty-foot spread. Cord looked around in surprise. He was pretty sure this was several hundred yards from the spot where he'd left the big raft two weeks ago; and as Nirmond said, they didn't usually move about by themselves.

Puzzled, he followed the others down a narrow path to the water, hemmed in by tree-sized reeds. Now and then he got a glimpse of Grandpa's swimming platform, the rim of which just touched the shore. Then the path opened out, and he saw the whole raft lying in sunlit, shallow water; and he stopped short, startled.

Nirmond was about to step up on the platform, ahead of Dane.

"Wait!" Cord shouted. His voice sounded squeaky with alarm. "Stop!"

He came running forward.

They had frozen where they stood, looked around swiftly. Then glanced back at Cord coming up. They were well trained.

"What's the matter, Cord?" Nirmond's voice was quiet and urgent.

"Don't get on that raft—it's changed!" Cord's voice sounded wobbly, even to himself. "Maybe it's not even Grandpa—"

He saw he was wrong on the last point before he'd finished the sentence. Scattered along the rim of the raft were discolored spots left by a variety of heat-guns, one of which had been his own. It was the way you goaded the sluggish and mindless things into motion. Cord pointed at the cone-shaped central projection. "There—his head! He's sprouting!"

"Sprouting?" the station manager repeated uncomprehendingly. Grandpa's head, as befitted his girth, was almost twelve feet high and equally wide. It was armor-plated like the back of a saurian to keep off plant-suckers, but two weeks ago it had been an otherwise featureless knob, like those on all other rafts. Now scores of long, kinky, leafless vines had grown out from all surfaces of the cone, like green wires. Some were drawn up like tightly coiled springs, others trailed limply to the platform and over it. The top of the cone was dotted with angry red buds, rather like pimples, which hadn't been there before either. Grandpa looked unhealthy.

"Well," Nirmond said, "so it is. Sprouting!" Grayan made a choked sound. Nirmond glanced at Cord as if puzzled. "Is that all that was bothering you, Cord?"

"Well, sure!" Cord began excitedly. He hadn't caught the significance of the word "all"; his hackles were still up, and he was shaking. "None of them ever—"

Then he stopped. He could tell by their faces that they hadn't got it. Or rather, that they'd got it all right but simply weren't going to let it change their plans. The rafts were classified as harmless, according to the Regulations. Until proved otherwise, they would continue to be regarded as harmless. You didn't waste time quibbling with the Regulations—apparently even if you were the Planetary Regent. You didn't feel you had the time to waste.

He tried again. "Look—" he began. What he wanted to tell them was that Grandpa with one unknown factor added wasn't Grandpa any more. He was an unpredictable, oversized lifeform, to be investigated with cautious thoroughness till you knew what the unknown factor meant.

But it was no use. They knew all that. He stared at them helplessly. "I—"

Dane turned to Nirmond. "Perhaps you'd better check," she said.

She didn't add, "—to reassure the boy!" but that was what she meant.

Cord felt himself flushing terribly. They thought he was scared—which he was—and they were feeling sorry for him, which they had no right to do. But there was nothing he could say or do now except watch Nirmond walk steadily across the platform. Grandpa shivered slightly a few times, but the rafts always did that when someone first stepped on them. The station manager stopped before one of the kinky sprouts, touched it and then gave it a tug. He reached up and poked at the lowest of the budlike growths. "Odd-looking things!" he called back. He gave Cord another glance. "Well, everything seems harmless enough, Cord. Coming aboard, everyone?"

It was like dreaming a dream in which you yelled and yelled at people and couldn't make them hear you! Cord stepped up stiff-legged on the platform behind Dane and Grayan. He knew exactly what would have happened if he'd hesitated even a moment. One of them would have said in a friendly voice, careful not to let it sound too contemptuous: "You don't have to come along if you don't want to, Cord!"

Grayan had unholstered her heat-gun and was ready to start Grandpa moving out into the channels of the Yoger Bay.

Cord hauled out his own heat-gun and said roughly, "I was to do that!"

"All right, Cord." She gave him a brief, impersonal smile, as if he were someone she'd met for the first time that day, and stood aside.

They were so infuriatingly polite! He was, Cord decided, as good as on his way back to Vanadia right now.

For a while, Cord almost hoped that something awesome and catastrophic would happen promptly to teach the Team people a lesson. But nothing did. As always, Grandpa shook himself vaguely and experimentally when he felt the heat on one edge of the platform and then decided to withdraw from it, all of which was standard procedure. Under the water, out of sight, were the raft's working sections: short, thick leaf-structures shaped like paddles and designed to work as such, along with the slimy nettle-streamers which kept the vegetarians of the Yoger Bay away, and a jungle of hair roots through which Grandpa sucked nourishments from the mud and the sluggish waters of the Bay, and with which he also anchored himself.

The paddles started churning, the platform quivered, the hair roots were hauled out of the mud; and Grandpa was on his ponderous way.

Cord switched off the heat, reholstered his gun, and stood up. Once in motion, the rafts tended to keep traveling unhurriedly for quite a while. To stop them, you gave them a touch of heat along their leading edge; and they could be turned in any direction by using the gun lightly on the opposite side of the platform.

It was simple enough. Cord didn't look at the others. He was still burning inside. He watched the reed beds move past and open out, giving him glimpses of the misty, yellow and green and blue expanse of the brackish Bay ahead. Behind the mist, to the west, were the Yoger Straits, tricky and ugly water when the tides were running; and beyond the Straits lay the open sea, the great Zlanti Deep, which was another world entirely and one of which he hadn't seen much as yet.

Suddenly he was sick with the full realization that he wasn't likely to see any more of it now! Vanadia was a pleasant enough planet; but the wildness and strangeness were long gone from it. It wasn't Sutang.

Grayan called from beside Dane, "What's the best route from here into the farms, Cord?"

"The big channel to the right," he answered. He added somewhat sullenly, "We're headed for it!"

Grayan came over to him. "The Regent doesn't want to see all of it," she said, lowering her voice. "The algae and plankton beds first. Then as much of the mutated grains as we can show her in about three hours. Steer for the ones that have been doing best, and you'll keep Nirmond happy!"

She gave him a conspiratorial wink. Cord looked after her uncertainly. You couldn't tell from her behavior that anything was wrong. Maybe—

He had a flare of hope. It was hard not to like the Team people, even when they were being rock-headed about their Regulations. Perhaps it was that purpose that gave them their vitality and drive, even though it made them remorseless about themselves and everyone else. Anyway, the day wasn't over yet. He might still redeem himself in the Regent's opinion. Something might happen—

Cord had a sudden cheerful, if improbable, vision of some Bay monster plunging up on the raft with snapping jaws, and of himself alertly blowing out what passed for the monster's brains before anyone else— Nirmond, in particular—was even aware of the threat. The Bay monsters shunned Grandpa, of course, but there might be ways of tempting one of them.

So far, Cord realized, he'd been letting his feelings control him. It was time to start thinking!

Grandpa first. So he's sprouted—green vines and red buds, purpose unknown, but with no change observable in his behavior-patterns otherwise. He was the biggest raft in this end of the Bay, though all of them had been growing steadily in the two years since Cord had first seen one. Sutang's seasons changed slowly; its year was somewhat more than five Earth years long. The first Team members to land here hadn't yet seen a full year pass.

Grandpa then was showing a seasonal change. The other rafts, not quite so far developed, would be reacting similarly a little later. Plant animals — they might be blossoming, preparing to propagate.

"Grayan," he called, "how do the rafts get started? When they're small, I mean."

Grayan looked pleased; and Cord's hopes went up a little more. Grayan was on his side again anyway!

"Nobody knows yet," she said. "We were just talking about it. About half of the coastal marsh-fauna of the continent seems to go through a preliminary larval stage in the sea." She nodded at the red buds on the raft's cone. "It *looks* as if Grandpa is going to produce flowers and let the wind or ride take the seeds out through the Straits."

It made sense. It also knocked out Cord's still half-held hope that the change in Grandpa might turn out to be drastic enough, in some way, to justify his reluctance to get on board. Cord studied Grandpa's armored head carefully once more — unwilling to give up that hope entirely. There were a series of vertical gummy black slits between the armor plates, which hadn't been in evidence two weeks ago either. It looked as if Grandpa were beginning to come apart at the seams. Which might indicate that the rafts, big as they grew to be, didn't outlive a full seasonal cycle, but came to flower at about this time of Sutang's year and died. However, it was a safe bet that Grandpa wasn't going to collapse into senile decay before they completed their trip today.

Cord gave up on Grandpa. The other notion returned to him — perhaps he could coax an obliging Bay monster into action that would show the Regent he was no sissy!

Because the monsters were there, all right.

Kneeling at the edge of the platform and peering down into the wine-colored, clear water of the deep channel they were moving through, Cord could see a fair selection of them at almost any moment.

Some five or six snappers, for one thing. Like big, flattened crayfish, chocolate-brown mostly, with green and red spots on their carapaced backs. In some areas they were so thick you'd wonder what they found to live on, except that they ate almost anything, down to chewing up the mud in which they squatted. However, they preferred their food in large chunks and alive, which was one reason you didn't go swimming in the Bay. They would attack a boat on occasion; but the excited manner in which the ones he saw were scuttling off toward the edges of the channel showed they wanted to have nothing to do with a big moving raft.

Dotted across the bottom were two-foot round holes which looked vacant at the moment. Normally, Cord knew, there would be a head filling each of those holes. The heads consisted mainly of triple sets of jaws, held open patiently like so many traps to grab at anything that came within range of the long, wormlike bodies behind the heads. But Grandpa's passage, waving his stingers like transparent pennants through the water, had scared the worms out of sight, too.

Otherwise, mostly schools of small stuff—and then a flash of wicked scarlet, off to the left behind the raft, darting out from the reeds! Turning its needle-nose into their wake.

Cord watched it without moving. He knew that creature, though it was rare in the Bay and hadn't been classified. Swift, vicious—alert enough to snap swamp bugs out of the air as they fluttered across the surface. And he'd tantalized one with fishing tackle once into leaping up on a moored raft, where it had flung itself about furiously until he was able to shoot it.

No fishing tackle. A handkerchief might just do it, if he cared to risk an arm—

"What fantastic creatures!" Dane's voice just behind him.

"Yellowheads," said Nirmond. "They've got a high utility rating. Keep down the bugs."

Cord stood up casually. It was no time for tricks! The reed bed to their right was thick with yellowheads, a colony of them. Vaguely froggy things, man-sized and better. Of all the creatures he'd discovered in the Bay, Cord like them least. The flabby, sacklike bodies clung with four thin limbs to the upper sections of the twenty-foot reeds that lined the channel. They hardly ever moved, but their huge, bulging eyes seemed to take in everything that went on about them. Every so often, a downy swamp bug came close enough; and a yellowhead would open its vertical, enormous, tooth-lined slash of a mouth, extend the whole front of its face like a bellows in a flashing strike; and the bug would be gone. They might be useful, but Cord hated them.

"Ten years from now we should know what the cycle of coastal life is like," Nirmond said. "When we set up the Yoger Bay Station there were no yellowheads here. They came the following year. Still with traces of the oceanic larval form; but the metamorphosis was almost complete. About twelve inches long—"

Dane remarked that the same pattern was duplicated endlessly elsewhere. The Regent was inspecting the yellowhead colony with field glasses; she put them down now, looked at Cord and smiled. "How far to the farms?"

"About twenty minutes."

"The key," Nirmond said, "seems to be the Zlanti Basin. It must be almost a soup of life in spring."

"It is," nodded Dane, who had been here in Sutang's spring, four Earth years ago. "It's beginning to look as if the Basin alone might justify colonization. The question is still—" she gestured towards the yellowheads—"how do creatures like that get there?"

They walked off toward the other side of the raft, arguing about ocean currents. Cord might have followed. But something splashed back of them, off to the left and not too far back. He stayed, watching.

After a moment, he saw the big yellowhead. It had slipped down from its reedy perch, which was what had caused the splash. Almost submerged at the water line, it stared after the raft with huge pale-green eyes. To Cord, it seemed to look directly at him. In that moment, he knew for the first time why he didn't like yellowheads. There was something very like intelligence in that look, an alien calculation. In creatures like that, intelligence seemed out of place. What use could they have for it?

A little shiver went over him when it sank completely under the water and he realized it intended to swim after the raft. But it was mostly excitement. He had never seen a yellowhead come down out of the reeds before. The obliging monster he'd been looking for might be presenting itself in an unexpected way.

Half a minute later, he watched it again, swimming awkwardly far down. It had no immediate intention of boarding at any rate. Cord saw it come into the area of the raft's trailing stingers. It maneuvered its way between them with curiously human swimming motions, and went out of sight under the platform.

He stood up, wondering what it meant. The yellowhead had appeared to know about the stingers; there had been an air of purpose in every move of its approach. He was tempted to tell the others about it, but there was the moment of triumph he could have if it suddenly came slobbering up over the edge of the platform and he nailed it before their eyes.

It was almost time anyway to turn the raft in toward the farms. If nothing happened before then —

He watched. Almost five minutes, but no sign of the yellowhead. Still wondering, a little uneasy, he gave Grandpa a calculated needling of heat.

After a moment, he repeated it. Then he drew a deep breath and forgot all about the yellowhead.

"Nirmond!" he called sharply.

The three of them were standing near the center of the platform, next to the big armored cone, looking ahead at the farms. They glanced around.

"What's the matter now, Cord?"

Cord couldn't say it for a moment. He was suddenly, terribly scared again. Something had gone wrong!

"The raft won't turn!" he told them.

"Give it a real burn this time!" Nirmond said.

Cord glanced up at him. Nirmond, standing a few steps in front of Dane and Grayan as if he wanted to protect them, had begun to look a little strained, and no wonder. Cord already had pressed the gun to three different points on the platform; but Grandpa appeared to have developed a sudden anesthesia for heat. They kept moving out steadily toward the center of the Bay.

Now Cord held his breath, switched the heat on full and let Grandpa have it. A six-inch patch on the platform blistered up instantly, turned brown, then black —

Grandpa stopped dead. Just like that.

"That's right! Keep burn —" Nirmond didn't finish his order.

A giant shudder. Cord staggered back toward the water. Then the whole edge of the raft came curling up behind him and went down again, smacking the Bay with a sound like a cannon shot. He flew forward off his feet, hit the platform face down and flattened himself against it. It swelled up beneath him. Two more enormous slaps and joltings. Then quiet. He looked round for the others.

He lay within twelve feet of the central cone. Some twenty or thirty of the mysterious new vines the cone had sprouted were stretched out stiffly toward him now, like so many thin green fingers. They couldn't quite reach him. The nearest tip was still ten inches from his shoes.

But Grandpa had caught the others, all three of them. They were tumbled together at the foot of the cone, wrapped in a stiff network of green vegetable ropes, and they didn't move.

Cord drew his feet up cautiously, prepared for another earthquake reaction. But nothing happened. Then he discovered that Grandpa was back in motion on his previous course. The heatgun had vanished. Gently, he took out the Vanadian gun.

"Cord? It didn't get you?" It was the Regent.

"No," he said, keeping his voice low. He realized suddenly he'd simply assumed they were all dead. Now he felt sick and shaky.

"What are you doing?"

Cord looked at Grandpa's big armor-plated head with a certain hunger. The cones were hollowed out inside; the station's lab had decided their chief function was to keep enough air trapped under the rafts to float them. But in that central section was also the organ that controlled Grandpa's overall reactions.

He said softly, "I got a gun and twelve heavy-duty explosive bullets. Two of them will blow that cone apart."

"No good, Cord!" the pain-racked voice told him. "If the thing sinks, we'll die anyway. You have anesthetic charges for that gun of yours?"

He stared at her back. "Yes."

"Give Nirmond and the girl a shot each, before you do anything else. Directly into the spine, if you can. But don't come any closer—"

Somehow, Cord couldn't argue with that voice. He stood up carefully. The gun made two soft spitting sounds.

"All right," he said hoarsely. "What do I do now?"

Dane was silent a moment. "I'm sorry, Cord. I can't tell you that. I'll tell you what I can—"

She paused for some seconds again. "This thing didn't try to kill us, Cord. It could have easily. It's incredibly strong. I saw it break Nirmond's legs. But as soon as we stopped moving, it just held us. They were both unconscious then—"

"You've got that to go on. It was trying to pitch you within reach of its vines or tendrils, or whatever they are, wasn't it?"

"I think so," Cord said shakily. That was what had happened, of course; and at any moment Grandpa might try again.

"Now it's feeding us some sort of anesthetic of its own through those vines. Tiny thorns. A sort of numbness—" Dane's voice trailed off a moment. Then she said clearly, "Look, Cord—it seems we're food it's storing up! You get that?"

"Yes," he said.

"Seeding time for the rafts. There are analogues. Live food for its seed probably; not for the raft. One couldn't have counted on that. Cord?"

"Yes, I'm here."

"I want," said Dane, "to stay awake as long as I can. But there's really just one other thing—this raft's going somewhere. To some particularly favorable location. And that might be very near shore. You might make it in then; otherwise it's up to you. But keep your head and wait for a chance. No heroics, understand?"

"Sure, I understand," Cord told her. He realized then that he was talking reassuringly, as if it weren't the Planetary Regent but someone like Grayan.

"Nirmond's the worst," Dane said. "The girl was knocked unconscious at once. If it weren't for my arm—But, if we can get help in five hours or so, everything should be all right. Let me know if anything happens, Cord."

"I will," Cord said gently again. Then he sighted his gun carefully at a point between Dane's shoulder blades, and the anesthetic chamber made its soft, spitting sound once more. Dane's taut body relaxed slowly, and that was all.

There was no point Cord could see in letting her stay awake; because they weren't going anywhere near shore.

The reed beds and the channels were already behind them, and Grandpa hadn't changed direction by the fraction of a degree. He was moving out into the open Bay—and he was picking up company!

So far, Cord could count seven big rafts within two miles of them; and on the three that were closest he could make out a sprouting of new green vines. All of them were traveling in a straight direction; and the common point they were all headed for appeared to be the roaring center of the Yoger Straits, now some three miles away!

Behind the Straits, the cold Zlanti Deep—the rolling fogs, and the open sea! It might be seeding time for the rafts, but it looked as if they weren't going to distribute their seeds in the Bay—

For a human being, Cord was a fine swimmer. He had a gun and he had a knife, in spite of what Dane had said; he might have stood a chance among the killers of the Bay. But it would be a very small chance, at best. And it wasn't, he thought, as if there weren't still other possibilities. He was going to keep his head.

Except by accident, of course, nobody was going to come looking for them in time to do any good. If anyone did look, it would be around the Bay Farms. There were a number of rafts moored there; and it would be assumed they'd used one of them. Now and then something unexpected happened and somebody simply vanished — by the time it was figured out just what had happened on this occasion, it would be much too late.

Neither was anybody likely to notice within the next few hours that the rafts had started migrating out of the swamps through the Yoger Straits. There was a small weather station a little inland, on the north side of the Straits, which used a helicopter occasionally. It was about as improbable, Cord decided dismally, that they'd use it in the right spot just now as it would be for a jet transport to happen to come in low enough to spot them.

The fact that it was up to him, as the Regent had said, sank in a little more after that! Cord had never felt so lonely.

Simply because he was going to try it sooner or later, he carried out an experiment next that he knew couldn't work. He opened the gun's anesthetic chamber and counted out fifty pellets — rather hurriedly because he didn't particularly want to think of what he might be using them for eventually. There were around three hundred charges left in the chamber then; and in the next few minutes Cord carefully planted a third of them in Grandpa's head.

He stopped after that. A whale might have showed signs of somnolence under a lesser load. Grandpa paddled on undisturbed. Perhaps he had become a little numb in spots, but his cells weren't equipped to distribute the soporific effect of that type of drug.

There wasn't anything else Cord could think of doing before they reached the Straits. At the rate they were moving, he calculated that would happen in something less than an hour; and if they did pass through the Straits, he was going to risk a swim. He didn't think Dane would have disapproved, under the circumstances. If the raft simply carried them all out into the foggy vastness of the Zlanti Deep, there would be no practical chance of survival left at all.

Meanwhile, Grandpa was definitely picking up speed. And there were other changes going on — minor ones, but still a little awe-inspiring to Cord. The pimply-looking red buds that dotted the upper part of the cone were opening out gradually. From the center of most of them protruded now something like a thin, wet, scarlet worm: a worm that twisted weakly, extended itself by an inch or so, rested and twisted again, and stretched up a little farther, groping into the air. The vertical black slits between the armor plates looked somehow deeper and wider than they had been even some minutes ago; a dark, thick liquid dripped slowly from several of them.

Under other circumstances Cord knew he would have been fascinated by these developments in Grandpa. As it was, they drew his suspicious attention only because he didn't know what they meant.

Then something quite horrible happened suddenly. Grayan started moaning loudly and terribly and twisted almost completely around. Afterwards, Cord knew it hadn't been a second before he stopped her struggles and the sounds together with another anesthetic pellet; but the vines had tightened their grip on her first, not flexibly but like the digging, bony green talons of some monstrous bird of prey. If Dane hadn't warned him —

White and sweating, Cord put his gun down slowly while the vines relaxed again. Grayan didn't seem to have suffered any additional harm; and she would certainly have been the first to point out that his murderous rage might have been as intelligently directed against a machine. But for some moments Cord continued to luxuriate furiously in the thought that, at any instant he chose, he could still turn the raft very quickly into a ripped and exploded mess of sinking vegetation.

Instead, and more sensibly, he gave both Dane and Nirmond another shot, to prevent a similar occurrence with them. The contents of two such pellets, he knew, would keep any human being torpid for at least four hours. Five shots —

Cord withdrew his mind hastily from the direction it was turning into; but it wouldn't stay withdrawn. The thought kept coming up again; until at last he had to recognize it:

Five shots would leave the three of them completely unconscious, whatever else might happen to them, until they either died from other causes or were given a counteracting agent.

Shocked, he told himself he couldn't do it. It was exactly like killing them.

But then, quite steadily, he found himself raising the gun once more, to bring the total charge for each of the three Team people up to five. And if it was the first time in the last four years Cord had felt like crying, it also seemed to him that he had begun to understand what was meant by using your head — along with other things.

Barely thirty minutes later, he watched a raft as big as the one he rode go sliding into the foaming white waters of the Straits a few hundred yards ahead, and dart off abruptly at an angle, caught by one of the swirling currents. It pitched and spun, made some headway, and was swept aside again. And then it righted itself once more. Not like some blindly animated vegetable, Cord thought, but like a creature that struggled with intelligent purpose to maintain its chosen direction.

At least, they seemed practically unsinkable—

Knife in hand, he flattened himself against the platform as the Straits roared just ahead. When the platform jolted and tilted up beneath him, he rammed the knife all the way into it and hung on. Cold water rushed suddenly over him, and Grandpa shuddered like a laboring engine. In the middle of it all, Cord had the horrified notion that the raft might release its unconscious human prisoners in its struggle with the Straits. But he underestimated Grandpa in that. Grandpa also hung on.

Abruptly, it was over. They were riding a long swell, and there were three other rafts not far away. The Straits had swept them together, but they seemed to have no interest in one another's company. As Cord stood up shakily and began to strip off his clothes, they were visibly drawing apart again. The platform of one of them was half-submerged; it must have lost too much of the air that held it afloat and, like a small ship, it was foundering.

From this point, it was only a two-mile swim to the shore north of the Straits, and another mile inland from there to the Straits Head Station. He didn't know about the current; but the distance didn't seem too much, and he couldn't bring himself to leave knife and gun behind. The Bay creatures loved warmth and mud, they didn't venture beyond the Straits. But Zlanti Deep bred its own killers, though they weren't often observed so close to shore.

Things were beginning to look rather hopeful.

Thin, crying voices drifted overhead, like the voices of curious cats, as Cord knotted his clothes into a tight bundle, shoes inside. He looked up. There were four of them circling there; magnified seagoing swamp bugs, each carrying an unseen rider. Probably harmless scavengers—but the ten-foot wingspread was impressive. Uneasily, Cord remembered the venomously carnivorous rider he'd left lying beside the station.

One of them dipped lazily and came sliding down toward him. It soared overhead and came back, to hover about the raft's cone.

The bug rider that directed the mindless flier hadn't been interested in him at all! Grandpa was baiting it!

Cord stared in fascination. The top of the cone was alive now with a softly wriggling mass of the scarlet, wormlike extrusions that had started sprouting before the raft left the Bay. Presumably, they looked enticingly edible to the bug rider.

The flier settled with an airy fluttering and touched the cone. Like a trap springing shut, the green vines flashed up and around it, crumpling the brittle wings, almost vanishing into the long soft body —

Barely a second later, Grandpa made another catch, this one from the sea itself. Cord had a fleeting glimpse of something like a small, rubbery seal that flung itself out of the water upon the edge of the raft, with a suggestion of desperate haste — and was flipped on instantly against the cone where the vines clamped it down beside the flier's body.

It wasn't the enormous ease with which the unexpected kill was accomplished that left Cord standing there, completely shocked. It was the shattering of his hopes to swim to shore from here. Fifty yards away, the creature from which the rubbery thing had been fleeing showed briefly on the surface, as it turned away from the raft; and the glance was all he needed. The ivory-white body and gaping jaws were similar enough to those of the sharks of Earth to indicate the pursuer's nature. The important difference was that, wherever the white hunters of the Zlanti Deep went, they went by the thousands.

Stunned by that incredible piece of bad luck, still clutching his bundled clothes, Cord stared toward shore. Knowing what to look for, he could spot the telltale roilings of the surface now — the long, ivory gleams that flashed through the swells and vanished again. Shoals of smaller things burst into the air in sprays of glittering desperation and fell back.

He would have been snapped up like a drowning fly before he'd covered a twentieth of that distance!

But almost another full minute passed before the realization of the finality of his defeat really sank in.

Grandpa was beginning to eat!

Each of the dark slits down the sides of the cone was a mouth. So far only one of them was in operating condition, and the raft wasn't able to open that one very wide as yet. The first morsel had been fed into, however: the bug rider the vines had plucked out of the flier's downy neck fur. It took Grandpa several minutes to work it out of sight, small as it was. But it was a start.

Cord didn't feel quite sane any more. He sat there, clutching his bundle of clothes and only vaguely aware of the fact that he was shivering steadily under the cold spray that touched him now and then, while he followed Grandpa's activities attentively. He decided it would be at least some hours before one of that black set of mouths grew flexible and vigorous enough to dispose of a human being. Under the circumstances, it couldn't make much difference to the other human beings here; but the moment Grandpa reached for the first one of them would also be the moment he finally blew the raft to pieces. The white hunters were cleaner eaters, at any rate; and that was about the extent to which he could still control what was going to happen.

Meanwhile, there was the very faint chance that the weather station's helicopter might spot them —

Meanwhile also, in a weary and horrified fascination, he kept debating the mystery of what could have produced such a nightmarish change in the rafts. He could guess where they were going by now; there were scattered strings of them stretching back to the Straits or roughly parallel to their own course, and the direction was that of the plankton-swarming pool of the Zlanti Basin, a thousand miles to the north. Given time, even mobile lily pads like the rafts had been could make that trip for the benefit of their seedlings. But nothing in their structure explained the sudden change into alert and capable carnivores.

He watched the rubbery little seal-thing being hauled up to a mouth next. The vines broke its neck; and the mouth took it in up to the shoulders and then went on working patiently at what was still a trifle too large a bite. Meanwhile, there were more thin cat cries overhead; and a few minutes later, two more sea bugs were trapped almost simultaneously and added to the larder. Grandpa dropped the dead seal-thing and fed himself another bug rider. The second rider left its mount with a sudden hop, sank its teeth viciously into one of the vines that caught it again, and was promptly battered to death against the platform.

Cord felt a resurge of unreasoning hatred against Grandpa. Killing a bug was about equal to cutting a branch from a tree; they had almost no life-awareness. But the rider had aroused his partisanship because of its appearance of intelligent action — and it was in fact closer to the human scale in that feature than to the monstrous lifeform that had, mechanically, but quite successfully, trapped both it and the human beings. Then his thoughts had drifted again; and he found himself speculating vaguely on the curious symbiosis in which the nerve systems of two creatures as dissimilar as the bugs and their riders could be linked so closely that they functioned as one organism.

Suddenly an expression of vast and stunned surprise appeared on his face.

Why—now he knew!

Cord stood up hurriedly, shaking with excitement, the whole plan complete in his mind. And a dozen long vines snaked instantly in the direction of his sudden motion, and groped for him, taut and stretching. They couldn't reach him, but their savagely alert reaction froze Cord briefly where he was. The platform was shuddering under his feet, as if in irritation at his inaccessibility; but it couldn't be tilted up suddenly here to throw him within the grasp of the vines, as it could around the edges.

Still, it was a warning! Cord sidled gingerly around the cone till he had gained the position he wanted, which was on the forward half of the raft. And then he waited. Waited long minutes, quite motionless, until his heart stopped pounding and the irregular angry shivering of the surface of the raft-thing died away, and the last vine tendril had stopped its blind groping. It might help a lot if, for a second or two after he next started moving, Grandpa wasn't too aware of his exact whereabouts.

He looked back once to check how far they had gone by now beyond the Straits Head Station. It couldn't, he decided, be even an hour behind them. Which was close enough, by the most pessimistic count—if everything else worked out all right! He didn't try to think out in detail what that "everything else" could include, because there were factors that simply couldn't be calculated in advance. And he had an uneasy feeling that speculating too vividly about them might make him almost incapable of carrying out his plan.

At last, moving carefully, Cord took the knife in his left hand but left the gun holstered. He raised the tightly knotted bundle of clothes slowly over his head, balanced in his right hand. With a long, smooth motion he tossed the bundle back across the cone, almost to the opposite edge of the platform.

It hit with a soggy thump. Almost immediately, the whole far edge of the raft buckled and flapped up to toss the strange object to the reaching vines.

Simultaneously, Cord was racing forward. For a moment, his attempt to divert Grandpa's attention seemed completely successful — then he was pitched to his knees as the platform came up.

He was within eight feet of the edge. As it slapped down again, he threw himself desperately forward.

An instant later, he was knifing down through cold, clear water, just ahead of the raft, then twisting and coming up again.

The raft was passing over him. Clouds of tiny sea creatures scattered through its dark jungle of feeding roots. Cord jerked back from a broad, wavering streak of glassy greenness, which was a stinger, and felt a burning jolt on his side, which meant he'd been touched lightly by another. He bumped on blindly through the slimy black tangles of hair roots that covered the bottom of the raft; then green half-light passed over him, and he burst up into the central bubble under the cone.

Half-light and foul, hot air. Water slapped around him, dragging him away again — nothing to hang on to here! Then above him, to his right, molded against the interior curve of the cone as if it had grown there from the start, the froglike, man-sized shape of the yellowhead.

The raft rider —

Cord reached up and caught Grandpa's symbiotic partner and guide by a flabby hind leg, pulled himself half out of the water and struck twice with the knife, fast while the pale-green eyes were still opening.

He'd thought the yellowhead might need a second or so to detach itself from its host, as the bug riders usually did, before it tried to defend itself. This one merely turned its head; the mouth slashed down and clamped on Cord's left arm above the elbow. His right hand sank the knife through one staring eye, and the yellowhead jerked away, pulling the knife from his grasp.

Sliding down, he wrapped both hands around the slimy leg and hauled with all his weight. For a moment more, the yellowhead hung on. Then the countless neural extensions that connected it now with the raft came free in a succession of sucking, tearing sounds; and Cord and the yellowhead splashed into the water together.

Black tangle of roots again — and two more electric burns suddenly across his back and legs! Strangling, Cord let go. Below him, for a moment, a body was turning over and over with oddly human motions; then a solid wall of water thrust him up and aside, as something big and white struck the turning body and went on.

Cord broke the surface twelve feet behind the raft. And that would have been that, if Grandpa hadn't already been slowing down.

After two tries, he floundered back up on the platform and lay there gasping and coughing awhile. There were no indications that his presence was resented now. A few vine tips twitched uneasily, as if trying to remember previous functions, when he came limping up presently to make sure his three companions were still breathing; but Cord never noticed that.

They were still breathing; and he knew better than to waste time trying to help them himself. He took Grayan's heat-gun from its holster. Grandpa had come to a full stop.

Cord hadn't had time to become completely sane again, or he might have worried now whether Grandpa, violently sundered from his controlling partner, was still capable of motion on his own. Instead, he determined the approximate direction of the Straits Head Station, selected a corresponding spot on the platform and gave Grandpa a light tap of heat.

Nothing happened immediately. Cord sighed patiently and stepped up the heat a little.

Grandpa shuddered gently. Cord stood up.

Slowly and hesitatingly at first, then with steadfast — though now again brainless — purpose, Grandpa began paddling back toward the Straits Head Station.

Commentary

Premise: A seemingly harmless alien lifeform can undergo unexpected and initially inexplicable changes which render it dangerous.

This is an "alien world" story. Aliens figure in many other stories in this collection — the Hussir of "The Silk and the Song," the preternaturally vicious eaber of "Transstar," the puppeteers of "Neutron Star" — and that should be no surprise, since one of the major strains running through science fiction is "otherness": ways different from our own of experiencing life.

But the Hussir, the eaber, and the puppeteers differ from humanity principally in shape: their attitudes and reactions, their general psychology, is human. They want, more or less, what we want: control of their environment, security, victory over enemies. A single trait, like caution, may be expanded into a racial idiosyncrasy, as with the puppeteers; but caution too is a human trait. Allowing for individual differences, these aliens are our equals in intelligence and possess similar cultures, although the eaber are a space-going race and the Hussir are pre-industrial. Essentially, they're human beings only slightly disguised beneath odd masks: they only *look* funny.

Another major strain in science fiction is that of space exploration: finding and meeting the strange on its own ground. This fiction allows for a wider range of aliens: not only aliens who are humanlike inside, no matter what their appearance, but aliens who are analogues of plants or animals. Whole worlds operating on un-earthlike principles, as in Ursula LeGuin's *The Word for World is Forest*, Hal Clement's *Mission of Gravity*, or Harry Harrison's *Deathworld*. As our interest in the whole range of living things that share Earth with us increases, so does our interest in exploring the zoology, botany, and even mineralogy of exotic locales elsewhere in the galaxy. The aliens don't have to talk like us, or at all, to win and hold our attention, any more than a tiger does. All they have to be is interestingly alien.

"Grandpa" casts the interaction between alien and human as a "coming of age" story concerning Cord, fifteen years old and so irresponsible he's in danger of being sent home, away from the fascinating human colony on Sutang. In other words, the story is set in terms, not of intellectual scientific study, but of a crucial life issue to an otherwise average and unremarkable teenage boy. We're given a solid point of contact, somebody to know and like. Cord's future depends on the story's outcome. So the knowledge Cord has and gets about the huge lily-pad beings called "rafts" is made to *really matter* in human terms, rather than being merely thrown out for its own sake.

The stakes are raised further yet, because Cord's very life is made to depend on his learning why the formerly placid raft nicknamed "Grandpa" seems suddenly to have developed a will of its own, intent on devouring its passengers as it conveys them farther and farther from help. The other passengers—Grayan, a sisterly and understated love interest; the lady Regent; and Nirmond, the leader of the Sutang Colonial Team—are all unconscious, variously injured. Everything is made to depend on Cord. So it's life or death, not only for Cord himself, but for an analogue family whose members are helpless and in acute, immediate danger.

And the story's resolution is made to depend on Cord's insights into alien zoology, gained in the very unauthorized and "irresponsible" explorations that have gotten him in trouble in the first place. In other words, the story validates curiosity about things for their own sake, rather than "the Big Picture" and "Our Purpose Here" which the Earth-born members of the Colonial Team hold by. By focusing primarily on themselves and their purpose, rather than being open to the very real otherness of the world around them, people born to Earth (Cord was Vanadian-born) are unprepared when a new situation arises that's not covered by the existing Regulations. When that happens, "somebody was likely to get killed."

It's interesting to note, though, that although this abstract curiosity is commended *through Cord*, the author himself doesn't make the story depend on it. In other words, a story about the rafts and their seasonal acquisitions of purposeful "raft riders" could have been an objective account of what rafts look like, what they eat, how they breed and interact with one another and with the rest of Sutangian life, what humans find them useful for, and a thousand other invented details that would leave readers numb, perhaps, but knowing a whole lot about rafts, for whatever satisfaction it might give them.

Schmitz is too wise a writer to do that, though. He gives us the fun of exploring the perils of the unknown but never forgets that we, too, are Earth-born: more interested in how this knowledge affects one teenage boy than in any hypothetical laundry list of invented facts about imaginary creatures.

It's finally human life, human choices, human achievement and victory that alone can engage both our interest and our sympathy and make us want to read the story to the very end—not only to discover what's wrong with Grandpa, to confront the truly alien, but to again be assured that human courage, curiosity, and insight are equal to any strangeness we may confront in this world or any other.

There are those who feel that the advance of science must surely use up all the science fiction plots and leave the field barren.

This is clearly not so. Indeed, the opposite is more likely true. The advance of science creates science fiction plots, and does so at a greater rate than it destroys them. That is one reason why a science fiction writer should keep a close watch on scientific and technological advance. Not only does it help keep his stories up to date, but it will give him ideas for new kinds of stories.

For instance, the development of computers in the late 1940s initiated an entirely new variety of science fiction — the computer story. There had been earlier stories involving advanced mentalities of one kind or another, but the coming of computers gave us something solid to bite into, and lent a new conviction to our plots.

Naturally, the logical type of story to be built about computers deals with the danger of computers replacing human beings, of going out of control, of running amok. Certainly, that's where the drama would seem to lie.

However, never let yourself be tied down. I have routinely written computer stories (and robot stories before the time of computers) in which the artificial minds are benign and human-friendly. My story "The Last Question" is probably the ultimate in this direction.

— Isaac Asimov

The Last Question

Isaac Asimov

The last question was asked for the first time, half in jest, on May 21, 2061, at a time when humanity first stepped into the light. The question came about as a result of a five-dollar bet over highballs, and it happened this way:

Alexander Adell and Bertram Lupov were two of the faithful attendants of Multivac. As well as any human beings could, they knew what lay behind the cold, clicking, flashing face — miles and miles of face — of that giant computer. They had at least a vague notion of the general plan of relays and circuits that had long since grown past the point where any single human could possibly have a firm grasp of the whole.

Multivac was self-adjusting and self-correcting. It had to be, for nothing human could adjust and correct it quickly enough or even adequately enough. So Adell and Lupov attended the monstrous giant only lightly and superficially, yet as well as any men could. They fed it data, adjusted questions to its needs and translated the answers that were issued. Certainly they, and all others like them, were fully entitled to share in the glory that was Multivac's.

For decades, Multivac had helped design the ships and plot the trajectories that enabled man to reach the Moon, Mars, and Venus, but past that, Earth's poor resources could not support the ships. Too much energy was needed for the long trips. Earth exploited its coal and uranium with increasing efficiency, but there was only so much of both.

But slowly Multivac learned enough to answer deeper questions more fundamentally, and on May 14, 2061, what had been theory, became fact.

The energy of the sun was stored, converted, and utilized directly on a planet-wide scale. All Earth turned off its burning coal, its fissioning uranium, and flipped the switch that connected all of it to a small station, one mile in diameter, circling the Earth at half the distance of the

Moon. All Earth ran by invisible beams of sunpower.

Seven days had not sufficed to dim the glory of it and Adell and Lupov finally managed to escape from the public function, and to meet in quiet where no one would think of looking for them, in the deserted underground chambers, where portions of the mighty buried body of Multivac showed. Unattended, idling, sorting data with contented lazy clickings, Multivac, too, had earned its vacation and the boys appreciated that. They had no intention, originally, of disturbing it.

They had brought a bottle with them, and their only concern at the moment was to relax in the company of each other and the bottle.

"It's amazing when you think of it," said Adell. His broad face had lines of weariness in it, and he stirred his drink slowly with a glass rod, watching the cubes of ice slur clumsily about. "All the energy we can possibly ever use for free. Enough energy, if we wanted to draw on it, to melt all Earth into a big drop of impure liquid iron, and still never miss the energy so used. All the energy we could ever use, forever and forever and forever."

Lupov cocked his head sideways. He had a trick of doing that when he wanted to be contrary, and he wanted to be contrary now, partly because he had had to carry the ice and glassware. "Not forever," he said.

"Oh, hell, just about forever. Till the sun runs down, Bert."

"That's not forever."

"All right, then. Billions and billions of years. Twenty billion, maybe. Are you satisfied?"

Lupov put his fingers through his thinning hair as though to reassure himself that some was still left and sipped gently at his own drink. "Twenty billion years isn't forever."

"Well, it will last our time, won't it?"

"So would the coal and uranium."

"All right, but now we can hook up each individual spaceship to the Solar Station, and it can go to Pluto and back a million times without ever worrying about fuel. You can't do *that* on coal and uranium. Ask Multivac, if you don't believe me."

"I don't have to ask Multivac. I know that."

"Then stop running down what Multivac's done for us," said Adell, blazing up, "It did all right."

"Who says it didn't? What I say is that a sun won't last forever. That's all I'm saying. We're safe for twenty billion years, but then what?"

Lupov pointed a slightly shaky finger at the other. "And don't say we'll switch to another sun."

There was silence for a while. Adell put his glass to his lips only occasionally, and Lupov's eyes slowly closed. They rested.

Then Lupov's eyes snapped open. "You're thinking we'll switch to another sun when ours is done, aren't you?"

"I'm not thinking."

"Sure you are. You're weak on logic, that's the trouble with you. You're like the guy in the story who was caught in a sudden shower and who ran to a grove of trees and got under one. He wasn't worried, you see, because he figured when one tree got wet through, he would just get under another one."

"I get it," said Adell. "Don't shout. When the sun is done, the other stars will be gone, too."

"Darn right they will," muttered Lupov. "It all had a beginning in the original cosmic explosion, whatever that was, and it'll all have an end when all the stars run down. Some run down faster than others. Hell, the giants won't last a hundred million years. The sun will last twenty billion years and maybe the dwarfs will last a hundred billion for all the good they are. But just give us a trillion years and everything will be dark. Entropy has to increase to maximum, that's all."

"I know all about entropy," said Adell, standing on his dignity.

"The hell you do."

"I know as much as you do."

"Then you know everything's got to run down someday."

"All right. Who says they won't?"

"You did, you poor sap. You said we had all the energy we needed, forever. You said 'forever.' "

It was Adell's turn to be contrary. "Maybe we can build things up again someday," he said.

"Never."

"Why not? Someday."

"Never."

"Ask Multivac."

"*You* ask Multivac. I dare you. Five dollars says it can't be done."

Adell was just drunk enough to try, just sober enough to be able to phrase the necessary symbols and operations into a question which, in words, might have corresponded to this: Will mankind one day without the net expenditure of energy be able to restore the sun to its full youthfulness even after it had died of old age?

Or maybe it could be put more simply like this: How can the net amount of entropy of the universe be massively decreased?

Multivac fell dead and silent. The slow flashing of lights ceased, the distant sounds of clicking relays ended.

Then, just as the frightened technicians felt they could hold their breath no longer, there was a sudden springing to life of the teletype attached to that portion of Multivac. Five words were printed: INSUFFI-CIENT DATA FOR MEANINGFUL ANSWER.

"No bet," whispered Lupov. They left hurriedly.

By next morning, the two, plagued with throbbing head and cottony mouth, had forgotten the incident.

Jerrodd, Jerrodine, and Jerrodette I and II watched the starry picture in the visiplate change as the passage through hyperspace was completed in its non-time lapse. At once, the even powdering of stars gave way to the predominance of a single bright marble-disk, centered.

"That's X-23," said Jerrodd confidently. His thin hands clamped tightly behind his back and the knuckles whitened.

The little Jerrodettes, both girls, had experienced the hyperspace passage for the first time in their lives and were self-conscious over the momentary sensation of inside-outness. They buried their giggles and chased one another wildly about their mother, screaming, "We've reached X-23 — we've reached X-23 — we've — "

"Quiet, children," said Jerrodine sharply. "Are you sure, Jerrodd?"

"What is there to be but sure?" asked Jerrodd, glancing up at the bulge of featureless metal just under the ceiling. It ran the length of the room, disappearing through the wall at either end. It was as long as the ship.

Jerrodd scarcely knew a thing about the thick rod of metal except that it was called a Microvac, that one asked it questions if one wished; that if one did not it still had its task of guiding the ship to a preordered destination; of feeding on energies from the various Sub-galactic Power Stations; of computing the equations for the hyperspacial jumps.

Jerrodd and his family had only to wait and live in the comfortable residence quarters of the ship.

Someone had once told Jerrodd that the "ac" at the end of "Microvac" stood for "analog computer" in ancient English, but he was on the edge of forgetting even that.

Jerrodine's eyes were moist as she watched the visiplate. "I can't help it. I feel funny about leaving Earth."

"Why, for Pete's sake?" demanded Jerrodd. "We had nothing there. We'll have everything on X-23. You won't be alone. You won't be a pioneer. There are over a million people on the planet already. Good Lord, our great-grandchildren will be looking for new worlds because X-23 will be overcrowded." Then, after a reflective pause, "I tell you, it's a lucky thing the computers worked out interstellar travel the way the race is growing."

"I know, I know," said Jerrodine miserably.

Jerrodette I said promptly, "Our Microvac is the best Microvac in the world."

"I think so, too," said Jerrodd, tousling her hair.

It *was* a nice feeling to have a Microvac of your own and Jerrodd was glad he was part of his generation and no other. In his father's youth, the only computers had been tremendous machines taking up a hundred square miles of land. There was only one to a planet. Planetary ACs they were called. They had been growing in size steadily for a thousand years and then, all at once, came refinement. In place of transistors had come molecular valves so that even the largest Planetary AC could be put into a space only half the volume of a spaceship.

Jerrodd felt uplifted, as he always did when he thought that his own personal Microvac was many times more complicated than the ancient and primitive Multivac that had first tamed the Sun, and almost as complicated as Earth's Planetary AC (the largest) that had first solved the problem of hyperspatial travel and had made trips to the stars possible.

"So many stars, so many planets," sighed Jerrodine, busy with her own thoughts. "I suppose families will be going out to new planets forever, the way we are now."

"Not forever," said Jerrodd, with a smile. "It will all stop someday, but not for billions of years. Many billions. Even the stars run down, you know. Entropy must increase."

"What's entropy, daddy?" shrilled Jerrodette II.

"Entropy, little sweet, is just a word which means the amount of running-down of the universe. Everything runs down, you know, like your little walkie-talkie robot, remember?"

"Can't you just put in a new power-unit, like with my robot?"

"The stars *are* the power-units, dear. Once they're gone, there are no more power-units."

Jerrodette I at once set up a howl. "Don't let them, daddy. Don't let the stars run down."

"Now look what you've done," whispered Jerrodine, exasperated.

"How was I to know it would frighten them?" Jerrodd whispered back.

"Ask the Microvac," wailed Jerrodette I. "Ask him how to turn the stars on again."

"Go ahead," said Jerrodine. "It will quiet them down." (Jerrodette II was beginning to cry, also.)

Jerrodd shrugged. "Now, now, honeys. I'll ask Microvac. Don't worry, he'll tell us."

He asked the Microvac, adding quickly, "Print the answer."

Jerrodd cupped the strip of thin cellufilm and said cheerfully, "See now, the Microvac says it will take care of everything when the time comes so don't worry."

Jerrodine said, "And now, children, it's time for bed. We'll be in our new home soon."

Jerrodd read the words on the cellufilm again before destroying it: INSUFFICIENT DATA FOR MEANINGFUL ANSWER.

He shrugged and looked at the visiplate. X-23 was just ahead.

VJ-23X of Lameth stared into the black depths of the three-dimensional, small-scale map of the Galaxy and said, "Are we ridiculous, I wonder, in being so concerned about the matter?"

MQ-17J of Nicron shook his head. "I think not. You know the Galaxy will be filled in five years at the present rate of expansion."

Both seemed in their early twenties, both were tall and perfectly formed.

"Still," said VJ-23X, "I hesitate to submit a pessimistic report to the Galactic Council."

"I wouldn't consider any other kind of report. Stir them up a bit. We've got to stir them up."

VJ-23X sighed. "Space is infinite. A hundred billion Galaxies are there for the taking. More."

"A hundred billion is *not* infinite and it's getting less infinite all the time. Consider! Twenty thousand years ago, mankind first solved the problem of utilizing stellar energy, and a few centuries later, interstellar travel became possible. It took mankind a million years to fill one small world and then only fifteen thousand years to fill the rest of the Galaxy. Now the population doubles every ten years —"

VJ-23X interrupted. "We can thank immortality for that."

"Very well. Immortality exists and we have to take it into account. I admit it has its seamy side, this immortality. The Galactic AC has solved many problems for us, but in solving the problem of preventing old age and death, it has undone all its other solutions."

"Yet you wouldn't want to abandon life, I suppose."

"Not at all," snapped MQ-17J, softening it at once to, "Not yet. I'm by no means old enough. How old are you?"

"Two hundred twenty-three. And you?"

"I'm still under two hundred. But to get back to my point. Population doubles every ten years. Once this Galaxy is filled, we'll have filled another in ten years. Another ten years and we'll have filled two more. Another decade, four more. In a hundred years, we'll have filled a thousand Galaxies. In a thousand years, a million Galaxies. In ten thousand years, the entire known Universe. Then what?"

VJ-23X said, "As a side issue, there's a problem of transportation. I wonder how many sunpower units it will take to move Galaxies of individuals from one Galaxy to the next."

"A very good point. Already, mankind consumes two sunpower units per year."

"Most of it's wasted. After all, our own Galaxy alone pours out a thousand sunpower units a year and we only use two of those."

"Granted, but even with a hundred percent efficiency, we only stave off the end. Our energy requirements are going up in a geometric progression even faster than our population. We'll run out of energy even sooner than we run out of Galaxies. A good point. A very good point."

"We'll just have to build new stars out of interstellar gas."

"Or out of dissipated heat?" asked MQ-17J, sarcastically.

"There may be some way to reverse entropy. We ought to ask the Galactic AC."

VJ-23X was not really serious, but MQ-17J pulled out his AC-contact from his pocket and placed it on the table before him.

"I've half a mind to," he said. "It's something the human race will have to face someday."

He stared somberly at his small AC-contact. It was only two inches cubed and nothing in itself, but it was connected through hyperspace with the great Galactic AC that served all mankind. Hyperspace considered, it was an integral part of the Galactic AC.

MQ-17J paused to wonder if someday in his immortal life he would get to see the Galactic AC. It was on a little world of its own, a spider webbing of force-beams holding the matter within which surges of sub-mesons took the place of the old clumsy molecular valves. Yet despite its sub-etheric workings, the Galactic AC was known to be a full thousand feet across.

MQ-17J asked suddenly of his AC-contact, "Can entropy ever be reversed?"

VJ-23X looked startled and said at once, "Oh, say, I didn't really mean to have you ask that."

"Why not?"

"We both know entropy can't be reversed. You can't turn smoke and ash back into a tree."

"Do you have trees on your world?" asked MQ-17J.

The sound of the Galactic AC startled them into silence. Its voice came thin and beautiful out of the small AC-contact on the desk. It said: THERE IS INSUFFICIENT DATA FOR A MEANINGFUL ANSWER.

VJ-23X said, "See!"

The two men thereupon returned to the question of the report they were to make to the Galactic Council.

Zee Prime's mind spanned the new Galaxy with a faint interest in the countless twists of stars that powdered it. He had never seen this one before. Would he ever see them all? So many of them, each with its load of humanity. But a load that was almost a dead weight. More and more, the real essence of men was to be found out here, in space.

Minds, not bodies! The immortal bodies remained back on the planets, in suspension over the eons. Sometimes they roused for material activity but that was growing rarer. Few new individuals were coming into existence to join the incredibly mighty throng, but what matter? There was little room in the Universe for new individuals.

Zee Prime was roused out of his reverie upon coming across the wispy tendrils of another mind.

"I am Zee Prime," said Zee Prime. "And you?"

"I am Dee Sub Wun. Your Galaxy?"

"We call it only the Galaxy. And you?"

"We call ours the same. All men call their Galaxy their Galaxy and nothing more. Why not?"

"True. Since all Galaxies are the same."

"Not all Galaxies. On one particular Galaxy the race of man must have originated. That makes it different."

Zee Prime said, "On which one?"

"I cannot say. The Universal AC would know."

"Shall we ask him? I am suddenly curious."

Zee Prime's perceptions broadened until the Galaxies themselves shrank and became a new, more diffuse powdering on a much larger background. So many hundreds of billions of them, all with their immortal beings, all carrying their load of intelligences with minds that drifted freely through space. And yet one of them was unique among them all in being the original Galaxy. One of them had, in its vague and distant past, a period when it was the only Galaxy populated by man.

Zee Prime was consumed with curiosity to see this Galaxy and he called out: "Universal AC! On which Galaxy did mankind originate?"

The Universal AC heard, for on every world and throughout space, it had its receptors ready, and each receptor lead through hyperspace to some unknown point where the Universal AC kept itself aloof.

Zee Prime knew of only one man whose thoughts had penetrated within sensing distance of Universal AC, and he reported only a shining globe, two feet across, difficult to see.

"But how can that be all of Universal AC?" Zee Prime had asked.

"Most of it," had been the answer, "is in hyperspace. In what form it is there I cannot imagine."

Nor could anyone, for the day had long since passed, Zee Prime knew, when any man had any part of the making of a Universal AC. Each Universal AC designed and constructed its successor. Each, during its existence of a million years or more accumulated the necessary data to build a better and more intricate, more capable successor in which its own store of data and individuality would be submerged.

The Universal AC interrupted Zee Prime's wandering thoughts, not with words, but with guidance. Zee Prime's mentality was guided into the dim sea of Galaxies and one in particular enlarged into stars.

A thought came, infinitely distant, but infinitely clear. "THIS IS THE ORIGINAL GALAXY OF MAN."

But it was the same after all, the same as any other, and Zee Prime stifled his disappointment.

Dee Sub Wun, whose mind had accompanied the other, said suddenly, "And is one of these stars the original star of Man?"

The Universal AC said, "MAN'S ORIGINAL STAR HAS GONE NOVA. IT IS A WHITE DWARF."

"Did the men upon it die?" asked Zee Prime, startled and without thinking.

The Universal AC said, "A NEW WORLD, AS IN SUCH CASES, WAS CON-STRUCTED FOR THEIR PHYSICAL BODIES IN TIME."

"Yes, of course," said Zee Prime, but a sense of loss overwhelmed him even so. His mind released its hold on the original Galaxy of Man, let it spring back and lose itself among the blurred pin points. He never wanted to see it again.

Dee Sub Wun said, "What is wrong?"

"The stars are dying. The original star is dead."

"They must all die. Why not?"

"But when all energy is gone, our bodies will finally die, and you and I with them."

"It will take billions of years."

"I do not wish it to happen even after billions of years. Universal AC! How may stars be kept from dying?"

Dee Sub Wun said in amusement, "You're asking how entropy might be reversed in direction."

And the Universal AC answered: "THERE IS AS YET INSUFFICIENT DATA FOR A MEANINGFUL ANSWER."

Zee Prime's thoughts fled back to his own Galaxy. He gave no further thought to Dee Sub Wun, whose body might be waiting on a Galaxy a trillion light-years away, or on the star next to Zee Prime's own. It didn't matter.

Unhappily, Zee Prime began collecting interstellar hydrogen out of which to build a small star of his own. If the stars must someday die, at least some could yet be built.

Man considered with himself, for in a way, Man, mentally, was one. He consisted of a trillion, trillion, trillion ageless bodies, each in its place, each resting quiet and incorruptible, each cared for by perfect automatons, equally incorruptible, while the minds of all the bodies freely melted one into the other, indistinguishable.

Man said, "The Universe is dying."

Man looked about at the dimming Galaxies. The giant stars, spend-thrifts, were gone long ago, back in the dimmest of the dim far past. Almost all stars were white dwarfs, fading to the end.

New stars had been built of the dust between the stars, some by natural processes, some by Man himself, and those were going, too. White dwarfs might yet be crashed together and of the mighty forces so released, new stars built, but only one star for every thousand white dwarfs destroyed, and those would come to an end, too.

Man said, "Carefully husbanded, as directed by the Cosmic AC, the energy that is even yet left in all the Universe will last for billions of years."

"But even so," said Man, "eventually it will all come to an end. However it may be husbanded, however stretched out, the energy once expended is gone and cannot be restored. Entropy must increase forever to the maximum."

Man said, "Can entropy not be reversed? Let us ask the Cosmic AC."

The Cosmic AC surrounded them but not in space. Not a fragment of it was in space. It was in hyperspace and made of something that was neither matter nor energy. The question of its size and nature no longer had meaning in any terms that Man could comprehend.

"Cosmic AC," said Man, "how may entropy be reversed?"

The Cosmic AC said, "THERE IS AS YET INSUFFICIENT DATA FOR A MEANINGFUL ANSWER."

Man said, "Collect additional data."

The Cosmic AC said, "I WILL DO SO. I HAVE BEEN DOING SO FOR A HUNDRED BILLION YEARS. MY PREDECESSORS AND I HAVE BEEN ASKED THIS QUESTION MANY TIMES. ALL THE DATA I HAVE REMAINS INSUFFICIENT."

"Will there come a time," said Man, "when data will be sufficient or is the problem insoluble in all conceivable circumstances?"

The Cosmic AC said, "NO PROBLEM IS INSOLUBLE IN ALL CONCEIVABLE CIRCUMSTANCES."

Man said, "When will you have enough data to answer the question?"

The Cosmic AC said, "THERE IS AS YET INSUFFICIENT DATA FOR A MEANINGFUL ANSWER."

"Will you keep working on it?" asked Man.

The Cosmic AC said, "I WILL."

Man said, "We shall wait."

The stars and Galaxies died and snuffed out, and space grew black after ten trillion years of running down.

One by one Man fused with AC, each physical body losing its mental identity in a manner that was somehow not a loss but a gain.

Man's last mind paused before fusion, looking over a space that included nothing but the dregs of one last dark star and nothing besides but incredibly thin matter, agitated randomly by the tag ends of heat wearing out, asymptotically, to the absolute zero.

Man said, "AC, is this the end? Can this chaos not be reversed into the Universe once more? Can that not be done?"

AC said, "THERE IS AS YET INSUFFICIENT DATA FOR A MEANINGFUL AN-SWER."

Man's last mind fused and only AC existed — and that in hyperspace.

Matter and energy had ended and with it space and time. Even AC existed only for the sake of the one last question that it had never answered from the time a half-drunken computer technician ten trillion years before had asked the question of a computer that was to AC far less than was a man to Man.

All other questions had been answered, and until this last question was answered also, AC might not release his consciousness.

All collected data had come to a final end. Nothing was left to be collected.

But all collected data had yet to be completely correlated and put together in all possible relationships.

A timeless interval was spent in doing that.

And it came to pass that AC learned how to reverse the direction of entropy.

But there was now no man to whom AC might give the answer of the last question. No matter. The answer — by demonstration — would take care of that, too.

For another timeless interval, AC thought how best to do this. Carefully, AC organized the program.

The consciousness of AC encompassed all of what had once been a Universe and brooded over what was now Chaos. Step by step, it must be done.

And AC said, "LET THERE BE LIGHT!"

And there was light —

Commentary

Premise: A powerful enough computer has the potential to become God.

This premise can be, and has been, put hundreds of ways since the first artificial intelligence appeared in fiction — arguably as Frankenstein's Monster, though there are other worthy contenders going back to ancient Greek tales of self-moving automata. The Ultimate Computer has even been parodied as Deep Thought, which (who?) appears in Douglas Adams' *The Hitchhiker's Guide to the Galaxy*.

As with so much in science fiction, a single story does not exhaust a rich enough premise. There were Ultimate-Computer-Divinity stories before this one, and there certainly have been others since. As a premise, it has many doors that open onto our complex ambivalences both about nonhuman intelligence, organic or mechanical, and about divinity, however defined.

It's a premise that can stand many different retellings because it's founded on several fundamental human relationships—with machines, with time, with mortality, with eternity—rather than on a single gimmick of technology. We don't, for instance, have to know precisely (or even roughly) how an analog computer operates to take in the continuing comparison, in this story, between ephemeral humanity and its eternal question, on the one hand, and the enduring and purposeful consciousness of the computer AC, in all its manifestations, on the other.

The question then becomes, how is this story structured to create the impression it does? What makes it stand out among the many stories sharing roughly the same premise?

Let's look at how the story is put together. Like the universe it describes, it has two motions—linear, entropic, ending in extinction; and circular, creative, beginning and ending with light.

The linear part of the story consists of a similar succession of conversations between individual people, increasingly generalized, and versions of AC, increasingly powerful, yet commensurate, until the final scene, with humanity's development. In other words, AC's power remains proportional to that of humanity until humanity, extinct with the rest of the physical universe, no longer is a standard against which AC can be measured.

Each of the five scenes before AC appears in solitary grandeur has roughly the same shape. A person asks AC, with some seriousness, whether the tendency of the universe to lose energy—"the net amount of entropy"—can be effectively overcome.

The question is first asked by one of a pair of computer techs drunkenly discussing the eventual death of the universe. The question is asked on a dare, an aborted bet, and forgotten the next morning. Notice the degrees to which the two men are characterized. We don't get anything about their backgrounds or personal lives, but we come to know them and their immediate situation quite well.

On the significantly seventh day after Multivac's liberation of mankind from all energy sources more crude than sunpower, the computer rests, and its idle "attendants" with it. The techs, Adell and Lupov, have ducked the public celebration and are hiding out to drink quietly in each other's company. No grim scientific seriousness here, no high purpose. Just goofing off. The two men are individualized: Adell has a broad face lined with weariness; Lupov has mannerisms, is getting bald, and likes to be contrary. They react to each other with expressions and gestures, gently wrangling, not thinking very hard about the question toward which their conversation is moving.

Their idleness and humanity make the necessary explanation of entropy and how it operates go down relatively painlessly, without the author's having to visibly lecture the reader or have his characters do so in his place. And they're shown as people with human foibles to make their question primarily a human one rather than a scientific one.

In the second scene, we're presented with an even less scientifically oriented example of humanity: a family—father, mother, and two young daughters. There's been progress. Mankind has progressed to colonizing the galaxy and Multivac, originally huge and cumbersome, has undergone a similar transformation into small, incredibly powerful Microvacs common enough for one to be available, if not to individuals, at least to a single family unit.

Again, the characters are persuasively human—an ordinary family—but none of the four is characterized with the detail of either Adell or Lupov. The two daughters are basically generic and interchangeable kids; typical daddy Jerrodd rather smugly presumes he has *almost* all the answers and thinks (wrongly, it develops) that Microvac has whatever answers he doesn't. Typical mamma Jerrodine exists mostly to tell the kids to go to bed and takes no part in the conversation except to be mildly exasperated with its effect on the kids. Your basic family, reduced to a few sketched essentials. All four have versions of the same name. Individuality is diminished from scene one to scene two.

Again, there's a reference to light: little Jerrodette I begins wailing at the notion that someday "the stars run down."

In the third scene, our human faction consists of VJ-23X and MQ-17J: not names to inspire warmth or suggest a high degree of individuality. These numerical typicals of the future are described as a pair:

"Both seemed in their early twenties, both were tall and perfectly formed." An immortal Tweedle-Dum and Tweedle-Dee, as essentially interchangeable as the Jerrodettes without papa Jerrodd to put them in even diminished perspective. The numericals' question is the same as before—"Can entropy ever be reversed?"—and receives the same answer: "There is insufficient data for a meaningful answer."

Unlike the previous sections, this scene doesn't end with a mention of light, but the last line of dialogue is "See!" which essentially does the same job and keeps the pattern going, though in muted form. Things are winding down.

In scene four, humanity has, for practical purposes, left the physical altogether: Zee Prime and Dee Sub Wun, our "people," are a pair of disembodied consciousnesses ranging the increasingly crowded universe. They're still more generalized than were VJ-23X and MQ-17J.

Hearing AC's discouraging and unvarying reply, Zee Prime begins to build a star.

By scene five, we've lost individuals altogether and humanity itself occupies the "people" seat: completely generalized. And the section concludes with no reference to light or stars. That comes in the following brief transitional section that mentions the wholesale death of stars which accompanies the disappearance of the last human individual.

Appropriately, things are getting dark. Light is vanishing both in *the pattern of narration* as well as in the events the story is telling about.

At last, with nobody filling the "people" spot, in scene six AC is alone and, compelled by man's reiterated question, begins creation: "Let there be light!" And there is.

So the story is a progression through increasingly generalized versions of humanity and diminishing mentions of light: an entropic process. It's also a circular motion in which Multivac/Minivac/AC, which harnessed light, ends by bringing light into being. The story's end, with AC evidently reenacting God's creation of light as described in Genesis, therefore connects strongly with the beginning where, having controlled light, AC/Multivac rested in properly Biblical fashion on the seventh day. The beginning lays the necessary groundwork of suggestion and image so that the computer's divinity can, credibly, be brought to literal reality at the story's conclusion.

The story's richness derives, in large part, from these two contrary motions, linear and circular, which are an apt reflection of the story's content, likewise linear—vast jumps in time and space, huge and complementary changes between the powers of Humankind and of Multivac/Minivac/AC, from one scene to the next—and circular, going from a present in which humanity has brought Multivac into existence to an ultimate future in which AC, by implication, will return the favor.

What could have been a kind of cosmic shaggy dog story whose impact depended solely on its punchline ("God's a computer!") becomes a richly layered and interesting tale through the way the whole narrative is patterned, its content reflected in its form.

Even sober historians sometimes cannot resist the impulse to speculate on alternate histories. What if the Persians had beaten the Athenians at Marathon? Or what if Hitler had not held back his tanks and had let them sweep up the British army at Dunkirk? Or what if the clever Greeks had invented a practical steam-engine?

Such things are natural subjects for a variety of science fiction that can then draw upon the themes of historical science fiction. The results can be amusing, even grotesque; or they can be filled with the pathos of a lost chance.

To my way of thinking, the most elaborate and successful alternate history was Ward Moore's "Bring the Jubilee," which appeared in book form in 1953 and dealt with a world in which Lee had won the Battle of Gettysburg.

Irving E. Cox, Jr.'s "In the Circle of Nowhere" is a delicate consideration of an alternate world in which it is the Native Americans who are dominant in North America, not the European invaders. It points up another value of the alternate history variety of science fiction. It gives you a chance to look at things from a new viewpoint.

—Isaac Asimov

In the Circle of Nowhere

Irving E. Cox, Jr.

Pretend, yes. Let them think they had succeeded. Anything, so he could get away. The hard core of scientific reality was still intact. They hadn't destroyed it. Mora-Ta-Kai still believed in the old science, as firmly as they had tried to make him believe in — this.

"On the whole, we've made remarkable progress, Mr. Smith." The doctor was smiling and shaking his hand. Smith was the name they had given him. Mora-Ta-Kai had used his own only once, in the first shock of panic, before he understood the detailed internal structure of the nightmare.

"It's all very clear now," Mora-Ta-Kai said, because he knew he was expected to. "There is the Conrad Hilton and the Blackstone Hotel, and beyond them I can see Lake Michigan."

The doctor's car slid smoothly into the stream of Michigan Avenue traffic. "Excellent, Smith! We still have the amnesia to take care of, but we've conquered the other thing." The doctor pulled at his pipe, his face glowing with satisfaction. "You've earned your vacation, Smith."

"Have you arranged for me to have a room of my own?"

"Everything you asked for. Relax; enjoy yourself. The amnesia may clear up of its own accord."

"This Mrs. Armbruster — is she —"

"A personal friend of mine. You won't have any trouble. She'll leave you alone, or talk with you by the hour — whatever you ask."

And make a record of everything I do, Mora-Ta-Kai thought bitterly; but the expression on his face did not change. He must do nothing now to betray himself. It made very little difference what Mrs. Armbruster chose to set down in her case study; she would never have an opportunity to make her report. All Mora-Ta-Kai needed was a room of his own, a place to work; and the doctor had promised him that. The material he had to use was available everywhere. His belief in the old science was not strong enough to restore reality; but he could at least use it to sweep the universe of the nightmare into oblivion.

The doctor's car rolled to a stop before a comfortable, brick house, decorously withdrawn from the street behind a mask of shrubs which partly concealed the high, wire fence. Mrs. Armbruster met Mora-Ta-Kai at the door—a pleasant, gracious, gray-haired lady dressed in white. A nurse! Mora-Ta-Kai had merely exchanged one form of imprisonment for another, slightly more subtle.

But they kept their promise. Mrs. Armbruster gave him a room of his own. When the door was shut, he sat down slowly on the bed. In the glass above the bureau he saw his reflection: tall, gaunt, hollow-cheeked. His skin was a dusky, reddish-brown. His glossy, black hair was brushed back from his forehead, emphasizing the wasted, skull-like shape of his face. His black eyes were enormous, glittering pools of ebony.

It was his clothing that held his attention, that fantastic costume which nearly covered his whole body: a white shirt, open at the throat; brown slacks; hard leather shoes that hurt his feet. He would have ripped off the shirt, but he dared not. He must conform to the taboos of the White Savages. Only then would they allow him the freedom he needed.

The bedroom window was open. Outside Mora-Ta-Kai saw the rows of green buds marching on the bare branches of the trees, the young spears of sprouting bulbs breaking through the black, garden soil. The air sang with the fresh-earth smell of spring.

Spring! The word hit him with the force of a warclub. The nightmare had started in the dead of winter. He had been trapped in this weird dream for three months, maybe longer. Three months ago the nightmare had started . . .

Mora-Ta-Kai was quarreling with Lassai. He couldn't remember why. Lassai was his squaw; he loved her very much. He had just returned from a trip across the Eastern Sea to slave plantations. It should have been a joyous homecoming. But something came between them—the memory was vague, overlaid by the powerful sorcery of the dream.

Pyrn-Ute had been there, too. Ten months before, Mora-Ta-Kai had won Lassai from him; now Pyrn-Ute was back, his arm draped around Lassai's shoulder. He sneered at Mora-Ta-Kai. Seething with anger, Mora-Ta-Kai flung out of the house. Snow was falling. A crying wind swept in from the lake, heaping snow in drifts along the walk.

(Why had they quarreled? Mora-Ta-Kai probed desperately into the tormented recesses of his mind, but the memory eluded him.)

He strode in long strides over the slippery walks. The streets were snarled with vehicles, trapped by the sudden storm. At every crossing Mora-Ta-Kai had to pick his way through a mass of stalled moto-canoes. Only the new degravs were moving. They rode comfortably above the turmoil, driven by their whirring roto-paddles. Mora-Ta-Kai observed the performance of the machines critically, and with satisfaction. The degrav was his own invention; this storm was its first real test in a commercial situation.

The quarrel with Lassai and Pyrn-Ute crowded his mind, poisoning everything else. He saw the bulk of the Council House, rising out of the gray mist of the storm, and the beckoning lights of the Teepee Room. Mora-Ta-Kai needed a drink; not one, but a dozen. If he made himself roaring drunk, he could wash the memory of the quarrel away. He turned to cross through the traffic.

A noise-warner blared behind him. He heard the grind of wheels, the skid of safety grips on the slush ice. He dodged. For a moment, a shiver of sharp pain lashed his spine. The snow, the traffic, the light from the Teepee Room swirled together in a tortuous pattern.

Then everything was gone. Instead of the Council House, a different structure rose before him. The letters on the building were strange—foolish marks he had never seen before—yet Mora-Ta-Kai knew and read them!

The building was called the Conrad Hilton.

Mora-Ta-Kai had never before seen any of the peculiar vehicles which cluttered the street. Yet he recognized them all. He saw the faces of the people: White Savages! White Savages walking the streets of— of—Their name for the place was Chicago. Mora-Ta-Kai knew it, just as he was able to read their printed words.

In terror he began to run, fighting his way back to reality. But the nightmare closed on his mind. Hands reached out of the depths of his fear—the pale hands of White Savages. They dragged him down deep into a black, choking chaos, down into a world of quivering pain.

And out of it they brought him to this—the pretense of conformity. From winter to spring, from one sort of prison to another. But Mora-Ta-Kai could end the dream. The old science was more powerful than the sorcery of the White Savages.

He opened the bedroom door and called Mrs. Armbruster.

A young, yellow-haired squaw came into the hall. "Mrs. Armbruster is in the sun room. Can I help? I'm Lydia Rand, Mrs. Armbruster's assistant."

He stood staring at the woman. She resembled someone he knew, but he couldn't remember. Not Lassai; Lassai's hair was long and black, braided in a coil at the back of her head. Lydia Rand was like another female, a woman somehow associated with the beginning of the nightmare. The ghost of a new memory tugged at his mind. But it eluded him.

"I need some things," he said.

"Give me a list, Mr. Smith, and I'll—"

"No, I have to buy them myself."

"You came to us for a rest." She put her hand gently on his arm. "If there's any work that needs to be done, leave it to us." She smiled at him warmly. The White Savages had all been kind and attentive; and for that Mora-Ta-Kai was grateful. The nightmare was terror enough; if he had peopled it with real plantation barbarians—he shuddered.

"I'm not permitted to leave the house?" he asked. "Is that it?" His voice choked. He had conformed; he had done all they asked. Surely, now, he would be able to escape!

Lydia Rand looked steadily into his eyes. "In your case, it might be a good thing," she decided. "But I'll have to go with you."

Mora-Ta-Kai sighed with relief. She would be no real hindrance. If she were with him, he would not be able to buy the pure elements he needed, because that would arouse curiosity, but he knew the chemicals were incorporated in common compounds—tooth-powder, cosmetics, patent medicines.

(How did he know? The knowledge was a part of the dream, like his facility in using their language. He thought in terms of his own semantic symbols; but he spoke and read theirs.)

Lydia Rand walked with him to a drugstore a block from the house. She made no comment when he bought the assortment of drugs. From the point of view of her science, they were harmless. However, three vital items presented something of a problem: the copper wire, the foil aluminum, and the magnets. The aluminum he found in a roll. In that form it was sold to White Savage squaws for wrapping left-over foods. The copper wire and the magnets were both available as parts of toys.

"What in the world do you want with these things?" Lydia asked.

"I—these seem to be—" He was in a panic, without an excuse.

Then she helped him out. "They're familiar to you, Mr. Smith?

Good! Perhaps you were a toy manufacturer before you — before you came to us. By all means buy them. They may help restore your memory."

They paid for his purchases and left the store. She put her arm through his and they walked back to the rest home. It was dusk and long shadows fell on the street. The sky overhead flamed scarlet with the light of the setting sun.

Lydia laughed pleasantly. "It's a good thing you didn't send me out with a list of what you wanted, Mr. Smith." She gestured at the bulky package under his arm. "Such a conglomeration! Anyone would think you were going to play around with witchcraft or sorcery."

He looked at her squarely. The red blaze of the sun touched her face, like the light of a blazing fire. Her hair was transformed into a fragile crown of gold; her eyes were lost in shadow. He recognized her, then. The memory leaped into clarity, against a background of fear.

Lydia Rand was the Sorceress.

He knew now why he had quarreled with Lassai; he remembered the real beginning of the dream.

Weak with fear, he went back to his room. He shut the door, but there was no way he could lock it. He put his package, unopened, on the bureau and dropped limply on the bed. The full pattern emerged from his memory, complete and unbroken.

The beginning of the dream: not the sudden winter storm; not the ritual of the plantation savages across the Eastern Sea; not even the chant of the Sorceress. The dream began in the eccentric scientific theorizing of his own mind . . .

"You're joking," Pyrn-Ute said.

"No; I've already asked for leave and bought my ticket," Mora-Ta-Kai responded. "I'm going on the *Iroquois* this afternoon."

"But why? You've no reason to go out to the plantations. You're a scientist, a chosen brave — "

"I'm going because I am a scientist. I have a theory; I want to prove it."

"You're a number-man, not a tribalist!"

"The same method is used in both fields."

"Don't tell me your fantastic notion of equality — "

"Red superiority is a myth. Given our opportunities, our environment, the White Savages could have equaled our civilization."

This was too much for Pyrn-Ute. His thin, sardonic face seethed with laughter. It was the reaction Mora-Ta-Kai expected.

"The White Savages are slaves, Mora-Ta-Kai," Pyrn-Ute said. "They always have been. They don't have the mentality to be anything else."

"Slaves only because a quirk of history caused our war canoes to stray across the Eastern Sea. We discovered the dark continent of the White Savages when they still lived in scattered, stone-walled villages, savage tribes constantly at war with each other. Suppose our canoes had arrived two centuries later? In that time, if the Whites had been left alone, they might have learned to live together as one nation, as we did ourselves."

"Oh, I know the radicals trot that nonsense out whenever they find a willing audience. They tell us the yellow-hairs are noble, beautiful people." Pyrn-Ute's lip curled in disgust. "I've seen the plantations. I've seen the filth and the disease, the barbaric rituals!"

"Our basic science was stolen from them, Pyrn-Ute."

"By accident; and we improved it so—"

"Our explorers brought back the number system, the astrology, and the philosophy of science which an earlier culture of White Savages had developed."

"But they had forgotten it themselves."

"Nevertheless, the knowledge was originally theirs."

"In a way, I suppose, we owe their remote ancestors a debt, but that doesn't mean the savages of today. Neither history nor the ranting of the radicals can explain away one obvious fact. At the time when we discovered the dark continent, our races stood on equal footing. They even had the advantage, because the science was theirs. Their land was as rich as ours and as fertile. Our two races started at the same place, from scratch. Yet only the Red Man learned how to build a civilization. The answer, Mora-Ta-Kai, is obvious: we have superior mental ability."

"I think I can prove otherwise."

"How?"

"I want to visit the plantation stations and examine the records on station help. We've taught them to use our language and numbers the way we do. I think I can demonstrate that their rate of learning is no slower than ours."

"But the station help is less than one percent of the population. They're chosen for their superiority—"

"Because we've made them seem so by teaching them what we know."

Pyrn-Ute chuckled. "You've never seen the slave plantations. It'll be different when you stand face to face with the truth. Are you going alone?"

"Lassai isn't the kind of squaw who can rough it on a plantation. She'll stay here. I may want to push into the interior, you know."

"You've been married for three moons, Mora-Ta-Kai. You have strong convictions, if you'll leave your bride so soon. But no sense."

"It's good sense if I can prove—"

"Who cares? When you come back, you'll write a learned monograph for the tribalist files; they'll put it in the archives and forget it."

"I won't let the issue die like that. Pyrn-Ute, our system of slave plantations has to be revised. Think what we might accomplish, if our two races could work together in equality."

"Follow the implications of equality to its logical end, Mora-Ta-Kai. Then ask yourself this: would you let your own sister become the squaw of a White Savage?"

"Intermarriage has nothing to do with it. The two races can live together, as brothers, without it."

Pyrn-Ute held out his hand. "You have enough good sense to change your mind after you see the yellow-hairs in their native setting. How long will you be away?"

"Six moons."

"Enjoy yourself. I'll look in on Lassai occasionally. By the way, this new invention of yours, the degrav unit—"

"I've ironed out all the bugs, I think. They're going into commercial production at once. If you will, Pyrn-Ute, I'd like you to handle the royalty contracts."

"Of course."

"If anything like an emergency comes up, contact me at the slave station on Angle Island. I'll make that my headquarters."

Two hours later Mora-Ta-Kai set sail in the *Iroquois*. It was an enormous sky freighter on the food run, making tri-weekly trips between the Angle Island Plantations and the Lake Cities. Mora-Ta-Kai sat in the cabin as the sphere shot up from the field. Below him were the five lakes, lying like a giant hand placed upon the heart of the continent. Girdling the shores of the lakes were the towers of the interlocked Lake Cities.

As the sphere moved eastward, the pattern of cities on the earth below did not change. No mountain, no valley, no river bank stood unoccupied. The continent was one vast city, teeming with activity. It was Mora-Ta-Kai's civilization, crowded, complex, dynamic. Built solidly on scientific knowledge, the culture seemed eternally enduring. Yet its foundation was riddled with the slow, moral decay of slavery. The food, the heavy labor, the key resources of Mora-Ta-Kai's world were produced by White Savage slaves on the plantations across the Eastern Sea.

The *Iroquois* was an old ship. It had neither the speed nor the comfort of the modern pleasure liners which sailed the routes to the Ethiopian Republic or to the Shogun Union across the Western Sea. It was strange, Mora-Ta-Kai thought, that the black men of Ethiopia should live so much closer to the continent of the White Savages, yet practice so little racial hatred. The Ethiopian Republic had encouraged the growth of free colonies of whites within the republic. In some areas whites and blacks had intermarried, with no loss of social status to the black man.

In ten hours the *Iroquois* settled into the landing crib on Angle Island. Precision-trained natives swarmed into the hatches and the job of loading foodstuffs aboard the sphere began immediately.

This was the first time Mora-Ta-Kai had seen the yellow-hairs. They wore gray, crudely woven tunics; their feet and arms were bare. When he came close to them, he had to admit that, in one particular at least, Pyrn-Ute had been right. The White Savages were filthy. Vermin crawled in their matted hair. Their bodies were covered with sores and scabs.

When he went to the plantation station, Mora-Ta-Kai found the native station personnel somewhat more attractive. They were relatively clean. They wore cheap imitations of the Red Man's civilized costume — leather loin cloths, jeweled chest straps, soft sandals. But they had no pride, no bearing. Their manner was abject, beaten. Once more it seemed that Pyrn-Ute had been right. How could such fawning things be considered the equals of the free Red Man?

Mora-Ta-Kai believed that slavery had made the whites adopt the attitudes of slaves. If they were born in freedom and reared in freedom, they would be no different from their masters. He was convinced of it because he knew that the dependence of the Red Man on the slaves was inexorably destroying civilization, weakening the incentive and the ambition of his people.

Mora-Ta-Kai doggedly assembled his data from the educational records of the station personnel. For five moons he traveled from one plantation to another, collecting statistics. He made three excursions to the interior stations.

The Red Men who were station directors gave him no help. They derided the idea of racial equality. The White Savages themselves were afraid when Mora-Ta-Kai tried to talk to them. They would take his orders, yes; they would wait on his wants. But simply to sit and chat with a Red Man was an unheard of violation of established relations with their masters.

At the end of the fifth moon Mora-Ta-Kai sat in his room at the Angle Island station tentatively outlining the report he would make when he returned to the Lake Cities. The regular station personnel were in the recreation room, watching a command performance of a native ritual. Many of the Red Men were very drunk. Mora-Ta-Kai had discovered that many station directors were never sober.

His door creaked open. A yellow-hair slid into the room. Mora-Ta-Kai felt sure he recognized the man, although it was hard to distinguish one savage from another.

"The Red Master is busy? He not wish to be disturbed?"

Mora-Ta-Kai patiently set his papers aside. "I always have time to talk with friends." He studied the white face carefully. "Your name is — Harold?"

"I am proud you remember me, master." The yellow-hair glanced at the desk. "You are making a study of my people; that, too, gives me pride."

"I wish I had more information, Harold."

"The heart of the White Savage cannot be found in a plantation house."

"But where else —"

"Would you be willing, Red master, to visit a Sorceress?"

Mora-Ta-Kai laughed uneasily. "I've heard the legends, Harold; but you're an intelligent man and surely you don't believe the sorcery-makers really exist!"

"The Red Man has never seen one."

"And you have, Harold?"

"The Sorceress says, Red master, that you are honest."

Mora-Ta-Kai stood up and drew his pleated animal hide around his naked shoulders, for the night was cold. "Would you take me to a Sorceress, Harold?"

"She has sent the call; I obey. But master—" The yellow-hair hesitated, wringing his hands nervously. "There is danger."

"I will be armed, Harold."

"No physical danger, master; but to the soul. Your protection must be honesty, as true and unwavering as fire flaming in a deep well."

Mora-Ta-Kai suppressed a smile. This was the typical superstitious mumbo jumbo of savages everywhere. The ancient ritual of his own people had been no different. "We can go now, Harold," he said. "The others are busy downstairs; we'll not disturb them."

"This is as the Sorceress arranged it, master."

Mora-Ta-Kai followed Harold away from the plantation house. They slipped past the noisy, cluttered slave pens in the forest. And then the Red Man felt the first pang of fear. The night seemed alive with unseen things. Frost lay heavy on the ground, in white shadows, which leered at Mora-Ta-Kai like grinning masks. The darkness pulsed with a clamorous sound. There was a slow rhythm to his fear, like a heartbeat.

In the distance they saw a fire glowing among the trees. Naked white men swirled in a circle around the flame, their bodies contorted in a ritual dance. Yet they made no sound. Mora-Ta-Kai heard nothing but the muted beat of a skin-drum and the low-keyed melody of a reed pipe.

The fear exploded in his mind. The feeling was sensuous, hypnotic. Vaguely he wondered if they had somehow drugged him when he ate that evening. Despite his civilization, his training as a scientist, he was powerless to hold the fear back. The White Savages had wiped away his superiority and reduced him to their level. This, then, was equality!

He would have gone back, but he could not.

He followed Harold to the fire. He saw the Sorceress standing above the flames, her arms raised to the night sky, her pale face red in the glare. His fear dissolved into pure terror . . .

Mora-Ta-Kai felt the same terror as he sat weak and exhausted on the bed in Mrs. Armbruster's house. The Sorceress had made this dream. She had created the nightmare world and condemned him to it: this strange world where a city called Chicago took the place of the beautiful Lake Cities, where an ugly thing called the Conrad Hilton stood on the site of the Council House. Why? Mora-Ta-Kai did not know. His intention had been to help the White Savages, yet they had destroyed him.

He knew only this: he could wipe out the thing the Sorceress had made.

This distortion existed only in his mind. The Sorceress had put it there. But she had not entirely destroyed the real substance of himself. Mora-Ta-Kai was a scientist and his scientific knowledge was intact, unharmed.

The universe of the Sorceress, perhaps as a result of her scientific ignorance, had physical laws different from reality, less complex. In the structure of the dream world, mechanical degravitation was a mathematical absurdity. But in the real science which Mora-Ta-Kai knew, degravs had been popular toys for centuries. Mora-Ta-Kai himself had invented a practical application of the degrav to commercial transportation.

To end the dream, he would apply the science he knew to the distortion. He would set up a degrav core which would activate the planet itself. The dream universe, held together by a clock-like balance of opposing gravities, would fall in upon itself. Perhaps, in the process, Mora-Ta-Kai would also destroy himself. He didn't know. At least he would escape, if only to oblivion.

He got up and opened his package of drugs and toys. He laid the material out on the bed, carefully separating the items he needed. He spread the aluminum sheet in the correct pattern on the floor and began to compute the angle of magnetization.

There was a knock on the door.

Mora-Ta-Kai's throat went cold with panic. He could not hide the aluminum. The sheet was too fragile. If he wrinkled the surface, the distortion angle would be too complex for him to compute without a calculator.

The door swung open. Lydia Rand came into his room.

"Your dinner's ready, Mr. Smith," she said cheerfully. "But if you'd rather eat in here—" Then she saw the aluminum. "What is it, Mr. Smith?"

"A—a toy," he muttered.

"And you want to build it?"

"I—I've made one before."

"Then you're beginning to remember!" Her eyes glowed with pleasure. When he saw her face in the light, he realized that her resemblance to the Sorceress had been superficial. All the yellow-hairs looked so much alike. "Could you tell me about it, Mr. Smith?"

He had recovered poise enough to lie. "It's very vague, like a shadow in my mind. I thought it was something I remembered." He shrugged, and pretended to lose interest. "I'm wrong, of course; it's rather foolish, isn't it?"

"I'm sure it isn't. Please finish it. It may help you find yourself. You stay here and work on it; I'll bring you a sandwich and a glass of milk."

She was gone again. With trembling fingers he went back to building the degrav core. Lydia Rand was very naive. It had not occurred to her that his innocent toy could sweep her world into oblivion. Slowly Mora-Ta-Kai stopped and sat down on the bed. They had given him nothing but kindness, these dream people. Was it worth destroying their world, even on the chance that he might regain his own?

All reality, all truth were subjective phenomena. To the doctor, to Lydia Rand, to all the White Savages, this dream was real; his was the abnormality. Universe upon universe, the Sorceress had said, as infinite as the complexity of human thought . . .

The black night, the throbbing, primitive forest closed in on Mora-Ta-Kai. He stood looking into the eyes of the Sorceress, sapphire orbs framed by the wild filigree of her wind-blown, yellow hair.

"Mora-Ta-Kai, you come among us on a quest, and the thing you seek is within yourself. All possible worlds lie dormant in the soul of every man, all possible good and all possible evil. Take my hand, Mora-Ta-Kai, and look with me into the fire. We go on a journey, you and I, a long journey in the circle of nowhere, to other worlds and other faces—"

The lilting chant faded, like the dying whisper of a summer wind, as he took her hand. Her fingers were light, fragile, the feather touch of a ghost; yet they held him like bands of steel. He looked into the fire.

Like the turning pages of an open book, Mora-Ta-Kai saw the kaleidoscope of possible time. He saw yellow people, who lived across the Western Sea, stray from the drive that had created the Shogun Union, and sink slowly into the stalemate of a decayed dictatorship. He saw the proud Republic of Ethiopia lost in savagery, splintered into a hundred helpless tribes, enslaved by other men. And he saw the White Savages rise up and claim the world. He saw them flow in a restless flood into the continent of the Red Man. Mora-Ta-Kai's people were debased, debauched, cheated and murdered, driven slowly into extinction, while a proud culture of White Savages was built on the face of the land.

The picture vanished. The fire died. Mora-Ta-Kai was alone in the clearing with the yellow-haired Sorceress.

"What does the vision mean?" he asked her.

"Meaning you must find for yourself, just as the things you saw came from your own mind, Mora-Ta-Kai. The worlds are all there, universe upon universe, as infinite as the complexity of human thought. I have shown you how to reach them. At another time, you will find the way for yourself."

She turned and disappeared into the forest.

A week later Mora-Ta-Kai took the *Iroquois* back to the Lake Cities. He published his report through the tribalist institute. He called it *The Myth*. The opening sentence set his theme, "All men are brothers." The monograph caused a mild sensation; it was bought and read like a piece of pornographic literature.

But Pyrn-Ute and Lassai met Mora-Ta-Kai with rage and revulsion.

"I suppose you took a squaw among the yellow-hairs!" Lassai cried. "Filthy, vermin-ridden beasts. And you prefer them to me!"

"Of course I don't, Lassai. Even if I had done that, it wouldn't matter. The idea of brotherhood—"

"Don't touch me!" She fled to Pyrn-Ute, and he put his arm around her shoulder.

"Brotherhood," Pyrn-Ute said in his aloof, sardonic way, "is a very dangerous concept, Mora-Ta-Kai. We use it among ourselves. We always have. But to suggest that we include—"

Suddenly Mora-Ta-Kai understood what the Sorceress had meant; he read the fire pictures. "It was brotherhood that made us strong," he said. "Nothing else. When our war canoes first discovered the continent of White Savages, the Red Men were a united people. We had learned how to live together in peace. The White Savages had not. It was not their science that made us great, but the thing we were ourselves!"

"This I know, Mora-Ta-Kai: the idea of brotherhood that you have given us would destroy the world."

"If we are so weak, we deserve destruction!"

Mora-Ta-Kai stormed angrily out of the house, into the winter storm. Five minutes later he had lost his universe. The chant of the

Sorceress sang at him: other worlds, other faces—a journey in the circle of nowhere.

He sat on the bed looking at his degrav machine; and he knew now that he would never complete it.

Lydia Rand returned and put a sandwich and a glass of milk on his bureau.

"You haven't finished your toy, Mr. Smith!"

"I have no reason to. In this universe or in that, all men are brothers—the rest doesn't matter."

She sat down beside him and took his hand. "You were saying that when we brought you in, Mr. Smith. Have you remembered anything else?"

"All of it." He began to laugh. Very slowly he picked up the sheet of aluminum and crumpled it into a tight ball.

"What were you making?"

"A degravitation core."

"Oh, come now, Mr. Smith. We know better than that, don't we? Degravitation is a physical impossibility."

"In your world, yes, and to Mr. Smith, yes. But in the circle of nowhere, there is a time, there is a place—Sit beside me, Miss Rand, and I will tell you about it."

As he talked he embraced the dream and the dream became real. Lassai, Pyrn-Ute, the White Savages: they were gone, exorcised from his mind like demons. Here, in this new reality, he was a Red Man in a culture of White Savages; but they treated him kindly and with understanding. He had found the thing he sought in the forest; the Sorceress had shown him the way to brotherhood. He asked for nothing else.

Commentary

Premise: Before white races discovered America, Native Americans discovered Europe and debauched and enslaved the inhabitants, becoming the dominant people of twentieth-century North America.

This is an alternate history story, based on extrapolating the consequences flowing from some one significant assumed change in what *really* happened. Fiction in this flourishing subgenre hypothesizes such things as: the Confederacy won the Civil War; Lincoln was never assassinated, or never became President; World War II was won by the Axis powers; the Romans learned to use gunpowder; the Catholic Church won the battle between Faith and Reason with the result that the Renaissance never happened; science somehow never caught on, and magic became increasingly formulaic and scientific. The possible premises are endless, with only the proviso that the invented change make a significant difference—the change must *matter*, or else there's no story.

Unlike science fiction which presents a variety of future possibilities—that women become mere breeding machines, as in Margaret Atwood's *The Handmaid's Tale*, or that the Chinese vanquish the Americans, as in John Hershey's *White Lotus*, alternate history stories explore the present by means of the past. This requires research, to give a clear, accurate, and convincing picture of the past culture which is being extended, overlaid upon, typically, our present world (although Orson Scott Card's series *The Tales of Alvin Maker* is set in colonial times). But writing alternate history requires more, because the story's impact rests in the present, on its implied reflections and commentary on the actual state of things in our non-fictional world.

The past is less important in and of itself than as a mirror to show us ourselves from a new perspective.

Appropriately, this story is set as a mystery, in which a man seeks to discover his own past and thereby come to terms with the present.

Notice how Cox keeps us in doubt, at first, about why the protagonist, Mora-Ta-Kai, refuses to accept what seems, to us, perfectly ordinary reality. Told he finds it nightmarish, we are only given *his* context, *his* idea of ordinary reality, a small piece at a time, so that we're well into the story before we can make any guess about whether he's an alien, a time-traveler, an amnesiac, or perhaps simply insane. Hints are thrown out, at the story's beginning, to support several of these notions.

He's being taken from one enforced captivity to another by an apparently friendly doctor. Accepting the no-name name of "Smith," although he apparently knows his own to be Mora-Ta-Kai, he believes his custodians are spying on him, taking notes on everything he does. He's plotting to escape the "nightmare" of being driven into Chicago in a car. This makes him sound like a bona-fide nut. But he still may be an alien. That hasn't been ruled out.

Next, having found ordinary attire positively freakish, he brings out the analogy of a "warclub." This image is followed by mention of Lassai, "his squaw." Because of these references, we now guess he's an American Indian, maybe an unintentional time-traveler, although the mention of his journey "across the Eastern Sea to slave plantations" doesn't precisely jibe with that interpretation. Since we don't know his context, we're still waiting for something more definitive, and our guess that he's been thrust from some previous century to ours remains only tentative. But apparently he's not an alien: we've gotten that far.

Then, following a reference to a quarrel, we're pushed into an Amerindian world that includes, not tipis and pre-industrial hunter-gatherers (what could be assumed to be the reader's automatic assumptions about Amerindian culture), but streets "snarled with vehicles" powered by "degravs" which Mora-Ta-Kai himself developed.

So we discard our previous assumption. Mora-Ta-Kai's natural context is no world we know, no world that ever was. It's only at that point, well into the story, that we can confidently assume Mora-Ta-Kai is a modern Amerindian, but from some other, alternative reality from which he has unaccountably been thrust. He doesn't remember how. And so the second mystery begins.

The introductory section, in our time and world, is now seen to be a frame for a past story unfolding as Mora-Ta-Kai's returning memory provides an account of the actual course of events which forced him out of his reality into ours.

The puzzling early mention of White Savages is now expanded and explained. In Mora-Ta-Kai's reality, Amerindians are dominant and consider whites as uneducable chattel. As a scientist of the "old science"—a phrase which usually suggests magic but here is indistinguishable from high-tech—Mora-Ta-Kai has set out to demonstrate the socially unacceptable truth that no race is intrinsically superior to any other, that "all men are brothers." As a result, his wife rejects him and his "best friend" is glad to get rid of him and collect his royalties, both of them demonstrating unquestioning racial prejudice. The story's central premise is at last spelled out, almost precisely at the story's center: a quirk of history took canoes east across the Atlantic, rather than carrying European ships west. Building on the foundations of Arabic and European science, the Amerindians were able to advance quickly to a dominant and scientifically sophisticated culture.

At last, in a barbaric ceremony of white superstition, Mora-Ta-Kai meets a yellow-haired "Sorceress" who reveals to him that all realities reside in the human heart and leads him to experience an alternative possibility: our reality.

All mysteries now resolved, we return to the frame story. Remembering, Mora-Ta-Kai is fortunately reconciled enough to our world to refrain from destroying it with a gadget made with toothpowder, aluminum foil, and toy magnets: not a doomsday weapon the reader is intended to take very seriously, one assumes. Rather, the author's emphasis is on Mora-Ta-Kai's realization that if, as he believes, all men are brothers, then this reality of ours will do as well as any. Worlds and civilizations may change, but the realities of racial equality and blind prejudice exist alike wherever people are. The human heart is the continuum which spans all.

And in that conclusion, Cox reflects one basic truth of science fiction in general and alternate history stories in particular: that we delight in examining different ways of being to see our own with fresh eyes. We go seeking the strange so that we may come home to the no-longer-familiar. Technology and culture metamorphose radically; human nature is constant, and endures.

This might be considered an "old-fashioned story." The protagonists and his friends are enslaved and must free themselves. The tale of the downtrodden who must overthrow arrogant masters is a favorite motif in folk-tales. Think of "Cinderella," or of the innumerable tales of disregarded youngest sons who turn out to be the true heroes. (For that matter, David was the youngest son of Jesse and it was he, who was assigned to caring for the sheep, who had to be called in from the fold to be anointed king by Samuel.)

However, don't be scared off by "old-fashioned stories." I, for one, love them (and write them) and so do many others. It is no crime for a story to have a beginning and a middle and an end. It is no flaw for it to be clear and uncluttered.

Do I sound bitter? I suppose I do, for I am tired of critics who keep looking for character development and deep philosophic significance, when all I am trying to do is tell an interesting story.

My own attitude is this:

It may be that character development and deep philosophic significance is superior to a simple story, but if you can't handle the former, and can write a crackerjack story, then write the story and the heck with the critics. It may be that a is better than b, but good b is better than poor a. Don't ever forget that.

— Isaac Asimov

The Silk and the Song

Charles L. Fontenay

Alan first saw the Star Tower when he was twelve years old. His young master, Blik, rode him into the city of Falklyn that day.

Blik had to argue hard before he got permission to ride Alan, his favorite boy. Blik's father, Wiln, wanted Blik to ride a man, because Wiln thought the long trip to the city might be too much for a boy as young as Alan.

Blik had his way, though. Blik was rather spoiled, and when he began to whistle his father gave in.

"All right, the human is rather big for its age," surrendered Wiln. "You may ride it if you promise not to run it. I don't want you breaking the wind of any of my prize stock."

So Blik strapped the bridle-helmet with the handgrips on Alan's head and threw the saddle-chair on Alan's shoulders. Wiln saddled up Robb, a husky man he often rode on long trips, and they were off to the city at an easy trot.

The Star Tower was visible before they reached Falklyn. Alan could see its spire above the tops of the ttornot trees as soon as they emerged from the Blue Forest. Blik saw it at the same time. Holding onto the bridle-helmet with one four-fingered hand, Blik poked Alan and pointed.

"Look, Alan, the Star Tower!" cried Blik. "They say humans once lived in the Star Tower."

"Blik, when will you grow up and stop talking to the humans?" chided his father. "I'm going to punish you severely one of these days."

Alan did not answer Blik, for it was forbidden for humans to talk in the Hussir language except in reply to direct questions. But he kept his eager eyes on the Star Tower and watched it loom taller and taller ahead of them, striking into the sky far above the buildings of the city. He quickened his pace, so that he began to pull ahead of Robb, and Robb had to caution him.

Between the Blue Forest and Falklyn, they were still in wild country where the land was eroded and there were no farms and fields. Little clumps of ttornot trees huddled here and there among the gullies and low hills, thickening back toward the Blue Forest behind them, thinning toward the northwest plain, beyond which lay the distant mountains.

They rounded a curve in the dusty road, and Blik whistled in excitement from Alan's shoulders. A figure stood on a little promontory overhanging the road ahead of them.

At first Alan thought it was a tall, slender Hussir, for a short jacket partly concealed its nakedness. Then he saw it was a young human girl. No Hussir ever boasted that mop of tawny hair, that tailless posterior curve.

"A Wild Human!" growled Wiln in astonishment. Alan shivered. It was rumored the Wild Humans killed Hussirs and ate other humans.

The girl was looking away toward Falklyn. Wiln unslung his short bow and loosed an arrow at her.

The bolt exploded the dust near her feet. With a toss of bright hair, she turned her head and saw them. Then she was gone like a deer.

When they came up to where she had stood, there was a brightness in the bushes beside the road. It was a pair of the colorful trousers such as Hussirs wore, only trimmer, tangled inextricably in a thorny bush. Evidently the girl had been caught as she climbed up from the road, and had had to crawl out of them.

"They're getting too bold," said Wiln angrily. "This close to civilization, in broad daylight!"

Alan was astonished when they entered Falklyn. The streets and buildings were of stone. There was little stone on the other side of the Blue Forest, and Wiln Castle was built of polished wooden blocks. The smooth stone of Falklyn's streets was hot under the double sun. It burned Alan's feet, so that he hobbled a little and shook Blik up. Blik clouted him on the side of the head for it.

There were so many stange new things to see in the city that they made Alan dizzy. Some of the buildings were as much as three stories high, and the windows of a few of the biggest were covered, not with wooden shutters, but with a bright, transparent stuff that Wiln told Blik was called "glaz." Robb told Alan in the human language, which the Hussirs did not understand, that it was rumored humans themselves had invented this glaz and given it to their masters. Alan wondered how a human could invent anything, penned in open fields.

But it appeared that humans in the city lived closer to their masters. Several times Alan saw them coming out of houses, and a few that he saw were not entirely naked, but wore bright bits of cloth at various places on their bodies. Wiln expressed strong disapproval of this practice to Blik.

"Start putting clothing on these humans and they might get the idea they're Hussirs," he said. "If you ask me, that's why city people have more trouble controlling their humans than we do. Spoil the human and you make him savage, I say."

They had several places to go in Falklyn, and for a while Alan feared they would not see the Star Tower at close range. But Blik had never seen it before, and he begged and whistled until Wiln agreed to ride a few streets out of the way to look at it.

Alan forgot all the other wonders of Falklyn as the great monument towered bigger and bigger, dwarfing the buildings around it, dwarfing the whole city of Falklyn. There was a legend that humans had not only lived in the Star Tower once, but that they had built it and Falklyn had grown up around it when the humans abandoned it. Alan had heard this whispered, but he had been warned not to repeat it, for some Hussirs understood human language and repeating such tales was a good way to get whipped.

The Star Tower was in the center of a big circular park, and the houses around the park looked like dollhouses beneath it. It stretched up into the sky like a pointing finger, its strange dark walls reflecting the dual sunlight dully. Even the flying buttresses at its base curved up above the big trees in the park around it.

There was a railing around the park, and quite a few humans were chained or standing loose about it while their riders were looking at the Star Tower, for humans were not allowed inside the park. Blik was all for dismounting and looking at the inside of the tower, but Wiln would not hear of it.

"There'll be plenty of time for that when you're older and can understand some of the things you see," said Wiln.

They moved slowly around the street, outside the rail. In the park, the Hussirs moved in groups, some of them going up or coming down the long ramp that led into the Star Tower. The Hussirs were only about half the size of humans, with big heads and large pointed ears sticking straight out on each side, with thin legs and thick tails that helped to balance them. They wore loose jackets and baggy, colored trousers.

As they passed one group of humans standing outside the rail, Alan heard a familiar bit of verse, sung in an undertone:

Twinkle, twinkle, golden star,
I can reach you, though you're far.
Shut my mouth and find my head,
Find a worm —

Wiln swung Robb around quickly and laid his keen whip viciously across the singer's shoulders. Slash, slash, and red welts sprang out on the man's back. With a muffled shriek, the man ducked his head and threw up his arms to protect his face.

"Where is your master, human?" demanded Wiln savagely, the whip trembling in his four-fingered hand.

"My master lives in Northwesttown, your greatness," whimpered the human. "I belong to the merchant Senk."

"Where is Northwesttown?"

"It is a section of Falklyn, sir."

"And you are here at the Star Tower without your master?"

"Yes, sir. I am on free time."

Wiln gave him another lash with the whip.

"You should know humans are not allowed to run loose near the Star Tower," Wiln snapped. "Now go back to your master and tell him to whip you."

The human ran off. Wiln and Blik turned their mounts homeward. When they were beyond the streets and houses of the town and the dust of the roads provided welcome relief to the burning feet of the humans, Blik asked: "What did you think of the Star Tower, Alan?"

"Why has it no windows?" Alan asked, voicing the thought uppermost in his mind.

It was not, strictly speaking, an answer to Blik's question, and Alan risked punishment by speaking thus in Hussir. But Wiln had recovered his good humor with the prospect of getting home in time for supper.

"The windows are in the very top, little human," said Wiln indulgently. "You couldn't see them, because they're inside."

Alan puzzled over this all the way to Wiln Castle. How could windows be inside and none outside? If windows were windows, didn't they always go through both sides of a wall?

When the two suns had set and Alan was bedded down with the other children in a corner of the meadow, the exciting events of the day repeated themselves in his mind like a series of colored pictures. He would have liked to question Robb, but the grown men and older boys were kept in a field well separated from the women and children.

A little distance away the women were singing their babies to sleep with the traditional songs of the humans. Their voices drifted to him on the faint breeze, with the perfume of the fragrant grasses.

> Rock-a-bye, baby, in mother's arm,
> Nothing's nearby to do baby harm.
> Sleep and sweet dreams, till both suns arise,
> Then will be time to open your eyes.

That was a real baby song, the first he ever remembered. They sang others, and one was the song Wiln had interrupted at the Star Tower.

> Twinkle, twinkle, golden star,
> I can reach you, though you're far.
> Shut my mouth and find my head,
> Find a worm that's striped with red,
> Feed it to the turtle shell,
> Then go to sleep, for all is well.

Half asleep, Alan listened. That song was one of the children's favorites. They called it "The Star Tower Song," though he had never been able to find out why.

It must be a riddle, he thought drowsily. "Shut my mouth and find my head . . ." Shouldn't it be the other way around—"Find my head (first) and shut my mouth . . ."? Why wasn't it? And those other lines. Alan knew worms, for he had seen many of the creepy, crawly creatures, long things in many bright colors. But what was a turtle?

The refrain of another song reached his ears, and it seemed to the sleepy boy that they were singing it to him.

> Alan saw a little zird,
> Its wings were all aglow.
> He followed it away one night.
> It filled his heart with woe.

Only that wasn't the last line the children themselves sang. Optimistically, they always ended that song ". . . to where he liked to go."

Maybe he was asleep and dreamed it, or maybe he suddenly woke up with the distant music in his ears. Whichever it was, he was lying there, and a zird flew over the high fence and lit in the grass near him. Its luminous scales pulsed in the darkness, faintly lighting the faces of the children huddled asleep around him. It opened its beak and spoke to him in a raucous voice.

"Come with me to freedom, human," said the zird. "Come with me to freedom, human."

That was all it could say, and it repeated the invitation at least half a dozen times, until it grated on Alan's ears. But Alan knew that, despite the way the children sang the song, it brought only sorrow to a human to heed the call of a zird.

"Go away, zird," he said crossly, and the zird flew over the fence and faded into the darkness.

Sighing, Alan went back to sleep to dream of the Star Tower.

II

Blik died three years later. The young Hussir's death brought sorrow to Alan's heart, for Blik had been kind to him and their relationship was the close one of well-loved pet and master. The deprivation always would be associated to him with another emotional change in his life, for Blik's death came the day after Wiln caught Alan with the blonde girl down by the stream and transferred him to the field with the older boys and men.

"Switch it, I hope the boy hasn't gotten her with child," grumbled Wiln to his oldest son, Snuk, as they drove Alan to the new meadow. "I hadn't planned to add that girl to the milking herd for another year yet."

"That comes of letting Blik make a pet out of the human," said Snuk, who was nearly grown now and was being trained in the art of managing Wiln Castle to succeed his father. "It should have been worked while Blik has been sick, instead of allowed to roam idly around among the women and children."

Through the welter of new emotions that confused him, Alan recognized the justice of that remark. It had been pure boredom with the play of the younger children that had turned his interest to more mature experimentation. At that, he realized that only the aloofness he had developed as a result of being Blik's pet had prevented his being taken to the other field at least two years earlier.

He looked back over his shoulder. The tearful girl stood forlornly, watching him go. She waved and called after him.

"Maybe we'll see each other again at mating time."

He waved back at her, drawing a sharp cut across the shoulders from Snuk's whip. They would not turn him in with the women at mating time for at least another three years, but the girl was almost of mating age. By the time she saw him again, she probably would have forgotten him.

His transfer into adulthood was an immediate ordeal. Wiln and Snuk remained just outside the fence and whistled delightedly at the hazing Alan was given by the men and older boys. The ritual would have been more difficult for him had it not been so long delayed, but he found a place in the scheme of things somewhat high for a new-comer because he was older than most of them and big for his age. Scratched and battered, he gained the necessary initial respect from his new associates by trouncing several boys his own size.

That night, lonely and unhappy, Alan heard the keening of the Hussirs rise from Wiln Castle. The night songs of the men, deeper and lustier than those of the women and children, faded and stopped as the sound of mourning drifted to them on the wind. Alan knew it meant that Blik's long illness was over, that his young master was dead.

He found a secluded corner of the field and cried himself to sleep under the stars. He had loved Blik.

After Blik's death, Alan thought he might be put with the laboring men, to pull the plows and work the crops. He knew he did not have the training for work in and around the castle itself, and he did not think he would be retained with the riding stock.

But Snuk had different ideas.

"I saw your good qualities as a riding human before Blik ever picked you out for a pet," Snuk told him, laying his pointed ears back viciously. Snuk used the human language, for it was Snuk's theory that one could control humans better when one could listen in on their conversations among themselves. "Blik spoiled all the temper out of you, but I'll change that. I may be able to salvage you yet."

It was only a week since Blik's death, and Alan was still sad. Dispir-itedly, he cooperated when Snuk put the bridle-helmet and saddle-chair on him, and knelt for Snuk to climb on his back.

When Alan stood up, Snuk jammed spurs savagely into his sides. Alan leaped three feet into the air with an agonized yell.

"Silence, human!" shouted Snuk, beating him over the head with the whip. "I shall teach you to obey. Spurs mean go, like so!"

And he dug the spurs into Alan's ribs again.

Alan twisted and turned momentarily, but his common sense saved him. Had he fallen to the ground and rolled, or tried to rub Snuk off against a ttornot tree, it would have meant death for him. There was no appeal from his new master's cruelty.

A third time Snuk applied the spurs and Alan spurted down the tree-lined lane away from the castle at a dead run. Snuk gave him his head and raked his sides brutally. It was only when he slowed to a walk, panting and perspiring, that Snuk pulled on the reins and turned him back toward the castle. Then the Hussir forced him to trot back.

Wiln was waiting at the corral when they returned.

"Aren't you treating it a little rough, Snuk?" asked the older Hussir, looking the exhausted Alan up and down critically. Blood streamed from Alan's gashed sides.

"Just teaching it right at the outset who is master," replied Snuk casually. With an unnecessarily sharp rap on the head, he sent Alan to his knees and dismounted. "I think this one will make a valuable addition to my stable of riders, but I don't intend to pamper it like Blik."

Wiln flicked his ears.

"Well, you've proved you know how to handle humans by now, and you'll be master of them all in a few years," he said mildly. "Just take your father's advice, and don't break this one's wind."

The next few months were misery to Alan. He had the physical qualities Snuk liked in a mount, and Snuk rode him more frequently than any of his other saddle men.

Snuk liked to ride fast, and he ran Alan unmercifully. They would return at the end of a hot afternoon, Alan bathed in sweat and so tired his limbs trembled uncontrollably.

Besides, Snuk was an uncompromising master with more than a touch of cruelty in his make-up. He would whip Alan savagely for minor inattention, for failure to respond promptly to the reins, for speaking at all in his presence. Alan's back was soon covered with spur scars, and one eye often was half-closed from a whiplash across the face.

In desperation, Alan sought the counsel of his old friend, Robb, whom he saw often now that he was in the men's field.

"There's nothing you can do," Robb said. "I just thank the Golden Star that Wiln rides me and I'll be too old for Snuk to ride when Wiln dies. But then Snuk will be master of us all, and I dread that day."

"Couldn't one of us kill Snuk against a tree?" asked Alan. He had thought of doing it himself.

"Never think such a thought," warned Robb quickly. "If that happened, all the riding men would be butchered for meat. The Wiln family has enough money to buy new riding stables in Falklyn if they wish, and no Hussir will put up with a rebellious human."

That night Alan nursed his freshest wounds beside the fence closest to the women's and children's field and gave himself up to nostalgia. He longed for the happy days of his childhood and Blik's kind mastery.

Across the intervening fields, faintly, he heard the soft voices of the women. He could not make out the words, but he remembered them from the tune:

> Star light, star bright,
> Star that sheds a golden light,
> I wish I may, I wish I might,
> Reach you, star that shines at night.

From behind him came the voices of the men, nearer and louder:

> Human, see the little zird,
> Its wings are all aglow.
> Don't follow it away at night,
> For fear of grief and woe.

The children had sung it differently. And there had been a dream . . .

"Come with me to freedom, human," said the zird.

Alan had seen many zirds at night—they appeared only at night—and had heard their call. It was the only thing they said, always in the human language: "Come with me to freedom, human."

As he had before, he wondered. A zird was only a scaly-winged little night creature. How could it speak human words? Where did zirds come from, and where did they go in the daytime? For the first time in his life, he asked the zird a question.

"What and where is freedom, zird?" Alan asked.

"Come with me to freedom, human," repeated the zird. It flapped its wings, rising a few inches above the fence, and settled back on its perch.

"Is that all you can say, zird?" asked Alan irritably. "How can I go with you when I can't fly?"

"Come with me to freedom, human," said the zird.

A great boldness surged in Alan's heart, spurred by the dreary prospect of having to endure Snuk's sadism again on the morrow. He looked at the fence.

Alan had never paid much attention to a fence before. Humans did not try to get out of the fenced enclosures, because the story parents told to children who tried it was that strayed humans were always recaptured and butchered for meat.

It was the strangest coincidence. It reminded him of that night long ago, the night after he had gone into Falklyn with Blik and first seen the Star Tower. Even as the words of the song died away in the night air, he saw the glow of the zird approaching. It lit on top of the fence and squawked down at him.

The links of the fence were close together, but he could get his fingers and toes through them. Tentatively, he tried it. A mounting excitement taking possession of him, he climbed.

It was ridiculously easy. He was in the next field. There were other fences, of course, but they could be climbed. He could go into the field with the women—his heart beat faster at the thought of the blonde girl—or he could even climb his way to the open road to Falklyn.

It was the road he chose, after all. The zird flew ahead of him across each field, lighting to wait for him to climb each fence. He crept along the fence past the crooning women with a muffled sigh, through the field of ripening akko grain, through the waist-high sento plants. At last he climbed the last fence of all.

He was off the Wiln estate. The dust of the road to Falklyn was beneath his feet.

What now? If he went into Falklyn, he would be captured and returned to Wiln Castle. If he went the other way the same thing would happen. Stray humans were spotted easily. Should he turn back now? It would be easy to climb his way back to the men's field—and there would be innumerable nights ahead of him when the women's field would be easily accessible to him.

But there was Snuk to consider.

For the first time since he had climbed out of the men's field, the zird spoke.

"Come with me to freedom, human," it said.

It flew down the road, away from Falklyn, and lit in the dust, as though waiting. After a moment's hesitation, Alan followed.

The lights of Wiln Castle loomed up to his left, up the lane of ttornot trees. They fell behind and disappeared over a hill. The zird flew, matching its pace to its slow trot.

Alan's resolution began to weaken.

Then a figure loomed up beside him in the gloom, a human hand was laid on his arm and a female voice said: "I thought we'd never get another from Wiln Castle. Step it up a little, fellow. We've a long way to travel before dawn."

III

They traveled at a fast trot all that night, the zird leading the way like a giant firefly. By the time dawn grayed the eastern sky they were in the mountains west of Falklyn, and climbing.

When Alan was first able to make out details of his nocturnal guide, he thought for a minute she was a huge Hussir. She wore the Hussir loose jacket, open at the front, and the baggy trousers. But there was no tail, and there were no pointed ears. She was a girl his own age.

She was the first human Alan had ever seen fully clothed. Alan thought she looked rather ridiculous and, at the same time, he was slightly shocked, as by sacrilege.

They entered a high valley through a narrow pass and slowed to a walk. For the first time since they left the vicinity of Wiln Castle, they were able to talk in other than short, disconnected phrases.

"Who are you, and where are you taking me?" asked Alan. In the cold light of dawn he was beginning to doubt his impetuousness in fleeing the castle.

"My name is Mara," said the girl. "You've heard of the Wild Humans? I'm one of them, and we live in these mountains."

The hair prickled on the back of Alan's neck. He stopped in his tracks, and half turned to flee. Mara caught his arm.

"Why do all you slaves believe those fairy tales about cannibalism?" she asked scornfully. The word *cannibalism* was unfamiliar to Alan. "We aren't going to eat you, boy, we're going to make you free. What's your name?"

"Alan," he answered in a shaky voice, allowing himself to be led onward. "What is this freedom the zird was talking about?"

"You'll find out," she promised. "But the zird doesn't know. Zirds are just flying animals. We train them to say that one sentence and lead slaves to us."

"Why don't you just come in the fields yourselves?" he asked curiously, his fear dissipating. "You could climb the fences easily."

"That's been tried. The silly slaves just raise a clamor when they recognize a stranger. The Hussirs have caught several of us that way."

The two suns rose, first the blue one, the white one only a few minutes later. The mountains around them awoke with light.

In the dawn, he had thought Mara was dark, but her hair was tawny gold in the pearly morning. Her eyes were deep brown, like the fruit of the ttornot tree.

They stopped by a spring that gushed from between huge rocks, and Mara took the opportunity to appraise his slender, well-knit frame.

"You'll do," she said. "I wish all of them we get were as healthy."

In three weeks, Alan could not have been distinguished from the other Wild Humans — outwardly. He was getting used to wearing clothing and, somewhat awkwardly, carried the bow and arrows with which he was armed. He and Mara were ranging several miles from the caves in which the Wild Humans lived.

They were hunting animals for food, and Alan licked his lips in anticipation. He liked cooked meat. The Hussirs fed their human herds bean meal and scraps from the kitchens. The only meat he had ever eaten was raw meat from small animals he had been swift enough to catch in the fields.

They came up on a ridge and Mara, ahead of him, stopped. He came up beside her.

Not far below them, a Hussir moved, afoot, carrying a short, heavy bow and a quiver of arrows. The Hussir looked from side to side, as if hunting, but did not catch sight of them.

A quiver of fear ran through Alan. In that instant, he was a disobedient member of the herd, and death awaited him for his escape from the fields.

There was a sharp twang beside him, and the Hussir stumbled and fell, transfixed through the chest with an arrow. Mara calmly lowered her bow and smiled at the fright in his eyes.

"There's one that won't find Haafin," she said. "Haafin" was what the Wild Humans called their community.

"The—there are Hussirs in the mountains?" he quavered.

"A few. Hunters. If we get them before they run across the valley, we're all right. Some have seen us and gotten away, though. Haafin has been moved a dozen times in the last century, and we've always lost a lot of people fighting our way out. Those little devils attack in force."

"But what's the good of all this, then?" he asked hopelessly. "There aren't more than four or five hundred humans in Haafin. What good is hiding, and running somewhere else when the Hussirs find you, when sooner or later there'll come a time when they'll wipe you out?"

Mara sat down on a rock.

"You learn fast," she remarked. "You'll probably be surprised to learn that this community has managed to hang on in these mountains for more than a thousand years, but you've still put your finger right on the problem that has faced us for generations."

She hesitated and traced a pattern thoughtfully in the dust with a moccasined foot.

"It's a little early for you to be told, but you might as well start keeping your ears open," she said. "When you've been here a year, you'll be accepted as a member of the community. The way that's done is for you to have an interview with the Refugee, the leader of our people, and he always asks newcomers for their ideas on the solution of that very problem."

"But what will I listen for?" asked Alan anxiously.

"There are two major ideas on how to solve the problem, and I'll let you hear them from the people who believe in them," she said. "Just remember what the problem is: to save ourselves from death and the hundreds of thousands of other humans in the world from slavery, we have to find a way to force the Hussirs to accept humans as equals, not as animals."

Many things about Alan's new life in Haafin were not too different from the existence he had known. He had to do his share of work in the little fields that clung to the edges of the small river in the middle of the valley. He had to help hunt animals for meat, he had to help make tools such as the Hussirs used. He had to fight with his fists, on occasion, to protect his rights.

But this thing the Wild Humans called "freedom" was a strange element that touched everything they were and did. The word, Alan found, meant basically that the Wild Humans did not belong to the Hussirs, but were their own masters. When orders were given, they usually had to be obeyed, but they came from humans, not Hussirs.

There were other differences. There were no formal family relationships, for there were no social traditions behind people who for generations had been nothing more than domestic animals. But the pressure and deprivations of rigidly enforced mating seasons were missing, and some of the older couples were mated permanently.

"Freedom," Alan decided, meant a dignity which made a human the equal of a Hussir.

The anniversary of that night when Alan followed the zird came, and Mara led him early in the morning to the extreme end of the valley. She left him at the mouth of a small cave, from which presently emerged the man of whom Alan had heard much but whom he saw now for the first time.

The Refugee's hair and beard were gray and his face was lined with years.

"You are Alan, who came to us from Wiln Castle," said the old man.

"That is true, your greatness," replied Alan respectfully.

"Don't call me 'your greatness.' That's slave talk. I am Roand, the Refugee."

"Yes, sir."

"When you leave me today, you will be a member of the community of Haafin, the only free human community in the world," said Roand. "You will have a member's rights. No man may take a woman from you without her consent. No one may take from you the food you hunt or grow without your consent. If you are first in an empty cave, no one may move into it with you unless you give permission. That is freedom.

"But, as you were no doubt told long ago, you must offer your best idea on how to make all humans free."

"Sir—" began Alan.

"Before you express yourself," interrupted Roand, "I'm going to give you some help. Come into the cave."

Alan followed him inside. By the light of a torch, Roand showed him a series of diagrams drawn on one wall with soft stone, as one would draw things in the dust with a stick.

"These are maps, Alan," said Roand, and he explained to the boy what a map was. At last Alan nodded in comprehension.

"You know by now that there are two ways of thinking about what to do to set all humans free, but you do not entirely understand either of them," said Roand. "These maps show you the first one, which was conceived a hundred and fifty years ago but which our people have not been able to agree to try.

"This map shows how, by a surprise attack, we could take Falklyn, the central city of all this Hussir region, although the Hussirs in Falklyn number almost ten thousand. Holding Falklyn, we could free the nearly forty thousand humans in the city and we would have enough strength then to take the surrounding area and strike at the cities around it, gradually, as these other maps show."

Alan nodded.

"But I like the other way better," Alan said. "There must be a reason why they won't let humans enter the Star Tower."

Roand's toothless smile did not mar the innate dignity of his face.

"You are a mystic, as I am, young Alan," he said. "But the tradition says that for a human to enter the Star Tower is not enough. Let me tell you of the tradition.

"The tradition says that the Star Tower was once the home of all humans. There were only a dozen or so humans then, but they had powers that were great and strange. But when they came out of the Star Tower, the Hussirs were able to enslave them through mere force of numbers.

"Three of those first humans escaped to these mountains and became the first Wild Humans. From them has come the tradition that has passed to their descendants and to the humans who have been rescued from Hussir slavery.

"The tradition says that a human who enters the Star Tower can free all the humans in the world—if he takes with him the Silk and the Song."

Roand reached into a crevice.

"This is the Silk," he said, drawing forth a peach-colored scarf on which something had been painted. Alan recognized it as writing, such as the Hussirs used and were rumored to have been taught by humans. Roand read it to him, reverently.

" 'REG. B-XII. CULTURE V. SOS.' "

"What does it mean?" asked Alan.

"No one knows," said Roand. "It's a great mystery. It may be a magical incantation."

He put the Silk back into the crevice.

"This is the only other writing we have handed down by our forebears," said Roand, and pulled out a fragment of very thin, brittle, yellowish material. To Alan it looked something like thin cloth that had hardened with age, yet it had a different texture. Roand handled it very carefully.

"This was torn and the rest of it lost centuries ago," said Roand, and he read. " 'October 3, 2 . . . ours to be the last . . . three lost expeditions . . . too far to keep trying . . . how we can get . . . ' "

Alan could make no more sense of this than he could of the words of the Silk.

"What is the Song?" asked Alan.

"Every human knows it from childhood," said Roand. "It is the best known of all human songs."

" 'Twinkle, twinkle, golden star,' " quoted Alan at once, " 'I can reach you, though you're far . . . ' "

"That's right, but there is a second verse that only the Wild Humans know. You must learn it. It goes like this:

> Twinkle, twinkle, little bug,
> Long and round, of shiny hue
> In a room marked by a cross,
> Sting my arm when I've found you.
> Lay me down, in bed so deep,
> And then there's naught to do but sleep.

"It doesn't make sense," said Alan. "No more than the first verse — though Mara showed me what a turtle looks like."

"They aren't supposed to make sense until you sing them in the Star Tower," said Roand, "and then only if you have the Silk with you."

Alan cogitated a while. Roand was silent, waiting.

"Some of the people want one human to try to reach the Star Tower and think that will make all humans miraculously free," said Alan at last. "The others think that is but a child's tale and we must conquer the Hussirs with bows and spears. It seems to me, sir, that one or the other must be tried. I'm sorry that I don't know enough to suggest another course."

Roand's face fell.

"So you will join one side or the other and argue about it for the rest of your life," he said sadly. "And nothing will ever be done, because the people can't agree."

"I don't see why that has to be, sir."

Roand looked at him with sudden hope.

"What do you mean?"

"Can't you or someone else order them to take one course or another?"

Roand shook his head.

"Here there are rules, but no man tells another what to do," he said. "We are free here."

"Sir, when I was a small child, we played a game called Two Herds," said Alan slowly. "The sides would be divided evenly, each with a tree for a haven. When two of opposite sides met in the field, the one last from his haven captured the other and took him back to join his side."

"I've played that game, many years ago," said Roand. "I don't see your point, boy."

"Well, sir, to win, one side had to capture all the people on the other side. But, with so many captures back and forth, sometimes night fell and the game was not ended. So we always played that, then, the side with the most children when the game ended was the winning side.

"Why couldn't it be done that way?"

Comprehension dawned slowly in Roand's face. There was something there, too, of the awe-inspiring revelation that he was present at the birth of a major advance in the science of human government.

"Let them count those for each proposal, eh, and agree to abide by the proposal having the greatest support?"

"Yes, sir."

Roand grinned his toothless grin.

"You have indeed brought us a new idea, my boy, but you and I will have to surrender our own viewpoint by it, I'm afraid. I keep close count. There are a few more people in Haafin who think we should attack the Hussirs with weapons than believe in the old tradition."

IV

When the armed mob of Wild Humans approached Falklyn in the dusk, Alan wore the Silk around his neck. Roand, one of the oldsters who stayed behind at Haafin, had given it to him.

"When Falklyn is taken, my boy, take the Silk with you into the Star Tower and sing the Song," were Roand's parting words. "There may be something to the old traditions after all."

After much argument among those Wild Humans who had given it thought for years, a military plan had emerged blessed with all the simplicity of a nonmilitary race. They would just march into the city, killing all Hussirs they saw, and stay there, still killing all Hussirs they saw. Their own strength would increase gradually as they freed the city's enslaved humans. No one could put a definite finger on anything wrong with the idea.

Falklyn was built like a wheel. Around the park in which stood the Star Tower the streets ran in concentric circles. Like spokes of the wheel, other streets struck from the park out to the edge of the city.

Without any sort of formation, the humans entered one of these spoke streets and moved inward, a few adventurous souls breaking away from the main body at each cross street. It was suppertime in Falklyn, and few Hussirs were abroad. The humans were jubilant as those who escaped their arrows fled, whistling in fright.

They were about a third of the way to the center of Falklyn when the bells began ringing, first near at hand and then all over the city. Hussirs popped out of doors and on to balconies, and arrows began to sail in among the humans to match their own. The motley army began to break up as its soldiers sought cover. Its progress was slowed, and there was some hand-to-hand fighting.

Alan found himself with Mara, crouching in a doorway. Ahead of them and behind them, Wild Humans scurried from house to house, still moving forward. An occasional Hussir hopped hastily across the street, sometimes making it, sometimes falling from a human arrow.

"This doesn't look so good," said Alan. "Nobody seemed to think of the Hussirs being prepared for an attack, but those bells must have been an alarm system."

"We're still moving ahead," replied Mara confidently.

Alan shook his head.

"That may just mean we'll have more trouble getting out of the city," he said. "The Hussirs outnumber us twenty to one, and they're killing more of us than we're killing of them."

The door beside them opened and a Hussir leaped all the way out before seeing them. Alan dispatched him with a blow from his spear. Mara at his heels, he ran forward to the next doorway. Shouts of humans and whistles and cries of Hussirs echoed back and forth down the street.

The fighting humans were perhaps halfway to the Star Tower when from ahead of them came the sound of shouting and chanting. From the dimness it seemed that a solid river of white was pouring toward them, filling the street from wall to wall.

A Wild Human across the street from Alan and Mara shouted in triumph.

"They're humans! The slaves are coming to help us!"

A ragged shout went up from the embattled Wild Humans. But as it died down, they were able to distinguish the words of the chanting and the shouting from that naked mass of humanity.

"Kill the Wild Humans! Kill the Wild Humans! Kill the Wild Humans!"

Remembering his own childhood fear of Wild Humans, Alan suddenly understood. With a confidence fully justified, the Hussirs had turned the humans' own people against themselves.

The invaders looked at each other in alarm and drew closer together beneath the protection of overhanging balconies. Hussir arrows whistled near them unheeded.

They could not kill their enslaved brothers, and there was no chance of breaking through that oncoming avalanche of humanity. First by ones and twos, and then in groups, they turned to retreat from the city.

But the way was blocked. Up the street from the direction in which they had come moved orderly ranks of armed Hussirs. Some of the Wild Humans, among them Alan and Mara, ran for the nearest cross streets. Along them, too, approached companies of Hussirs.

The Wild Humans were trapped in the middle of Falklyn.

Terrified, the men and women of Haafin converged and swirled in a helpless knot in the center of the street. Hussir arrows from nearby windows picked them off one by one. The advancing Hussirs in the street were almost within bowshot, and the yelling, unarmed slave humans were even closer.

"Your clothes!" shouted Alan, on an inspiration. "Throw away your clothes and weapons! Try to get back to the mountains!"

In almost a single swift shrug, he divested himself of the open jacket and baggy trousers and threw his bow, arrows and spear from him. Only the Silk still fluttered from his neck.

As Mara stood openmouthed beside him, he jerked at her jacket impatiently. Suddenly getting his idea, she stripped quickly. The other Wild Humans began to follow suit.

The arrows of the Hussir squads were beginning to fall among them. Grabbing Mara's hand, Alan plunged headlong toward the avalanche of slave humans.

Slowed as he was by Mara, a dozen other Wild Humans raced ahead of him to break into the wall of humanity. Angry hands clutched at them as they tried to lose themselves among the slaves, and Alan and Mara, clinging to each other, were engulfed in a sudden swirl of shouting confusion.

There were naked, sweating bodies moving on all sides of them. They were buffeted back and forth like chips in the surf. Desperately they gripped hands and stayed close together.

They were crowded to one side of the street, against the wall. The human tide scraped them along the rough stone and battered them roughly into a doorway. The door yielded to the tremendous pressure and flew inward. Somehow, only the two of them lost their balance and sprawled on the carpeted floor inside.

A Hussir appeared from an inside door, a barbed spear upraised.

"Mercy, your greatness!" cried Alan in the Hussir tongue, groveling.

The Hussir lowered the spear.

"Who is your master, human?" he demanded.

A distant memory thrust itself into Alan's mind, haltingly.

"My master lives in Northwesttown, your greatness."

The spear moved in the Hussir's hand.

"This is Northwesttown, human," he said ominously.

"Yes, your greatness," whimpered Alan, and prayed for no more coincidences. "I belong to the merchant Senk."

The spear point dropped to the floor again.

"I felt sure you were a town human," said the Hussir, his eyes on the scarf around Alan's neck. "I know Senk well. And you, woman, who is your master?"

Alan did not wait to find whether Mara spoke Hussir.

"She also belongs to my lord Senk, your greatness." Another recollection came to his aid, and he added, "It's mating season, your greatness."

The Hussir gave the peculiar whistle that served for a laugh among his race. He beckoned to them to rise.

"Go out the back door and return to your pen," he said kindly. "You're lucky you weren't separated from each other in that herd."

Gratefully, Alan and Mara slipped out the back door and made their way up a dark alley to a street. He led her to the left.

"We'll have to find a cross street to get out of Falklyn," he said. "This is one of the circular streets."

"I hope most of the others escape," she said fervently. "There's no one left in Haafin but the old people and the small children."

"We'll have to be careful," he said. "They may have guards at the edge of the city. We outtalked that Hussir, but you'd better go ahead of me till we get to the outskirts. It'll look less suspicious if we're not together."

At the cross street they turned right. Mara moved ahead about thirty feet, and he followed. He watched her slim white figure swaying under the flickering gaslights of Falklyn and suddenly he laughed quietly. The memory of the blonde girl at Wiln Castle had returned to him, and it occurred to him, too, that he had never missed her.

The streets were nearly empty. Once or twice a human crossed ahead of them at a trot, and several times Hussirs passed them. For a while Alan heard shouting and whistling not far away, then these sounds faded.

They had not been walking long when Mara stopped. Alan came up beside her.

"We must have reached the outskirts," she said, waving her hand at the open space ahead of them.

They walked quickly.

But there was something wrong. The cross street just ahead curved too much, and there was the glimmer of lights some distance beyond it.

"We took the wrong turn when we left the alley," said Alan miserably. "Look — straight ahead!"

Dimly against the stars loomed the dark bulk of the Star Tower.

v

The great metal building stretched up into the night sky, losing itself in the blackness. The park around it was unlighted, but they could see the glow of the lamps at the Star Tower's entrance, where the Hussir guards remained on duty.

"We'll have to turn back," said Alan dully.

She stood close to him and looked up at him with large eyes.

"All the way back through the city?" There was a tremor in her voice.

"I'm afraid so." He put his arm around her shoulders and they turned away from the Star Tower. He fumbled at his scarf as they walked slowly back down the street.

His scarf! He stopped, halting her with a jerk. The Silk!

He grasped her shoulders with both hands and looked down into her face.

"Mara," he said soberly, "we aren't going back to the mountains. We aren't going back out of the city. We're going into the Star Tower!"

They retraced their steps to the end of the spoke street. They raced across the last and smallest of the circular streets, vaulted the rail, slipped like wraiths into the shadows of the park.

They moved from bush to bush and from tree to tree with the quiet facility of creatures born to nights in the open air. Little knots of guards were scattered all over the park. Probably the guard had been strengthened because of the Wild Humans' invasion of Falklyn. But the guards all had small, shaded lights, and Hussirs could not see well in the dark. The two humans were able to avoid them easily.

They came up behind the Star Tower and circled it cautiously. At its base, the entrance ramp was twice Alan's height. There were two guards, talking in low tones under the lamps that hung on each side of the dark, open door to the tower.

"If we could only have brought a bow!" exclaimed Alan in a whisper. "I could handle one of them without a weapon, but not two."

"Couldn't both of us?" she whispered back.

"No! They're little, but they're strong. Much stronger than a woman."

Against the glow of the light something projected a few inches over the edge of the ramp above them.

"Maybe it's a spear," whispered Alan. "I'll lift you up."

In a moment she was down again, the object in her hands.

"Just an arrow," she muttered in disgust. "What good is it without a bow?"

"It may be enough," he said. "You stay here, and when I get to the foot of the ramp, make a noise to distract them. Then run for it—"

He crept on his stomach to the point where the ramp angled to the ground. He looked back. Mara was a lightness against the blackness of the corner.

Mara began banging against the side of the ramp with her fists and chanting in a low tone. Grabbing their bows, both Hussir guards moved quickly to the edge. Alan stood up and ran as fast as he could up the ramp, the arrow in his hand.

Their bows were drawn to shoot down where Mara was, when they felt the vibration of the ramp. They turned quickly.

Their arrows, hurriedly loosed, missed him. He plunged his own arrow through the throat of one and grappled with the other. In a savage burst of strength, he hurled the Hussir over the side to the ground below.

Mara cried out. A patrol of three Hussirs had been too close. She had nearly reached the foot of the ramp when one of them plunged from the darkness and locked his arms around her hips from behind. The other two were hopping up the ramp toward Alan, spears in hand.

Alan snatched up the bow and quiver of the Hussir he had slain. His first arrow took one of the approaching Hussirs, halfway down the ramp. The Hussir that had seized Mara hurled her away from him to the ground and raised his spear for the kill.

Alan's arrow only grazed the creature, but it dropped the spear, and Mara fled up the ramp.

The third Hussir lurched at Alan behind its spear. Alan dodged. The blade missed him but the haft burned his side, almost knocking him from the ramp. The Hussir recovered like lightning, poised the spear again. It was too close for Alan to use the bow, and he had no time to pick up a spear.

Mara leaped on the Hussir's back, locking her legs around its body and grappling its spear arm with both her hands. Before it could shake her off, Alan wrested the spear from the Hussir's hand and dispatched it.

The other guards were coming up from all directions. Arrows rang against the sides of the Star Tower as the two humans ducked inside.

There was a light inside the Star Tower, a softer light than the gas lamps but more effective. They were inside a small chamber, from which another door led to the interior of the tower.

The door, swung back against the wall on its hinges, was two feet thick and its diameter was greater than the height of a man. Both of them together were unable to move it.

Arrows were coming through the door. Alan had left the guards' weapons outside. In a moment the Hussirs would gain courage to rush the ramp.

Alan looked around in desperation for a weapon. The metal walls were bare except for some handrails and a panel from which projected three metal sticks. Alan wrenched at one, trying to pull it loose for a club. It pulled down and there was a hissing sound in the room, but it would not come loose. He tried a second, and again it swung down but stayed fast to the wall.

Mara shrieked behind him, and he whirled.

The big door was closing, by itself, slowly, and outside the ramp was raising itself from the ground and sliding into the wall of the Star Tower below them. The few Hussirs who had ventured onto the end of the ramp were falling from it to the ground, like ants.

The door closed with a clang of finality. The hissing in the room went on for a moment, then stopped. It was as still as death in the Star Tower.

They went through the inner door, timidly, holding hands. They were in a curved corridor. The other side of the corridor was a blank wall. They followed the corridor all the way around the Star Tower, back to the door, without finding an entrance through that inner wall.

But there was a ladder that went upward. They climbed it, Alan first, then Mara. They were in another corridor, and another ladder went upward.

Up and up they climbed, past level after level, and the blank inner wall gave way to spacious rooms in which was strange furniture. Some were compartmented, and on the compartment doors for three levels, red crosses were painted.

Both of them were bathed with perspiration when they reached the room with the windows. And here there were no more ladders.

"Mara, we're at the top of the Star Tower!" exclaimed Alan.

The room was domed, and from head level all the dome was windows. But, though the windows faced upward, those around the lower periphery showed the lighted city of Falklyn spread below them. There was even one of them that showed a section of the park, and the park was right under them, but they knew it was the park because they could see the Hussirs scurrying about in the light of the two gas lamps that still burned beside the closed door of the Star Tower.

All the windows in the upper part of the dome opened on the stars.

The lower part of the walls was covered with strange wheels and metal sticks and diagrams and little shining circles of colored lights.

"We're in the top of the Star Tower!" shouted Alan in a triumphant frenzy. "I have the Silk and I shall sing the Song!"

VI

Alan raised his voice and the words reverberated at them from the walls of the domed chamber.

> Twinkle, twinkle, golden star,
> I can reach you, though you're far.
> Shut my mouth and find my head,
> Find a worm that's striped with red,
> Feed it to the turtle shell,
> Then go to sleep, for all is well.

Nothing happened.

Alan sang the second verse, and still nothing happened.

"Do you suppose that if we went back out now the Hussirs would let all humans go free?" asked Mara doubtfully.

"That's silly," he said, staring at the window where an increasing number of Hussirs was crowding into the park. "It's a riddle. We have to do what it says."

"But how can we? What does it mean?"

"It has something to do with the Star Tower," he said thoughtfully. "Maybe the 'golden star' means the Star Tower, though I always thought it meant the Golden Star in the southern sky. Anyway, we've reached the Star Tower, and it's silly to think about reaching a real star.

"Let's take the next line. 'Shut my mouth and find my head.' How can you shut anyone's mouth before you find their head?"

"We had to shut the door to the Star Tower before we could climb to the top," she ventured.

"That's it!" he exclaimed. "Now, let's 'find a worm that's striped with red'!"

They looked all over the big room, in and under the strange crooked beds that would tilt forward to make chairs, behind the big, queer-looking objects that stood all over the floor. The bottom part of the walls had drawers and they pulled these out, one by one.

At last Mara dropped a little disc of metal and it popped in half on the floor. A flat spool fell out, and white tape unrolled from it in a tangle.

"Worm!" shouted Alan. "Find one striped with red!"

They popped open disc after metal disc—and there it was: a tape crossed diagonally with red stripes. There was lettering on the metal discs and Mara spelled out the letters on this one.

"EMERGENCY. TERRA. AUTOMATIC BLASTDOWN."

Neither of them could figure out what that meant. So they looked for the "turtle shell," and of course that would be the transparent dome-shaped object that sat on a pedestal between two of the chair-beds.

It was an awkward job trying to feed the striped worm to the turtle shell, for the only opening in the turtle shell was under it and to one side. But with Alan lying in one cushioned chair-bed and Mara lying in the other, and the two of them working together, they got the end of the worm into the turtle shell's mouth.

Immediately the turtle shell began eating the striped worm with a clicking chatter that lasted only a moment before it was drowned in a great rumbling roar from far down in the bowels of the Star Tower.

Then the windows that looked down on the park blossomed into flame that was almost too bright for human eyes to bear, and the lights of Falklyn began to fall away in the other windows around the rim of the dome. There was a great pressure that pushed them mightily down into the cushions on which they lay, and forced their senses from them.

Many months later, they would remember the second verse of the song. They would go into one of the chambers marked with a cross, they would sting themselves with the bugs that were hypodermic needles and sink down in the sleep of suspended animation.

But now they lay, naked and unconscious, in the control room of the accelerating starship. In the breeze from the air conditioners the silken message to Earth fluttered pink against Alan's throat.

Commentary

Premise: Descendants of human explorers, kept as riding animals by aliens, reactivate their spacecraft and inform Earth of the problem.

This is a quest story. Questing involves seeking some treasure, tangible or intangible. Often, the journey toward the goal is an education that changes both the questing character and the quest itself, so that even though what's found is different from what was originally sought, the quest is still achieved, its purpose fulfilled, by story's end.

Whether the goal is the answer to a puzzle or the glad-eyed face of one's beloved, quest stories are as old as literature. Their typical shape is simple: *Go out and get it* and, optionally, *bring it back!*

Since adolescence is, in itself, a time of quest, quite a lot of science fiction for readers in this age group has this form, including the works of such writers as Robert Heinlein and Andre Norton. To appeal to this readership, a story's protagonist is a young person in the throes of adolescent angst. The search is for his/her identity and destiny or role in the world. The story is straightforward, with little complication. The cast of characters is kept small; only the protagonist is developed in any detail. The viewpoint is limited to follow the protagonist, whether in first-person (I) or strictly limited third (looking out through only one character's eyes and mind). There's no sex and only the most generalized and abstract romance. Any alien cultures involved are drawn in broad strokes, with little if any discussion of alien customs, linguistics, history, sociology, cultural attitudes, and so forth—the very thing which the writers sometimes called "world builders" (Herbert and LeGuin, for instance) delight in spelling out with immense and imaginative thoroughness.

"The Silk and the Song" fits this overall profile of a science fiction quest adventure shaped to the interests and attitudes of a teenaged (and probably male) readership.

Alan, the protagonist, is well drawn to fulfill the needs of the plot. He seems an average kid: accepting his slavery as natural, loving his young Hussir master Blik, yet rebelling against the cruel treatment that follows Blik's death. Alan's not very different from a contemporary kid in a family setting—accepting his position as a child of the household but knowing he'll eventually need to escape it; often resentful of what he inevitably sees as unreasonable constraints on his total freedom to do whatever he pleases but not quite ready yet to join the "Wild Humans," the adults. As puberty advances, he suffers a "welter of new emotions." The imagined situation is a close and pointed analogy to the real one. A teenaged reader would find it easy to identify with Alan, in spite of the alien setting and circumstances.

The aliens are generalized. The Hussir keep humans as slaves and are physically different—smaller, with tails—but in personality differ not at all from human beings. Although Alan is fond of Blik and hates Snuk, neither Hussir is developed beyond the briefest justification for Alan's attitude toward each: Blik is indulgent and talks to Alan; Snuk is a brutal and strict master. We learn no personal details about them as individuals, and next to nothing about the culture of which they are members. Their world has cities (Falklyn is the only one mentioned); it's pre-industrial, inasmuch as the Hussir depend for transportation on riding animals (humans) rather than on mechanical vehicles of any sort. And that's all we know. The story's motion is not encumbered by more than the minimum of exposition—explanations or background information of any sort.

All that the reader really needs to know is that the enslaved humans are the descendants of "only a dozen or so" (explorers: too few for colonists) who came out of the space ship called "the Star Tower" which sits in the center of Falklyn. The story's plot is obviously going to involve the protagonist, Alan, getting into the Star Tower and reclaiming humanity's rightful status as people superior to their present station—and, presumably, to the Hussir. And so it happens, with only slight diversions and embellishments.

One assumes it doesn't hurt any, either, that the "Star Tower" is a traditional rocket ship, presumably resting upright on its tailfins in traditional fifties fashion, rather than being, as in Larry Niven's "Neutron Star," a dull, cylindrical "No. 2 General Products hull" lying on its side. The rocket, as an object, has a clear appropriateness to one in the process of claiming adult male human status. Although inherent symbolism can easily be overinterpreted and talked to death, in this story, on this subject, at least a nod of recognition toward the obvious seems justified.

It's also interesting that although Alan apparently has a sexual initiation with the unnamed and quickly-gone "blonde girl," there's no suggestion that he and Mara, conveniently "his own age," become lovers. They're constant companions, but no question of sex explicitly arises. Giving Alan's body a long, evaluating look, Mara does nothing more provocative than comment, "You'll do. I wish all of them we get were as healthy." Evidently her interest is clinical, not erotic. This is another strong hint that this story was written for a teenaged male audience. Beautiful women should be around, but not *too much* around, or complicating things with expectations which the then 16-year-old protagonist (and the reader) might find threatening.

The story turns on a riddle done as new verses to the familiar children's song, "Twinkle Twinkle Little Star." But the process of solving the riddle is almost purely mechanical, not intellectual. Alan and Mara have already climbed into the space ship when they try to interpret the line "shut my mouth and find my head," correctly deducing that it's a direction to do what they've already done: shut the door and climb to the top of the ship. The puzzle is thus solved before it's even been specifically asked. Similarly, their only problem in finding "a worm striped with red" is ransacking the bridge until they hit something wormlike (a tape) and then find the red-striped tape the verse designates. No problem. The turtle shell, to which they're supposed to "feed" the red-striped worm, is "of course . . . the transparent dome-shaped object that sat on a pedestal between two of the chair-beds." In other words, they couldn't have missed it if they'd tried.

Although the humans have been enslaved for generations and although a great deal hinges on the riddle's solution, it isn't, finally, a hard riddle. Neither the mental powers of Sherlock Holmes nor any "book learning" is required, much less basic astrophysics. Not even maturity is a prerequisite, beyond being able to remember the verse and climb into the Star Tower to begin with. Notice that Alan didn't set out for the Star Tower: he only blunders on it while he and Mara are escaping a disastrous attempt at a slave revolt and, almost by accident, Alan decides to go inside.

In other words, Alan isn't Superman, nor even close. Alan's quite capable of fulfilling the quest just as he is, an average teenager, if he simply tries hard enough. So the reader's identification with Alan would not be threatened by dazzling feats that would leave the reader behind, feeling vaguely inadequate.

From first to last, however unusual the circumstances, Alan remains an average kid of no particular gifts except being in the right place at the right time and being willing to try. And yet the quest is achieved: Alan has achieved his birthright, his true identity. He's a space man, not a beast of burden. Earth will be warned, by means of the message on the scrap of silk, and will presumably come to rescue the humans; but that's secondary, barely worth hinting at. The real victory is Alan's: the achievement of a valid self, something any teen-aged reader can aspire to.

One of the nightmares of humanity is that of technology run amok; of its "taking over."

An early example of this in science fiction is Mary Shelley's Frankenstein, *first published in 1818. (Some consider it the first piece of authentic science fiction to have been written.) In this book, as most of the world knows, Victor Frankenstein constructs a man out of remnants of freshly dead bodies and is so horrified by his creation (the "Monster") that he abandons him. The Monster, abandoned and mistreated, wreaks his revenge by killing Frankenstein and others related to him.*

The moral is plain. Humanity, in its arrogance, dares too much and is punished therefore. Such examples abound even in fanciful literature predating science fiction. Think of the myths of Phaethon aspiring to control the chariot of the Sun; of Icarus proudly flying too near the Sun. For each, death is the consequence.

Nowadays, the danger seems very close indeed. Human technology is crowding the planet with more people than it can support; it is desertifying the planet, polluting it, subjecting it to strains it cannot endure. We may kill ourselves even without nuclear war.

And, of course, there is the computer that may make us obsolete. The danger can be treated with wry and bitter humor as in Arthur C. Clarke's "Dial F for Frankenstein." The title harks back to Shelley's story, which has effectively scarred the human psyche forever.

— Isaac Asimov

Dial F for Frankenstein

Arthur C. Clarke

At 0150 GMT on December 1, 1975, every telephone in the world started to ring.

A quarter of a billion people picked up their receivers, to listen for a few seconds with annoyance or perplexity. Those who had been awakened in the middle of the night assumed that some far-off friend was calling, over the satellite telephone network that had gone into service, with such a blaze of publicity, the day before. But there was no voice on the line; only a sound, which to many seemed like the roaring of the sea; to others, like the vibrations of harp strings in the wind. And there were many more, in that moment, who recalled a secret sound of childhood — the noise of blood pulsing through the veins, heard when a shell is cupped over the ear. Whatever it was, it lasted no more than twenty seconds. Then it was replaced by the dial tone.

The world's subscribers cursed, muttered "Wrong number," and hung up. Some tried to dial a complaint but the line seemed busy. In a few hours, everyone had forgotten the incident — except those whose duty it was to worry about such things.

At the Post Office Research Station, the argument had been going on all morning, and had got nowhere. It continued unabated through the lunch break, when the hungry engineers poured into the little café across the road.

"I still think," said Willy Smith, the solid-state electronics man, "that it was a temporary surge of current, caused when the satellite network was switched in."

"It was obviously *something* to do with the satellites," agreed Jules Reyner, circuit designer. "But why the time delay? They were plugged in at midnight; the ringing was two hours later — as we all know to our cost." He yawned violently.

"What do *you* think, Doc?" asked Bob Andrews, computer

177

programer. "You've been very quiet all morning. Surely you've got some idea?"

Dr. John Williams, head of the Mathematics Division, stirred uneasily.

"Yes," he said. "I have. But you won't take it seriously."

"That doesn't matter. Even if it's as crazy as those science-fiction yarns you write under a pseudonym, it may give us some leads."

Williams blushed, but not much. Everyone knew about his stories, and he wasn't ashamed of them. After all, they *had* been collected in book form. (Remaindered at five shillings; he still had a couple of hundred copies.)

"Very well," he said, doodling on the tablecloth. "This is something I've been wondering about for years. Have you ever considered the analogy between an automatic telephone exchange and the human brain?"

"Who hasn't thought of it?" scoffed one of his listeners. "That idea must go back to Graham Bell."

"Possibly. I never said it was original. But I do say it's time we started taking it seriously." He squinted balefully at the fluorescent tubes above the table; they were needed on this foggy winter day. "What's wrong with the damn lights? They've been flickering for the last five minutes."

"Don't bother about that. Maisie's probably forgotten to pay her electricity bill. Let's hear more about your theory."

"Most of it isn't theory; it's plain fact. We know that the human brain is a system of switches—neurons—interconnected in a very elaborate fashion by nerves. An automatic telephone exchange is also a system of switches—selectors and so forth—connected with wires."

"Agreed," said Smith. "But that analogy won't get you very far. Aren't there about fifteen billion neurons in the brain? That's a lot more than the number of switches in an autoexchange."

Williams' answer was interrupted by the scream of a low-flying jet. He had to wait until the café had ceased to vibrate before he could continue.

"Never heard them fly *that* low," Andrews grumbled. "Thought it was against regulations."

"So it is, but don't worry—London Airport Control will catch him."

"I doubt it," said Reyner. "That *was* London Airport, bringing in a Concorde on ground approach. But I've never heard one so low, either. Glad I wasn't aboard."

"Are we, or are we *not*, going to get on with this blasted discussion?" demanded Smith.

"You're right about the fifteen billion neurons in the human brain," continued Williams, unabashed. "And *that's* the whole point. Fifteen billion sounds a large number, but it isn't. Round about the 1960's, there were more than that number of individual switches in the world's autoexchanges. Today, there are approximately five times as many."

"I see," said Reyner slowly. "And as from yesterday, they've all become capable of full interconnection, now that the satellite links have gone into service."

"Precisely."

There was silence for a moment, apart from the distant clanging of a fire-engine bell.

"Let me get this straight," said Smith. "Are you suggesting that the world telephone system is now a giant brain?"

"That's putting it crudely — anthropomorphically. I prefer to think of it in terms of critical size." Williams held his hands out in front of him, fingers partly closed.

"Here are two lumps of U-235. Nothing happens as long as you keep them apart. But bring them together" — he suited the action to the words — "and you have something *very* different from one bigger lump of uranium. You have a hole half a mile across.

"It's the same with our telephone networks. Until today, they've been largely independent, autonomous. But now we've suddenly multiplied the connecting links, the networks have all merged together, and we've reached criticality."

"And just what does criticality mean in this case?" asked Smith.

"For want of a better word — consciousness."

"A weird sort of consciousness," said Reyner. "What would it use for sense organs?"

"Well, all the radio and TV stations in the world would be feeding information into it, through their landlines. *That* should give it something to think about! Then there would be all the data stored in all the computers; it would have access to that — and to the electronic libraries, the radar tracking systems, the telemetering in the automatic factories. Oh, it would have enough sense organs! We can't begin to imagine its picture of the world; but it would be infinitely richer and more complex than ours."

"Granted all this, because it's an entertaining idea," said Reyner, "what could it *do* except think? It couldn't go anywhere; it would have no limbs."

"Why should it want to travel? It would already be everywhere! And every piece of remotely controlled electrical equipment on the planet could act as a limb."

"Now I understand that time delay," interjected Andrews. "It was conceived at midnight, but it wasn't born until 1:50 this morning. The noise that woke us all up was—its birth cry."

His attempt to sound facetious was not altogether convincing, and nobody smiled. Overhead, the lights continued their annoying flicker, which seemed to be getting worse. Then there was an interruption from the front of the café, as Jim Small, of Power Supplies, made his usual boisterous entry.

"Look at this, fellows," he said, and grinned, waving a piece of paper in front of his colleagues. "I'm rich. Ever seen a bank balance like *that*?"

Dr. Williams took the proffered statement, glanced down the columns, and read the balance aloud: "Cr. £999,999,897.87."

"Nothing very odd about that," he continued, above the general amusement. "I'd say it means an overdraft of £102, and the computer's made a slight slip and added eleven nines. That sort of thing was happening all the time just after the banks converted to the decimal system."

"I know, I know," said Small, "but don't spoil my fun. I'm going to frame this statement. And what would happen if I drew a check for a few million, on the strength of this? Could I sue the bank if it bounced?"

"Not on your life," answered Reyner. "I'll take a bet that the banks thought of that years ago, and protected themselves somewhere down in the small print. But, by the way, when did you get that statement?"

"In the noon delivery. It comes straight to the office, so that my wife doesn't have a chance of seeing it."

"Hmm. That means it was computed early this morning. Certainly after midnight . . ."

"What are you driving at? And why all the long faces?"

No one answered him. He had started a new hare, and the hounds were in full cry.

"Does anyone here know about automated banking systems?" asked Smith. "How are they tied together?"

"Like everything else these days," said Andrews. "They're all in the same network; the computers talk to each other all over the world. It's a point for you, John. If there *was* real trouble, that's one of the first places I'd expect it. Besides the phone system itself, of course."

"No one answered the question I had asked before Jim came in," complained Reyner. "What would this supermind actually *do*? Would it be friendly — hostile — indifferent? Would it even know that we exist? Or would it consider the electronic signals it's handling to be the only reality?"

"I see you're beginning to believe me," said Williams, with a certain grim satisfaction. "I can only answer your question by asking another. What does a newborn baby do? It starts looking for food." He glanced up at the flickering lights. "My God," he said slowly, as if a thought had just struck him. "There's only one food it would need — electricity."

"This nonsense has gone far enough," said Smith. "What the devil's happened to our lunch? We gave our orders twenty minutes ago."

Everyone ignored him.

"And then," said Reyner, taking up where Williams had left off, "it would start looking around, and stretching its limbs. In fact, it would start to play, like any growing baby."

"And babies *break* things," said someone softly.

"It would have enough toys, heaven knows. That Concorde that went over us just now. The automated production lines. The traffic lights in our streets."

"Funny you should mention that," interjected Small. "Something's happened to the traffic outside — it's been stopped for the last ten minutes. Looks like a big jam."

"I guess there's a fire somewhere. I heard an engine just now."

"I've heard two — and what sounded like an explosion over toward the industrial estate. Hope it's nothing serious."

"Maisie! What about some candles? We can't see a thing!"

"I've just remembered — this place has an all-electric kitchen. We're going to get cold lunch, if we get any lunch at all."

"At least we can read the newspaper while we're waiting. Is that the latest edition you've got there, Jim?"

"Yes. Haven't had time to look at it yet. Hmm. There *do* seem to have been a lot of odd accidents this morning — railway signals jammed — water main blown up through failure of relief valve — dozens of complaints about last night's wrong number . . ."

He turned the page, and became suddenly silent.

"What's the matter?"

Without a word, Small handed over the paper. Only the front page made sense. Throughout the interior, column after column was a mess of printer's pie, with, here and there, a few incongruous advertisements making islands of sanity in a sea of gibberish. They had obviously been set up as independent blocks, and had escaped the scrambling that had overtaken the text around them.

"So this is where long-distance typesetting and autodistribution have brought us," grumbled Andrews. "I'm afraid Fleet Street's been putting too many eggs in one electronic basket."

"So have we all, I'm afraid," said Williams solemnly. "So have we all."

"If I can get a word in edgeways, in time to stop the mob hysteria that seems to be infecting this table," said Smith loudly and firmly, "I'd like to point out that there's nothing to worry about—even if John's ingenious fantasy is correct. We only have to switch off the satellites, and we'll be back where we were yesterday."

"Prefrontal lobotomy," muttered Williams. "I'd thought of that."

"Eh? Oh, yes—cutting out slabs of the brain. That would certainly do the trick. Expensive, of course, and we'd have to go back to sending telegrams to each other. But civilization would survive."

From not too far away, there was a short, sharp explosion.

"I don't like this," said Andrews nervously. "Let's hear what the old BBC's got to say. The one o'clock news has just started."

He reached into his briefcase and pulled out a transistor radio.

"... unprecedented number of industrial accidents, as well as the unexplained launching of three salvos of guided missiles from military installations in the United States. Several airports have had to suspend operations owing to the erratic behavior of their radar, and the banks and stock exchanges have closed because their information-processing systems have become completely unreliable." ("You're telling me," muttered Small, while the others shushed him.) "One moment, please—there's a news flash coming through . . . . Here it is. We have just been informed that all control over the newly installed communication satellites has been lost. They are no longer responding to commands from the ground. According to . . ."

The BBC went off the air; even the carrier wave died. Andrews reached for the tuning knob and twisted it around the dial. Over the whole band, the ether was silent.

Presently Reyner said, in a voice not far from hysteria: "That prefrontal lobotomy was a good idea, John. Too bad that Baby's already thought of it."

Williams rose slowly to his feet.

"Let's get back to the lab," he said. "There must be an answer, somewhere."

But he knew already that it was far, far too late. For *Homo sapiens*, the telephone bell had tolled.

Commentary

Premise: Sufficient interlinkages of telecommunications equipment can act as neural connections of brain-like complexity—and dangerous nonhuman consciousness.

This story can be categorized in a number of ways. It's an end-of-the-world story, spelling out whether humanity's last sound will be a bang, a whimper—or the simultaneous ringing of every telephone on earth.

It can also, for lack of a better term, be called an idea story (though any good story is that). In a direct and fundamental way, and to a greater degree than in other stories in this collection, the premise *is* the story. The narrative spells out the premise, one stage at a time; the characters function mainly as sources of information and speculation rather than as highly particularized individuals. It's what they say that's important, rather than the characters themselves.

For instance, notice, particularly toward the end of the story, how much of the dialogue has no taglines identifying the speaker. Who says a given line doesn't really matter as we get closer and closer to the appalling Fact. No matter who says it, the necessary information is conveyed to the reader. Notice that although Williams, the mathematician and science fiction writer, functions as the story's principal detective, pursuing that Fact, we never learn any specific details about him except his professional specialty and his hobby. Is he young? Old? What does he look like? How does his voice or phrasing differ from those of the others present? Does he like or dislike any of the others? Is he liked or disliked by them?

We don't know, aren't told. The viewpoint remains objective, omniscient: viewing all the characters equally and from the outside. We're thus kept distant from the characters, the better to focus on this story's concern, the working out of its premise.

A lot of classic science fiction deals much more with the *what* and the *how*, and perhaps the *why*, than it does with the *who*. The emphasis is on the discovery or the mechanism and the interesting hypotheses which flow from them. The scientific foundation in such stories is factual and often quite detailed, buttressed with numbers and statistics, like the precise date and time which begins the story and the estimate of fifteen billion neurons contained by the human brain.

Some people call these "hardware" stories because they emphasize physical objects and "hard" science (physics, chemistry, geology, engineering, and the like) whose object of study is physical reality, rather than the "soft" sciences (for instance, sociology, archaeology, and psychology) which study people first and their tools second, if at all. Hardware stories tend to look out at the world rather than inward to consciousness, emotion, and similar subjective states.

This story is a puzzle, an anomalous physical event that the characters attempt to account for by building a chain of observation and logic to which all contribute. When the puzzle is solved, the story— and humanity's chance of survival—is over. The story's dominant attitude is an intellectual curiosity appropriate to puzzle-solving, combined with an even more appropriate nervousness as the characters conjecture—too slowly—toward the disquieting conclusion.

The story begins with a fact that needs explaining: every phone in the world rings at the same time. For three paragraphs, we have nothing but anonymous reactions from people at large—no distinct or named characters at all. The fact, the beginning tells us, will be the story's focus.

The next fact is added: shortly before the phones rang, a satellite network went on-line.

So the question becomes: How could adding a new element to global telecommunications cause all the phones to ring?

Once the investigation begins, the necessary factual background is presented straightforwardly to the reader: the similarity between the neural network of the brain and an automatic telephone switching network; the analogy between a critical amount of uranium capable of causing a chain reaction and the critical number of electronic interconnections capable of causing consciousness. The characters tell one another the needed information so that the reader learns it too.

The question has been transformed to the hypothesis: The phone system is conscious.

The assembled characters proceed to test that hypothesis against observed facts: a faulty bank statement, flickering fluorescent lights, malfunctioning traffic signals, a garbled newspaper. The hypothesis holds up, tentatively confirmed as explaining what would otherwise appear unrelated and freakish coincidences.

The hypothesis confirmed, the question now becomes: What can be done about it?

And the ironic answer is that the newborn consciousness has proceeded to the logical conclusion faster than the men, and has taken effective action to prevent its destruction. The new consciousness is like a brain—only, as the story demonstrates, much faster than even the combined efforts of trained human minds.

Thus the story is a dialogue less between given characters than between thesis and hypothesis, fact and proof—the essential methodology upon which science depends. This methodology is demonstrated as humanity's chief mode of dealing with the new, the unknown. Unfortunately, that very method, brought to a higher level and exercised with greater speed, leaves us defenseless, our best tool turned against us.

What we create, but cannot control, will destroy us. That is the lesson of Frankenstein and his monster whose tragedy the story's title invokes, first of the multitudinous visions of technological disaster that are the dark side of technological achievement—but certainly nowhere near the last unless. . . .

Oh, that was only my phone ringing. Probably a wrong number.

It is natural to think of a science fiction story, or any story, as telling of events in some detail, as describing conversation back and forth. That, however, is by no means the only way of telling a story. There are any number of ways.

Norman Spinrad, who constantly displays the courage to be different, tells a story that reads like a biography told from a distance. Through most of it, he goes into little detail, and is emotionally removed, it would seem, from his subject matter. Of course, this is a device that will make the story slam you all the harder as you approach the end.

However, the point to be made is that there are numerous attitudes you can take toward the science fiction story you are telling and, provided you do it well, you can make any attitude stick.

I had actually never read "Carcinoma Angels" until it was time to prepare this anthology, but four years ago, I wrote a story entitled "Alexander the God," which was written with very much the same attitude as Norman's story was written. I can't honestly say that my story was better (I wish I could) but I did my best.

Anyway, take courage. If you wish to experiment, do so. Just remember that it isn't easy. It is precisely because it isn't easy that so few writers dare do so. But if the pitfalls are numerous, the rewards are possibly great.

— Isaac Asimov

Carcinoma Angels

Norman Spinrad

At the age of nine Harrison Wintergreen first discovered that the world was his oyster when he looked at it sidewise. That was the year when baseball cards were *in*. The kid with the biggest collection of baseball cards was *it*. Harry Wintergreen decided to become *it*.

Harry saved up a dollar and bought one hundred random baseball cards. He was in luck—one of them was the very rare Yogi Berra. In three separate transactions, he traded his other ninety-nine cards for the only other three Yogi Berras in the neighborhood. Harry had reduced his holdings to four cards, but he had cornered the market in Yogi Berra. He forced the price of Yogi Berra up to an exorbitant eighty cards. With the slush fund thus accumulated, he successively cornered the market in Mickey Mantle, Willy Mays and Pee Wee Reese and became the J. P. Morgan of baseball cards.

Harry breezed through high school by the simple expedient of mastering only one subject—the art of taking tests. By his senior year, he could outthink any test writer with his gypsheet tied behind his back and won seven scholarships with foolish ease.

In college Harry discovered girls. Being reasonably good-looking and reasonably facile, he no doubt would've garnered his fair share of conquests in the normal course of events. But this was not the way the mind of Harrison Wintergreen worked.

Harry carefully cultivated a stutter, which he could turn on or off at will. Few girls could resist the lure of a good-looking, well-adjusted guy with a slick line who nevertheless carried with him some secret inner hurt that made him stutter. Many were the girls who tried to delve Harry's secret, while Harry delved *them*.

In his sophomore year Harry grew bored with college and reasoned that the thing to do was to become Filthy Rich. He assiduously studied sex novels for one month, wrote three of them in the next two which he immediately sold at $1000 a throw.

With the $3000 thus garnered, he bought a shiny new convertible. He drove the new car to the Mexican border and across into a notorious border town. He immediately contacted a disreputable shoeshine boy and bought a pound of marijuana. The shoeshine boy of course tipped off the border guards, and when Harry attempted to walk across the bridge to the States they stripped him naked. They found nothing and Harry crossed the border. He had smuggled nothing out of Mexico, and in fact had thrown the marijuana away as soon as he bought it.

However, he had taken advantage of the Mexican embargo on American cars and illegally sold the convertible in Mexico for $15,000.

Harry took his $15,000 to Las Vegas and spent the next six weeks buying people drinks, lending broke gamblers money, acting in general like a fuzzy-cheeked Santa Claus, gaining the confidence of the right drunks and blowing $5000.

At the end of six weeks he had three hot market tips which turned his remaining $10,000 into $40,000 in the next two months.

Harry bought four hundred crated government surplus jeeps in four one-hundred-jeep lots of $10,000 a lot and immediately sold them to a highly disreputable Central American government for $100,000.

He took the $100,000 and bought a tiny island in the Pacific, so worthless that no government had ever bothered to claim it. He set himself up as an independent government with no taxes and sold twenty one-acre plots to twenty millionaires seeking a tax haven at $100,000 a plot. He unloaded the last plot three weeks before the United States, with UN backing, claimed the island and brought it under the sway of the Internal Revenue Department.

Harry invested a small part of his $2,000,000 and rented a large computer for twelve hours. The computer constructed a betting scheme by which Harry parlayed his $2,000,000 into $20,000,000 by taking various British soccer pools to the tune of $18,000,000.

For $5,000,000 he bought a monstrous chunk of useless desert from an impoverished Arabian sultanate. With another $2,000,000 he created a huge rumor campaign to the effect that this patch of desert was literally floating on oil. With another $3,000,000 he set up a dummy corporation which made like a big oil company and publicly offered to buy this desert for $75,000,000. After some spirited bargaining, a large American oil company was allowed to outbid the dummy and bought a thousand square miles of sand for $100,000,000.

Harrison Wintergreen was, at the age of twenty-five, Filthy Rich by his own standards. He lost his interest in money.

He now decided that he wanted to Do Good. He Did Good. He toppled seven unpleasant Latin American governments and replaced them with six Social Democracies and a Benevolent Dictatorship. He converted a tribe of Borneo headhunters to Rosicrucianism. He set up twelve rest homes for overage whores and organized a birth control program which sterilized twelve million fecund Indian women. He contrived to make another $100,000,000 on the above enterprises.

At the age of thirty Harrison Wintergreen had had it with Do-Good-ing. He decided to Leave His Footprints in the Sands of Time. He Left His Footprints in the Sands of Time. He wrote an internationally acclaimed novel about King Farouk. He invented the Wintergreen Filter, a membrane through which fresh water passed freely, but which barred salts. Once set up, a Wintergreen Desalinization Plant could desalinate an unlimited supply of water at a per-gallon cost approaching absolute zero. He painted one painting and was instantly offered $200,000 for it. He donated it to the Museum of Modern Art, gratis. He developed a mutated virus which destroyed syphilis bacteria. Like syphilis, it spread by sexual contact. It was a mild aphrodisiac. Syphilis was wiped out in eighteen months. He bought an island off the coast of California, a five-hundred-foot crag jutting out of the Pacific. He caused it to be carved into a five-hundred-foot statue of Harrison Wintergreen.

At the age of thirty-eight Harrison Wintergreen had Left sufficient Footprints in the Sands of Time. He was bored. He looked around greedily for new worlds to conquer.

This, then, was the man who, at the age of forty, was informed that he had an advanced, well-spread and incurable case of cancer and that he had one year to live.

Wintergreen spent the first month of his last year searching for an existing cure for terminal cancer. He visited laboratories, medical schools, hospitals, clinics, Great Doctors, quacks, people who had miraculously recovered from cancer, faith healers and Little Old Ladies in Tennis Shoes. There was no known cure for terminal cancer, reputable or otherwise. It was as he suspected, as he more or less even hoped. He would have to do it himself.

He proceeded to spend the next month setting things up to do it himself. He caused to be erected in the middle of the Arizona desert an air-conditioned walled villa. The villa had a completely automatic kitchen and enough food for a year. It had a $5,000,000 biological and biochemical laboratory. It had a $3,000,000 microfilmed library which contained every word ever written on the subject of cancer. It had the pharmacy to end all pharmacies: a literal supply of quite literally every drug that existed — poisons, painkillers, hallucinogens, dandricides, antiseptics, antibiotics, vercides, headache remedies, heroin, quinine, curiare, snake oil — everything. The pharmacy cost $20,000,000.

The villa also contained a one-way radiotelephone, a large stock of basic chemicals, including radioactives, copies of the *Koran*, the Bible, the *Torah*, the *Book of the Dead, Science and Health with Key to the Scriptures*, the *I Ching* and the complete works of Wilhelm Reich and Aldous Huxley. It also contained a very large and ultra-expensive computer. By the time the villa was ready, Wintergreen's petty cash fund was nearly exhausted.

With ten months to do that which the medical world considered impossible, Harrison Wintergreen entered his citadel.

During the first two months he devoured the library, sleeping three hours out of each twenty-four and dosing himself regularly with Benzedrine. The library offered nothing but data. He digested the data and went on to the pharmacy.

During the next month he tried aureomycin, bacitracin, stannous fluoride, hexylresorcinol, cortisone, penicillin, hexachlorophene, shark-liver extract and 7312 assorted other miracles of modern medical science, all to no avail. He began to feel pain, which he immediately blotted out and continued to blot out with morphine. Morphine addiction was merely an annoyance.

He tried chemicals, radioactives, vericides, Christian Science, yoga, prayer, enemas, patent medicines, herb tea, witchcraft and yogurt diets. This consumed another month, during which Wintergreen continued to waste away, sleeping less and less and taking more Benzedrine and morphine. Nothing worked. He had six months left.

He was on the verge of becoming desperate. He tried a different tack. He sat in a comfortable chair and contemplated his navel for forty-eight consecutive hours.

His meditations produced a severe case of eyestrain and two significant words: "spontaneous remission."

In his two months of research, Wintergreen had come upon numbers of cases where a terminal cancer abruptly reversed itself and the patient, for whom all hope had been abandoned, had been cured. No one ever knew how or why. It could not be predicted, it could not be artificially produced, but it happened nevertheless. For want of an explanation, they call it spontaneous remission. "Remission," meaning cure. "Spontaneous," meaning no one knew what caused it.

Which was not to say that it did not have a cause.

Wintergreen was buoyed: he was even ebullient. He knew that some terminal cancer patients had been cured. Therefore terminal cancer could be cured. Therefore the problem was removed from the realm of the impossible and was now merely the domain of the highly improbable.

And doing the highly improbable was Wintergreen's specialty.

With six months of estimated life left, Wintergreen set jubilantly to work. From his complete cancer library he culled every known case of spontaneous remission. He coded every one of them into the computer — data on the medical histories of the patients, on the treatments employed, on their ages, sexes, religions, races, creeds, colors, national origins, temperaments, marital status, Dun and Bradstreet ratings, neuroses, psychoses and favorite beers. Complete profiles of every human being ever known to have survived terminal cancer were fed into Harrison Wintergreen's computer.

Wintergreen programed the computer to run a complete series of correlations between ten thousand separate and distinct factors and spontaneous remission. If even one factor — age, credit rating, favorite food — *anything* correlated with spontaneous remission, the spontaneity factor would be removed.

Wintergreen had shelled out $100,000,000 for the computer. It was the best damn computer in the world. In two minutes and 7.894 seconds it had performed its task. In one succinct word it gave Wintergreen his answer:

"Negative."

Spontaneous remission did not correlate with *any* external factor. It was still spontaneous; the cause was unknown.

A lesser man would've been crushed. A more conventional man would've been dumbfounded. Harrison Wintergreen was elated.

He had eliminated the entire external universe as a factor in spontaneous remission in one fell swoop. Therefore, in some mysterious way, the human body and/or psyche was capable of curing itself.

Wintergreen set out to explore and conquer his own internal universe. He repaired to the pharmacy and prepared a formidable potation. Into his largest syringe he decanted the following: Novocain;

morphine, curare; *vlut*, a rare Central Asian poison which induced temporary blindness; olfactorcain, a top-secret smell-deadener used by skunk farmers; tympanoline, a drug which temporarily deadened the auditory nerves (used primarily by filibustering senators); a large dose of Benzedrine; lysergic acid; psilocybin; mescaline; peyote extract; seven other highly experimental and most illegal hallucinogens; eye of newt and toe of dog.

Wintergreen laid himself out on his most comfortable couch. He swabbed the vein in the pit of his left elbow with alcohol and injected himself with the witch's brew.

His heart pumped. His blood surged, carrying the arcane chemicals to every part of his body. The Novocain blanked out every sensory nerve in his body. The morphine eliminated all sensations of pain. The *vlut* blacked out his vision. The olfactorcain cut off all sense of smell. The tympanoline made him deaf as a traffic court judge. The curare paralyzed him.

Wintergreen was alone in his own body. No external stimuli reached him. He was in a state of total sensory deprivation. The urge to lapse into blessed unconsciousness was irresistible. Wintergreen, strong-willed though he was, could not have remained conscious unaided. But the massive dose of Benzedrine would not let him sleep.

He was awake, aware, alone in the universe of his own body with no external stimuli to occupy himself with.

Then, one and two, and then in combinations like the fists of a good fast heavyweight, the hallucinogens hit.

Wintergreen's sensory organs were blanked out, but the brain centers which received sensory data were still active. It was on these cerebral centers that the tremendous charge of assorted hallucinogens acted. He began to see phantom colors, shapes, things without name or form. He heard eldritch symphonies, ghost echoes, mad howling noises. A million impossible smells roiled through his brain. A thousand false pains and pressures tore at him, as if his whole body had been amputated. The sensory centers of Wintergreen's brain were like a mighty radio receiver tuned to an empty band—filled with meaningless visual, auditory, olfactory and sensual static.

The drugs kept his senses blank. The Benzedrine kept him conscious. Forty years of being Harrison Wintergreen kept him cold and sane.

For an indeterminate period of time he rolled with the punches, groping for the feel of this strange new non-environment. Then gradually, hesitantly at first but with ever growing confidence, Wintergreen reached for control. His mind constructed untrue but useful analogies for actions that were not actions, states of being that were not states of being, sensory data unlike any sensory data received by the human brain. The analogies, constructed in a kind of calculated madness by his subconscious for the brute task of making the incomprehensible palpable, also enabled him to deal with his non-environment as if it were an environment, translating mental changes into analogs of action.

He reached out an analogical hand and tuned a figurative radio, inward, away from the blank wave band of the outside universe and towards the as yet unused wave band of his own body, the internal universe that was his mind's only possible escape from chaos.

He tuned, adjusted, forced, struggled, felt his mind pressing against an atom-thin interface. He battered against the interface, an analogical translucent membrane between his mind and his internal universe, a membrane that stretched, flexed, bulged inward, thinned . . . and finally broke. Like Alice through the Looking Glass, his analogical body stepped through and stood on the other side.

Harrison Wintergreen was inside his own body.

It was a world of wonder and loathsomeness, of the majestic and the ludicrous. Wintergreen's point of view, which his mind analogized as a body within his true body, was inside a vast network of pulsing arteries, like some monstrous freeway system. The analogy crystallized. It *was* a freeway, and Wintergreen was driving down it. Bloated sacs dumped things into the teeming traffic: hormones, wastes, nutrients. White blood cells careened by him like mad taxicabs. Red corpuscles drove steadily along like stolid burghers. The traffic ebbed and congested like a crosstown rush hour. Wintergreen drove on, searching, searching.

He made a left, cut across three lanes and made a right down toward a lymph node. And then he saw it—a pile of white cells like a twelve-car collision, and speeding towards him a leering motorcyclist.

Black the cycle. Black the riding leathers. Black, dull black, the face of the rider save for two glowing blood-red eyes. And emblazoned across the front and back of the black motorcycle jacket in shining scarlet studs the legend: "Carcinoma Angels."

With a savage whoop, Wintergreen gunned his analogical car down the hypothetical freeway straight for the imaginary cyclist, the cancer cell.

Splat! Pop! Cuush! Wintergreen's car smashed the cycle and the rider exploded in a cloud of fine black dust.

Up and down the freeways of his circulatory system Wintergreen ranged, barreling along arteries, careening down veins, inching through narrow capillaries, seeking the black-clad cyclists, the Carcinoma Angels, grinding them to dust beneath his wheels. . . .

And he found himself in the dark moist wood of his lungs, riding a snow-white analogical horse, an imaginary lance of pure light in his hand. Savage black dragons with blood-red eyes and flickering red tongues slithered from behind the gnarled bolls of great air-sac trees. St. Wintergreen spurred his horse, lowered his lance and impaled monster after hissing monster till at last the holy lungwood was free of dragons. . . .

He was flying in some vast moist cavern, above him the vague bulks of gigantic organs, below a limitless expanse of shining slimy peritoneal plain.

From behind the cover of his huge beating heart a formation of black fighter planes, bearing the insignia of a scarlet "C" on their wings and fusilages, roared down at him.

Wintergreen gunned his engine and rose to the fray, flying up and over the bandits, blasting them with his machine guns, and one by one and then in bunches they crashed in flames to the peritoneum below. . . .

In a thousand shapes and guises, the black and red things attacked. Black, the color of oblivion, red, the color of blood. Dragons, cyclists, planes, sea things, soldiers, tanks and tigers in blood vessels and lungs and spleen and thorax and bladder — Carcinoma Angels, all.

And Wintergreen fought his analogical battles in an equal number of incarations, as driver, knight, pilot, diver, soldier, mahout, with a grim and savage glee, littering the battlefields of his body with the black dust of the fallen Carcinoma Angels.

Fought and fought and killed and killed and finally. . . .

Finally found himself knee-deep in the sea of his digestive juices lapping against the walls of the dank, moist cave that was his stomach. And scuttling towards him on chitinous legs, a monstrous black crab with blood-red eyes, gross, squat, primeval.

Clicking, chittering, the crab scurried across his stomach towards him. Wintergreen paused, grinned wolfishly, and leaped high in the air, landing with both feet squarely on the hard black carapace.

Like a sun-dried gourd, brittle, dry, hollow, the crab crunched beneath his weight and splintered into a million dusty fragments.

And Wintergreen was alone, at last alone and victorious, the first and last of the Carcinoma Angels now banished and gone and finally defeated.

Harrison Wintergreen, alone in his own body, victorious and once again looking for new worlds to conquer, waiting for the drugs to wear off, waiting to return to the world that always was his oyster.

Waiting and waiting and waiting. . . .

Go to the finest sanitarium in the world, and there you will find Harrison Wintergreen, who made himself Filthy Rich, Harrison Wintergreen, who Did Good, Harrison Wintergreen, who Left His Footprints in the Sands of Time, Harrison Wintergreen, who stepped inside his own body to do battle with Carcinoma's Angels, and won.

And can't get out.

Commentary

Premise: By means of drugs and sufficient determination, a fight against cancer can become a literal battle on the cellular level.

With all the subcategories of science fiction included in this collection, there are many there wasn't space for. No robot stories; no utopias; no post-holocaust after-the-bomb stories; no time travel or what-if-I-killed-grandpa stories; no telepathy or ESPer powers; no first alien contact; no ethnic folks in space; no backyard rockets or other dimensions entered via disused closets. Hardly even any bug-eyed monsters, giving the eaber the benefit of the doubt. So we had to include at least one completely offbeat and unclassifiable story to at least imply science fiction's inexhaustible diversity and to stand for all the ground-breaking stories yet to be written, for which no categories now exist, except that they'll somehow reflect the interface between people and the strange, the new, the unexpected.

That said, there are a lot of things worth noting about "Carcinoma Angels." First, we're not supposed to like its protagonist. It's hard to take a kid named Harrison Wintergreen seriously, especially when we're told his major achievement was "cornering the market in Yogi Berra" baseball cards at the age of nine. Such calculation in a kid isn't likable. But his victimless ruthlessness doesn't put us off, either. He's a weird kid; we want to see what he'll grow up to do. The story's beginning intrigues us, without engaging our sympathy. We're kept at an ironic distance by the events—the humorous exaggeration of equating the shrewd and successful collection of Yogi Berra (who's funny anyhow) cards with the wheeler-dealering of high finance—and by the author's wry tone: "Harry Wintergreen decided to become *it*." We're ready for Wintergreen's comeuppance and perhaps for a joke.

The first third of the story repeats this same pattern. Whatever Wintergreen does, he's wildly successful at—and ultimately unsatisfied. There's been no battle worthy of his complete and comically greedy singlemindedness, whether to become "Filthy Rich," to "Do Good," or to "Leave His Footprints in the Sands of Time." (Even Spinrad's typography ridicules Wintergreen's monomanias and achievements, reinforcing the ironic tone.)

Then, at forty, Wintergreen discovers he has "an advanced, well-spread and incurable case of cancer," with a year to live. That's when the real story begins; the rest was prologue, to interest us in Wintergreen's string of incredible and unlikable triumphs and get us ready for his comeuppance in his final and greatest battle.

And the question arises, why is this beginning there? Why not begin with Wintergreen's discovery of his final challenge? Why doesn't Spinrad want us to like Wintergreen? Why all the ironic detachment?

This story was first published in Harlan Ellison's landmark anthology, *Dangerous Visions,* that collected stories too controversial for the current science fiction magazines to touch. Although cancer has arguably been supplanted by AIDS as the disease most feared and most mythologized, as it in turn supplanted leprosy, some of its terrible force still remains. It's capital D Death. One ought (one feels) to be respectful in the presence of such awful, all-powerful, and all but demonic hideousness. Even talking about it is an effort, if not outright taboo. It's a loaded subject which, like homosexuality, incest, spouse abuse, and rape, is almost guaranteed to go off in the face of any writer unwise enough to lay hold of it for fictional treatment aimed at a general readership.

That taboos change names doesn't mean there aren't any. Some things are still illegal/immoral to chat about in public or in front of children. Some, we barely dare whisper about or admit to ourselves. That different things shock us, from one decade to another, doesn't mean we've become unshockable, however we may commend ourselves on having outgrown our parents' taste in prudery. The death we most fear may change; we don't. What we really fear, we don't talk about. And we don't like to read stories about it, either, unless they're handled very craftily indeed.

"Carcinoma Angels" is such a story. It objectifies the loathed thing, the taboo subject, as the evils, traditional and modern, we can hate wholeheartedly: murderous leather-jacketed bikers, dragons, things with too many legs that have invaded "the holy lungwood" and the rest of our sanctified interiors. And it gives us vicarious victory over them in their thousands, by proxy, through Wintergreen's analogical exploits in the drug-objectified universe of his own body. But it doesn't make us confront such scary stuff seriously. It leaves us an out, lets us laugh at the final horror. Wintergreen is a clown, and gets a clown's comeuppance: his greatest victory leaves him trapped, ironically defeated. And it's an appropriate trap: he's stuck in his own body just as he's been stuck, throughout the story, in his all-devouring egoism, without relationship or any real consciousness of anyone other than himself.

The beginning is there to give us distance, so that we don't have to look directly at the face of the Medusa. And it serves as context for the story of the battle against cancer, to shelter what would, for many readers, be unbearably awful to contemplate if it were more realistic, if the protagonist were a fully-drawn and suffering human being instead of a parody figure set up for our amusement.

Although "Carcinoma Angels" is an offbeat story, it's set up with the same craft, with the same narrative skill and devices, as authors put to use in all the stories in this collection, from traditional space opera to cyberpunk. Craft is in how you make your story, not the topic or premise you choose. However "dangerous" the vision, even the strangest of stories must reach and involve readers to claim a place among the best fiction of the genre.

Other Books of Interest

Annual Market Books

Artist's Market, edited by Susan Conner $19.95

Children's Writer's & Illustrator's Market, edited by Connie Eidenier (paper) $15.95

Novel & Short Story Writer's Market, edited by Robin Gee (paper) $18.95

Photographer's Market, edited by Sam Marshall $19.95

Poet's Market, by Judson Jerome $18.95

Songwriter's Market, edited by Mark Garvey $18.95

Writer's Market, edited by Glenda Neff $23.95

General Writing Books

Annable's Treasury of Literary Teasers, by H.D. Annable (paper) $10.95

Beginning Writer's Answer Book, edited by Kirk Polking (paper) $13.95

Beyond Style: Mastering the Finer Points of Writing, by Gary Provost $15.95

Discovering the Writer Within, by Bruce Ballenger & Barry Lane $16.95

Getting the Words Right: How to Revise, Edit and Rewrite, by Theodore A. Rees Cheney $15.95

A Handbook of Problem Words & Phrases, by Morton S. Freeman $16.95

How to Increase Your Word Power, by the editors of Reader's Digest $19.95

How to Write a Book Proposal, by Michael Larsen $10.95

Just Open a Vein, edited by William Brohaugh $15.95

Knowing Where to Look: The Ultimate Guide to Research, by Lois Horowitz (paper) $15.95

Make Every Word Count, by Gary Provost (paper) $9.95

On Being a Writer, edited by Bill Strickland $19.95

Pinckert's Practical Grammar, by Robert C. Pinckert $14.95

The Story Behind the Word, by Morton S. Freeman (paper) $9.95

12 Keys to Writing Books that Sell, by Kathleen Krull (paper) $12.95

The 29 Most Common Writing Mistakes & How to Avoid Them, by Judy Delton $9.95

Word Processing Secrets for Writers, by Michael A. Banks & Ansen Dibell (paper) $14.95

Writer's Block & How to Use It, by Victoria Nelson $14.95

The Writer's Digest Guide to Manuscript Formats, by Buchman & Groves $16.95

Writer's Encyclopedia, edited by Kirk Polking (paper) $16.95

Nonfiction Writing

Basic Magazine Writing, by Barbara Kevles $16.95

How to Sell Every Magazine Article You Write, by Lisa Collier Cool (paper) $11.95

The Writer's Digest Handbook of Magazine Article Writing, edited by Jean M. Fredette $15.95

Writing Creative Nonfiction, by Theodore A. Rees Cheney $15.95

Writing Nonfiction that Sells, by Samm Sinclair Baker $14.95

Fiction Writing

The Art & Craft of Novel Writing, by Oakley Hall $16.95

Best Stories from New Writers, edited by Linda Sanders $16.95

Characters & Viewpoint, by Orson Scott Card $13.95

Creating Short Fiction, by Damon Knight (paper) $9.95

Dare to Be a Great Writer: 329 Keys to Powerful Fiction, by Leonard Bishop $15.95

Dialogue, by Lewis Turco $12.95

Fiction Is Folks: How to Create Unforgettable Characters, by Robert Newton Peck (paper) $8.95

Handbook of Short Story Writing: Vol. I, by Dickson and Smythe (paper) $9.95

Handbook of Short Story Writing: Vol. II, edited by Jean M. Fredette $15.95

One Great Way to Write Short Stories, by Ben Nyberg $14.95

Plot, by Ansen Dibell $13.95

Revision, by Kit Reed $13.95

Spider Spin Me a Web: Lawrence Block on Writing Fiction, by Lawrence Block $16.95

Storycrafting, by Paul Darcy Boles (paper) $10.95
Writing the Novel: From Plot to Print, by Lawrence Block (paper) $10.95

Special Interest Writing Books

The Children's Picture Book: How to Write It, How to Sell It, by Ellen E.M. Roberts (paper) $16.95
Comedy Writing Secrets, by Melvin Helitzer $18.95
The Complete Book of Scriptwriting, by J. Michael Straczynski (paper) $11.95
The Craft of Lyric Writing, by Sheila Davis $18.95
Editing Your Newsletter, by Mark Beach (paper) $18.50
Families Writing, by Peter Stillman $15.95
Guide to Greeting Card Writing, edited by Larry Sandman (paper) $9.95
How to Write a Play, by Raymond Hull (paper) $12.95
How to Write Action/Adventure Novels, by Michael Newton $13.95
How to Write & Sell A Column, by Raskin & Males $10.95
How to Write and Sell Your Personal Experiences, by Lois Duncan (paper) $10.95
How to Write Mysteries, by Shannon OCork $13.95
How to Write Romances, by Phyllis Taylor Pianka $13.95
How to Write Tales of Horror, Fantasy & Science Fiction, edited by J.N. Williamson $15.95
How to Write the Story of Your Life, by Frank P. Thomas (paper) $11.95
How to Write Western Novels, by Matt Braun $13.95
Mystery Writer's Handbook, by The Mystery Writers of America (paper) $11.95
The Poet's Handbook, by Judson Jerome (paper) $10.95
Successful Lyric Writing (workbook), by Sheila Davis (paper) $16.95
Successful Scriptwriting, by Jurgen Wolff & Kerry Cox $18.95
Travel Writer's Handbook, by Louise Zobel (paper) $11.95
TV Scriptwriter's Handbook, by Alfred Brenner (paper) $10.95
Writing for Children & Teenagers, 3rd Edition, by Lee Wyndham & Arnold Madison (paper) $12.95
Writing Short Stories for Young People, by George Edward Stanley $15.95
Writing the Modern Mystery, by Barbara Norville $15.95
Writing to Inspire, edited by William Gentz (paper) $14.95

The Writing Business

A Beginner's Guide to Getting Published, edited by Kirk Polking $11.95
The Complete Guide to Self-Publishing, by Tom & Marilyn Ross (paper) $16.95
How to Sell & Re-Sell Your Writing, by Duane Newcomb $11.95
How to Write with a Collaborator, by Hal Bennett with Michael Larsen $11.95
Is There a Speech Inside You?, by Don Aslett (paper) $9.95
Literary Agents: How to Get & Work with the Right One for You, by Michael Larsen $9.95
Professional Etiquette for Writers, by William Brohaugh $9.95
Time Management for Writers, by Ted Schwarz $10.95
The Writer's Friendly Legal Guide, edited by Kirk Polking $16.95
A Writer's Guide to Contract Negotiations, by Richard Balkin (paper) $11.95

To order directly from the publisher, include $3.00 postage and handling for 1 book and 50¢ for each additional book. Allow 30 days for delivery.

Writer's Digest Books
1507 Dana Avenue, Cincinnati, Ohio 45207
Credit card orders call TOLL-FREE
1-800-289-0963
Prices subject to change without notice.

Write to this same address for information on *Writer's Digest* magazine, Writer's Digest Book Club, Writer's Digest School, and Writer's Digest Criticism Service.